Stochastic Choice Theory

Models of stochastic choice are studied in decision theory, discrete choice econometrics, behavioral economics, and psychology. Numerous experiments show that perception of stimuli is not deterministic but stochastic (randomly determined). A growing body of evidence indicates that the same is true of economic choices. Whether trials are separated by days or minutes, the fraction of choice reversals is substantial. *Stochastic Choice Theory* offers a systematic introduction to these models, unifying insights from various fields. It explores mathematical models of stochastic choice, which have a variety of applications in game theory, industrial organization, labor economics, marketing, and experimental economics. Offering a systematic introduction to the field, this book builds up from scratch without any prior knowledge requirements and surveys recent developments, bringing readers to the frontier of research.

Tomasz Strzalecki is Henry Lee Professor of Economics at Harvard University. He is a leading decision theorist contributing to the areas of stochastic choice, temporal preferences, and ambiguity aversion. He is a fellow of the Econometric Society and a recipient of the Sloan Fellowship.

Econometric Society Monographs Series

Editors:

Andrea Prat, Columbia University
Stéphane Bonhomme, University of Chicago

The Econometric Society is an international society for the advancement of economic theory in relation to statistics and mathematics. The Econometric Society Monographs series is designed to promote the publication of original research contributions of high quality in mathematical economics and theoretical and applied econometrics.

Books in the Series

Continued on page following the index

Stochastic Choice Theory

Tomasz Strzalecki

Harvard University

CAMBRIDGE
UNIVERSITY PRESS

CAMBRIDGE
UNIVERSITY PRESS

Shaftesbury Road, Cambridge CB2 8EA, United Kingdom

One Liberty Plaza, 20th Floor, New York, NY 10006, USA

477 Williamstown Road, Port Melbourne, VIC 3207, Australia

314–321, 3rd Floor, Plot 3, Splendor Forum, Jasola District Centre,
New Delhi – 110025, India

103 Penang Road, #05–06/07, Visioncrest Commercial, Singapore 238467

Cambridge University Press is part of Cambridge University Press & Assessment,
a department of the University of Cambridge.

We share the University's mission to contribute to society through the pursuit of
education, learning and research at the highest international levels of excellence.

www.cambridge.org
Information on this title: www.cambridge.org/9781009512763

DOI: 10.1017/9781009512749

First published 2025

A catalogue record for this publication is available from the British Library

Library of Congress Cataloging-in-Publication Data
Names: Strzalecki, Tomasz, author.
Title: Stochastic choice theory / Tomasz Strzalecki, Harvard University, Massachusetts.
Description: Cambridge, United Kingdom ; New York, NY : Cambridge
University Press, 2025. | Series: Econometric society monographs |
Includes bibliographical references and index.
Identifiers: LCCN 2024011555 (print) | LCCN 2024011556 (ebook) |
ISBN 9781009512763 (hardback) | ISBN 9781009512749 (ebook)
Subjects: LCSH: Econometrics. | Economics – Psychological aspects. |
Stochastic processes.
Classification: LCC HB139 .S87 2025 (print) | LCC HB139 (ebook) | DDC
330.01/5195–dc23/eng/20240426
LC record available at https://lccn.loc.gov/2024011555
LC ebook record available at https://lccn.loc.gov/2024011556

ISBN 978-1-009-51276-3 Hardback
ISBN 978-1-009-51278-7 Paperback

Contents

Figures

Tables

Preface

I wanted to keep this book relatively short, so I had to make some compromises. To focus on the conceptual description of the theory and the directions of its development, I made math as simple as I could. If you get interested in this topic, please be mindful that this monograph will *not* build much "muscle." If you find a decision theory class near you, take it!

You should have paper and pencil with you and try to work out the details yourself. I sometimes ask you (why?) questions, but there are a lot of other points where you might want to slow things down. This material, like most of theory, has a fractal-like nature and you can zoom in at any little bit and discover a whole universe. Material with an asterisk may be omitted at first reading.

To save on some technicalities, I state some results as Theorem.[†] The dagger means that additional technical details or definitions are needed because not all terms are properly defined. Fully formal statements are contained in the original source. You should not use any daggers in your job market paper!

Acknowledgments

Much of how I think about stochastic choice has been shaped by talking to my coauthors on these topics: Mira Frick, Drew Fudenberg, Ryota Iijima, and Philipp Strack. I thank Ricky Li and Christopher Turansick for thorough proofreading and help working out the details of some results and examples. I thank two anonymous reviewers for helpful criticism.

For helpful comments, I am grateful to Jetlir Duraj, Alex Frankel, Jake Furst, Anthony Marley, Frank Pinter, Mauricio Ribeiro, Terry Rockafellar, Nicola Rosaia, Brit Sharoni, Juuso Toikka, and Christopher Walker. I thank many great colleagues in decision theory for inspiration.

I thank my parents for prodding me to finish this project. Above all, I am grateful to my wife Kristin for her support and patience in the last few years as this project took shape.

These notes are based on the Hotelling Lectures I gave at the 2017 Econometric Society European Meeting in Lisbon. I thank the Society for giving me this opportunity. I have also learned a great deal from my past students at Harvard and various mini courses. None of the above people or institutions are responsible for any mistakes or omissions.

PART I

STATIC CHOICE

CHAPTER 1

Random Utility

1.1 THE ANALYST AND THE AGENT

The main character in this book is the *analyst*. She is a researcher: an econometrician, an experimental economist, and so on. The analyst has access to data about the behavior of an *agent* (or a population of agents) summarized by a stochastic choice function (SCF) ρ. The analyst wants to understand ρ to predict the agent's behavior in a new situation, for example, forecast demand for a new product. A benevolent analyst wants to be able to measure the agent's welfare.[1]

This book focuses on nonstrategic situations, where the data are, for example, the occupational choices in a population or response frequencies in a laboratory or field experiment. Our agents don't play games with each other or with the analyst. Of course, strategic interactions are prevalent in economics, but it's worthwhile to first see how much we can understand about individual behavior. We assume that the analyst is passively studying the agent. The analyst's decisions (which will be unmodeled here) may ultimately impact the agent as new products get introduced or new contracts or mechanisms get designed, but our agents are not strategic enough to take this into account.[2]

Many analysts model the agent as a utility-maximizing creature and make various other more specific assumptions. Each model puts some restrictions on the class of behaviors that are allowed. We will try to understand these restrictions and the ways the various classes connect to each other.

Understanding the relationships between models is interesting in its own right but can also serve some practical purposes. The analyst often has to pick a particular model and it's good to know what the possible trade-offs between these models are.

---

[1] I will refer to the analyst as "she/her," or sometimes "us." I use "they/them" for the agent(s).

[2] In fact, the situation of the mechanism designer is similar to the situation of our analyst: She has some information about behavior in various situations and picks a situation (mechanism) to induce the agent to behave in a desired way.

1.2 DETERMINISTIC CHOICE

We start with deterministic choice because this will be the basis for much of what is to come in this book. This will also establish notation used throughout.

Let X be the set of all possible alternatives that our agent might be facing. Typical elements are denoted $x, y \in X$ and may stand for things such as brand choices, employment status, number of children, market entry decisions, or choosing which perceptual stimulus is stronger in a lab experiment.

The analyst observes the agent's choices in multiple-choice situations. The data of the analyst is a *choice function* that says what the agent does in each situation. We will treat the choice function as observable to the analyst – we will assume that she can collect this data by observing how people behave in real life or by designing a lab or field experiment.

In decision theory and consumer theory, a choice situation is typically summarized by the *menu* (a subset of X) the agent is choosing from (e.g., the actual menu at the restaurant, or the set of insurance plans an employer offers, or the budget set in consumer theory).

Let $\mathcal{A}$ be the collection of all nonempty and finite subsets of X, with typical elements A, B, C, which we call *menus*.[3] A single-valued *choice function* is a mapping $\chi : \mathcal{A} \to X$ such that $\chi(A) \in A$. That is, for each menu $A \in \mathcal{A}$, the analyst observes what is chosen. The condition $\chi(A) \in A$ just means that the agent cannot choose items outside of the menu.

The "revealed preference" exercise of Samuelson (1938) seeks to rationalize such observations by preference maximization and to uncover the preference relation from the observed data.

A binary relation $\succsim$ on X is a *preference* if it is:

- complete ($x \succsim y$ or $y \succsim x$ for all $x, y \in X$) and
- transitive ($x \succsim y$ and $y \succsim z$ implies $x \succsim z$ for all $x, y, z \in X$).

Moreover, the relation is a *strict preference* if it also satisfies the following property:

- $x \succsim y$ and $y \succsim x$ implies $x = y$ for all $x, y \in X$.

The last requirement (called *antisymmetry*) means that the agent is never indifferent between two distinct options.

We say that a strict preference $\succsim$ *represents* χ whenever, for each $A \in \mathcal{A}$, $\chi(A)$ is the highest ranked element of A according to $\succsim$. The key here is that

---

[3] In introductory microeconomics and consumer theory, X is typically an infinite set of consumption bundles ($X = \mathbb{R}^n_+$, where n is the number of goods) and the agent is choosing how much of each good to consume (the menu is an infinite set). The analysis then quickly assumes differentiability and convexity and characterizes optimality by first-order conditions. In discrete choice theory, the analysis is somewhat different: The menu is finite (discrete) and the optimality conditions are a set of inequalities instead of equalities. We allow X to be infinite, but the menu will always be finite, although there is some work on stochastic choice with infinite menus (see, e.g., Bandyopadhyay, Dasgupta, and Pattanaik (1999)).

the agent maximizes *the same* preference on X irrespective of which menu they are facing. If the preference is allowed to depend on the menu, we can explain every possible choice function and our model is not falsifiable (so there is no way of testing if it's true).

There are χs that cannot be represented by any $\succsim$; they are sometimes called "irrational," "behavioral," or "boundedly rational."

The key test for deterministic preference maximization is known under many names, such as Sen's α condition (Sen, 1971), Arrow's IIA (Arrow, 1959), or Chernoff's condition (Chernoff, 1954). The axiom imposes consistency conditions on choices from various menus.

Axiom 1.1 (Sen's α). If $x \in A \subseteq B$, then $x = \chi(B)$ implies $x = \chi(A)$.

This axiom says that if alternative x beats all things in a menu, it must also beat all things in a subset of the menu.

Proposition 1.2. *A choice function χ satisfies Sen's α if and only if there exists a strict preference relation that represents it. Moreover, $\succsim$ is unique.*

A simple proof is, for example, in Osborne and Rubinstein (2020). The assumption that $\mathcal{A}$ contains all menus can be relaxed as long as it contains all pairs and triples.

Decision theorists are attracted to results like Proposition 1.2 because they provide an exact translation between two languages:

- what is observable (the choice function χ) and
- what is a mathematical *representation* (the preference $\succsim$).

This exact translation helps us understand the connections between the two ways of describing choice. It also offers a test of "rationality": If our agent violates Sen's α, then they cannot be maximizing a complete and transitive preference.

To deal with indifferences, economists often consider a multivalued *choice correspondence* $\chi : \mathcal{A} \to \mathcal{A}$ such that $\chi(A) \subseteq A$. The idea behind multivalued choice is that from any given menu, the agent sometimes chooses one alternative and sometimes another (the set of those choices must be a subset of the menu). The analyst records both of these choices and interprets this as indifference. For choice correspondences, an additional condition, known as Sen's β, is needed to characterize preference maximization. Conditions α and β combined are called weak axiom of revealed preferences (WARP). For details, see Chapter 2 of Kreps (1988) and Chapter 1 of Mas-Colell, Whinston, Green, et al. (1995). We will not deal with choice correspondences because the theory of stochastic choice provides a more precise way of modeling the situation where the agent makes different choices from the same menu.

So far, we have two languages: the observables (choice function χ) and the representation (preference relation $\succsim$). To make the math easier, economists often use yet another language to represent choices – the utility functions. This allows them to use familiar tools from optimization theory, such as first- and second-order conditions, Hamilton–Jacobi–Bellman equations, and so on.

A preference $\succsim$ is represented by a *utility function* $U : X \to \mathbb{R}$ whenever

$$x \succsim y \text{ if and only if } U(x) \geq U(y).$$

We will interchangeably write $U : X \to \mathbb{R}$ and $U \in \mathbb{R}^X$ for the same object, thanks to the useful notation in mathematics that says that if X and Y are sets, then Y^X is the collection of all functions from X to Y.

If $\succsim$ is complete and transitive and X is finite or countable, then a utility representation of $\succsim$ always exists. A classic counterexample when X is uncountable are lexicographic preferences. Since we often have to deal with uncountable X, for example, consumption bundles (as in price theory) or lotteries (Chapter 4), typically continuity is assumed to get a representation.[4]

For any preference, there is a multitude of utility representations: If U represents $\succsim$, then any monotone transform $\phi(U)$ also represents $\succsim$.

Proposition 1.3. *Functions U_1, U_2 represent the same preference $\succsim$ on X if and only if there exists a strictly increasing function $\phi : R_1 \to \mathbb{R}$ such that $U_2(x) = \phi(U_1(x))$ for all $x \in X$, that is, $U_2 = \phi \circ U_1$. Here R_1 is the range of U_1 defined by $\{U_1(x) : x \in X\}$.*

This is called *ordinal uniqueness*, that is, utility is unique up to the ordering of alternatives but its scale does not have any meaning. In particular, if $u(x) - u(y) > u(z) - u(w)$, then we are tempted to say that x is preferred to y "more intensely" than z is to w, but this statement does not have any meaning in terms of choices because we can always take a different utility function that represents the same preferences where the inequality is reversed. Later in Section 4.1, we will see stricter "cardinal" uniqueness results.

1.3   STOCHASTIC CHOICE

As mentioned earlier, if the agent is alternating choices from the same menu, the classical approach is to ignore the frequency of such choices and treat them as indifferent. This means that a person who chooses x from menu $\{x, y\}$ 99% of the time and another person who chooses y 99% of the time are classified as the same type.

In this book we will take the choice frequencies seriously and try to extract information from them. To do this, we need to enrich the set of observables: For each menu A and item $x \in A$, let $\rho(x, A)$ be the frequency with which a choice of x from A was observed.[5] In reality, we will have a finite sample of n observations, but we will think of $\rho(x, A)$ as the limiting frequency as

---

[4] For the finite and countable cases, see Propositions 3.2 and 3.3 of Kreps (1988). For uncountable X, see Theorems 3.5 and 3.7 of Kreps (1988) or Chapter 9 of Ok (2014).

[5] The recent paper of Ok and Tserenjigmid (2022) compares the choice-correspondence approach to the choice-frequency approach.

$n \to \infty$.[6] A stochastic choice function collects these limiting frequencies as a function of the menu.

For any finite set Z, let $\Delta(Z)$ denote the set of *probability distributions* over Z, that is, functions $p : Z \to [0, 1]$ such that $\sum_{z \in Z} p(z) = 1$. For each menu A, the values of $\rho(\cdot, A)$ form a probability distribution over A, so we can think of the SCF as a map that takes a menu A and maps it into $\Delta(A)$.

Definition 1.4. An *stochastic choice function* (SCF) is a mapping

$$\rho : \mathcal{A} \to \Delta(X)$$

such that $\sum_{x \in A} \rho(x, A) = 1$ for all $A \in \mathcal{A}$.

Sometimes not all menus are observed, in which case the domain of ρ is smaller. For example, in experiments often there are just binary menus. To simplify notation in this case, we will write $\rho(x, y) := \rho(x, \{x, y\})$ when $x \neq y$ and define $\rho(x, x) := 0.5$.

In discrete choice econometrics the menu is often fixed but what varies are the attributes of these alternatives. The first three parts of the book focus on menu variation and the last part of the book focuses on attribute variation. However, the distinction between the two approaches is not clear cut; for example, for lotteries, each alternative is characterized by a vector of attributes (probabilities of each payoff).

If our analyst is observing a single individual who faces the problem repeatedly (as it happens in some within-subject experiments), then $\rho(x, A)$ is the fraction of times the agent chose x from A. Stochastic choice functions can also capture population-level data. For example, McFadden (1974) studied transportation choices of the Bay area population. In this situation, $\rho(x, A)$ is the fraction of the population choosing x from A. In such applications, choice has two sources of stochastic variation: Individual randomness (how much choice varies if a given person is sampled over and over again) and heterogeneity of preferences (how much choice varies across people).

While it's easy to imagine that preference heterogeneity leads to nontrivial choice frequencies in the aggregate data, it's less obvious why the choices of a single individual should be stochastic. Yet, stochastic choice is routinely observed. This was established first and foremost, in the context of discrimination between perceptual stimuli (Fechner, 1860; Thurstone, 1927). The following example discusses perception of weight, but similar experiments are used in the study of other senses: hearing, touch, vision, and so on.[7]

---

[6] Taking limiting frequencies as a primitive is routine in econometrics for the purpose of estimation and identification of parameters. We will talk about this more in Chapter 2.

[7] For example, in some experiments, in each trial the subject faces a screen where a fraction of dots is moving in a coherent direction (left or right), while others are moving randomly, and the agent is incentivized to guess the correct direction of motion (see, e.g., Newsome, Britten, and Movshon (1989), Bogacz, Brown, Moehlis, Holmes, and Cohen (2006), and Drugowitsch, Moreno-Bote, Churchland, Shadlen, and Pouget (2012)). A similar design was used by Dean and Neligh (2023).

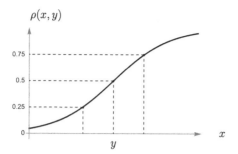

Figure 1.1 An S-shaped psychometric function.

Example 1.5 (Perception Task). Let $X = \mathbb{R}_+$ be a collection of weights (the weights all look the same, or the experimental subject's view is obstructed). The subject is facing a series of binary menus $A_i := \{x_i, y_i\}$, $i = 1, \ldots, n$, where x_i, y_i are drawn i.i.d. from some distribution $\pi \in \Delta(X)$. The subject is tasked with picking the heavier of the two objects: There is a positive payoff for a correct guess and zero for incorrect. The analyst records the subject's choice over many i.i.d. trials. In the limit, we get $\rho(x, y)$.

It is interesting to examine $\rho(x, y)$ as a function of x for a fixed value of the reference weight y. This is called a *psychometric function*; in fact we have a family of psychometric functions indexed by y. $\triangle$

Numerous experiments in psychology and psychophysics can be summarized by the following stylized facts (see Woodrow (1933) and Gescheider (1997)). First, psychometric functions are typically S-shaped. This means that if x is close to y, it is hard for the subject to discriminate between them and accuracy is low. If x is far from y, the accuracy improves. It is typical to use the cumulative distribution function (CDF) of the normal distribution Φ to model psychometric functions.

Another stylized fact is *diminishing sensitivity*: A given weight difference between x and y may be big enough for the subject to notice when both x and y are small, but not big enough when x and y are both large. One way to state this stylized fact is to say that the family of psychometric functions $\rho(\cdot, y)$ gets flatter as y grows.[8] Diminishing sensitivity has been incorporated into many psychological theories, such as Prospect Theory (Kahneman and Tversky, 1979) and Salience Theory (Bordalo, Gennaioli, and Shleifer, 2012).

Yet another stylized fact is *payoff-monotonicity*, which says that the error rate diminishes if the payoff for guessing correctly increases. There is some debate about this between economists (who think that incentives matter) and psychologists (who think they don't).

---

[8] This is often operationalized as the requirement that the interquartile range, depicted in Figure 1.1 is an increasing function of y. This is related to the Weber–Fechner law, which was originally formulated in terms of *just noticeable differences*, a theoretical construct that is inconsistent with our first stylized fact (S-shaped psychometric functions).

The final stylized fact is *frequency-dependence*, which says that $\rho(x, y)$ depends on the distribution π of weights across trials. Intuitively, this is because the agent gets attuned to the range of weight variation, so that the same weight difference can be perceptible if all weights in the experiment are in some small range but may go unnoticed if the weights vary a lot from trial to trial. Notice that frequency-dependence implies that we should more accurately be talking about $\rho^\pi(x, y)$, where π is fixed in a given batch of trials and the analyst runs several batches each with a different π.

While it may be unsurprising that perception of physical stimuli is random, there is a body of experimental evidence showing that economic choices are random as well. Mosteller and Nogee (1951) were first to show that choices between lotteries show substantial switching. This is true whether trials are separated by days (Tversky, 1969; Hey and Orme, 1994) or minutes (Camerer, 1989; Ballinger and Wilcox, 1997; Agranov and Ortoleva, 2017; Agranov, Healy, and Nielsen, 2023). This is true even in questions that offer dominated options.

We will now discuss various reasons why individual choices fluctuate. Each of them corresponds to a particular *representation* of ρ.

1.4 REPRESENTATIONS

The easiest case is population heterogeneity. For example, in the Hotelling (1929) model, consumers' or voters' bliss points are distributed along a line. More generally, we are given a probability distribution over utility functions that specifies the frequency of each utility in the population. This is called a *random utility* representation and our formal analysis of stochastic choice will begin with it. Each individual's utility function is deterministic, but choices appear random to the analyst as she only observes aggregate data. This model is at the heart of discrete choice econometrics. The heterogeneity of tastes is important for firms (e.g., to choose the product mix, which is something they can't do based on knowing just the average demand) and to policymakers (who care about distributional effects).

What about stochastic choices of a single agent? Here there are more possible mechanisms, all of which will be discussed in detail later on:

1. *Random utility*. Instead of a distribution of utilities in the population, we now have a distribution of utility realizations for a fixed agent.[9] In perception tasks, perceptions are random. For example, Thurstone (1927) assumed that the perceived stimulus equals true stimulus plus a normally distributed error, which leads to what is now known as the *probit model*. In choice tasks, the tastes of the agent fluctuate from trial to trial.

2. *Learning*. Here the agent's tastes are fixed, but their information evolves as they learn new things. The agent gets a noisy signal of the true state of the world and updates their beliefs using the Bayes rule. The agent's information

---

[9] This is similar to Harsanyi's purification in game theory (Harsanyi, 1973a).

is private and unobservable to the analyst, so observed choices are stochastic. The main two variants of the model are when information is exogenous (passive learning) or chosen by the agent (active learning), also known as "rational inattention."

3. *Random consideration.* The agent's tastes and information might be fixed, but they may not always be paying attention to the same objects in the menu. If the attention process is random, it will lead the agent to consider different subsets of the menu (called consideration sets) from trial to trial, thereby generating random choices.

Notice that 2 and 3 offer two different models of attention (endogenously choosing the information vs. being exogenously restricted to a subset of the menu). We will treat them in separate chapters.

In all of these stories above, choices are actually deterministic from the point of view of the agent. They know what their craving is today, or what they learned so far, or which options they are considering. Observed choices appear stochastic to the analyst as a result of the informational asymmetry between the two characters. In the following two stories, choices are random even in the agent's eyes, so both our characters are on the same footing.

4. *Trembling hands*: The agent cannot perfectly control their choice: There is a random implementation error or decision error. In some models, this error is exogenous; however, in others, the agent may control mistakes at a cost. Observed randomness is then the result of a balance between the importance of choosing correctly and the cost of doing so.

5. *Deliberate randomization.* The agent likes to randomize. They view each menu A as the set of probability distributions $\Delta(A)$ and pick a favorite distribution according to some preference that may capture nonlinear probability weighting, a wish to hedge their bets, or aversion to regret.

This book starts with random utility. This is by far the most popular model to study population-level data: Almost all of discrete choice econometrics and demand system theory stem from this model. Moreover, much of the classical decision theory work on stochastic choice is about random utility. A good understanding of this model is also a prerequisite for the other models.

1.5   RANDOM UTILITY

There are three equivalent ways to formulate the model mathematically: (1) a probability distribution over preferences, (2) a probability distribution over utility functions, and (3) a random utility function. It may seem like excessive formalism to define all three here but going forward it will be convenient to seamlessly switch between them, depending on the application or context, so I want you to get comfortable with all three.

Let $\mathcal{P}$ be the set of all strict preferences over a finite set X. Let $\mu \in \Delta(\mathcal{P})$ be a probability distribution over strict preferences. Depending on our interpretation of ρ, μ is either the distribution of preferences in the population or the probability that governs the evolution of the preferences of the individual. For any $A \in \mathcal{A}$ and $x \in A$, let

$$N(x, A) := \{\succsim \in \mathcal{P} : x \succsim y \text{ for all } y \in A\}$$

be the set of preferences that rationalize the choice of x from A.

Definition 1.6. $\rho : \mathcal{A} \to \Delta(X)$ is represented by a *distribution over preferences* if there exists $\mu \in \Delta(\mathcal{P})$ such that $\rho(x, A) = \mu(N(x, A))$ for all $A \in \mathcal{A}$ and $x \in A$.

Notice that if we observe choices from only one menu, then any ρ has such a representation. For all $x \in A$, we can just define the probability that x is ranked highest in A to be equal $\rho(x, A)$; the relative ranking of non-top items does not matter. It is the nontrivial menu variation that gives content to the representation.

1.5.1 Invariance of μ

The key assumption is that the distribution μ does not depend on the menu A – it is a structural invariant of the model. If μ is allowed to depend on the choice set in an arbitrary way, then any SCF ρ can be trivially explained (why?).

A possible complication occurs if the invariance assumption is actually satisfied by the data-generating process but violated in the observed sample because of the way the sample is collected. For example, the distribution of preferences between two brands of orange juice can be different depending on whether the menu of choices is Whole Foods or Walmart because of self-selection: Different people choose to go to these stores.

For now, we will assume that the data-generating process and our sample are free of such effects. This assumption will let the analyst estimate μ based on choices from some incomplete set of menus $\mathcal{A}^*$ and predict choice from a new menu $A \notin \mathcal{A}^*$, for example, when a new product is introduced.

1.5.2 Equivalent Definitions

A slightly different object than a distribution over preferences is a distribution over *utilities*. Our set N becomes

$$N(x, A) := \{U \in \mathbb{R}^X : U(x) \geq U(y) \text{ for all } y \in A\}$$
$$= \{U \in \mathbb{R}^X : U(x) = \max_{y \in A} U(y)\}.$$

Now N stands for the set of utility functions that rationalize the choice of x from A.

When X is finite, it is without loss of generality to consider discrete measures over $\mathbb{R}^X$, but sometimes it is convenient to use continuous distributions that admit a density. In general, let $\Delta(\mathbb{R}^X)$ be the set of *Borel probability measures* over $\mathbb{R}^X$. (For the purpose of understanding this book, you can just think of this as containing all discrete and continuous distributions.)

Definition 1.7. $\rho : \mathcal{A} \to \Delta(X)$ is represented by a *distribution over utilities* if there exists $\mu \in \Delta(\mathbb{R}^X)$ such that $\rho(x, A) = \mu(N(x, A))$ for all $A \in \mathcal{A}$ and $x \in A$.

Yet another way to model this is to let utility be a random variable. Let $(\Omega, \mathcal{F}, \mathbb{P})$ be a probability space, that is, $\mathcal{F}$ is a σ-algebra and $\mathbb{P}$ is a probability measure. (If you are not familiar with measure-theoretic probability, you can rely on your intuitive understanding of random variables.) Utility is a random function, that is, $\widetilde{U} : \Omega \to \mathbb{R}^X$ is $\mathcal{F}$-measurable. I will try to put a tilde on every random variable (function, element, etc.). We can think of Ω as things that are observable to the agent but unobservable to the analyst. The event N is now written as

$$N(x, A) := \{\omega \in \Omega : \widetilde{U}_\omega(x) \geq \widetilde{U}_\omega(y) \text{ for all } y \in A\}$$
$$= \Big\{\omega \in \Omega : \widetilde{U}_\omega(x) = \max_{y \in A} \widetilde{U}_\omega(y)\Big\}.$$

Definition 1.8. $\rho : \mathcal{A} \to \Delta(X)$ has a *random utility* representation if there exists a random variable $\widetilde{U} : \Omega \to \mathbb{R}^X$ such that $\rho(x, A) = \mathbb{P}(N(x, A))$ for all $A \in \mathcal{A}$ and $x \in A$.

I have not made a distinction between the three different definitions of the set $N(x, A)$ and I will not do so in the future. I do make a notational distinction between $\mathbb{P}$, which is the probability measure on the probability space Ω that caries the random utility $\widetilde{U}$, and μ, which is the probability distribution (a.k.a. the law) of the random variable $\widetilde{U}$.

The following is an easy adaptation of Theorem 3.1 in Block and Marschak (1960) (see also Regenwetter and Marley (2001)).

Proposition 1.9. *The following are equivalent for a finite X:*

    (i) ρ *is represented by a distribution over preferences,*
    (ii) ρ *is represented by a distribution over utilities, and*
    (iii) ρ *has a random utility representation.*

Given this result, we will write $\rho \sim RU$ whenever any of the conditions above holds.

Proof. $(i) \Rightarrow (ii)$: Suppose that ρ is represented by a distribution over preferences $\mu \in \Delta(\mathcal{P})$. For each preference $\succsim$, pick a utility function $U_{\succsim}$ that represents $\succsim$. Define the distribution over utilities $\hat{\mu} \in \Delta(\mathbb{R}^X)$ by setting $\hat{\mu}(U_{\succsim}) := \mu(\succsim)$ for all $\succsim \in \mathcal{P}$ and $\hat{\mu}(U) := 0$ otherwise. We have

$$\rho(x, A) = \mu(\{\succsim \in \mathcal{P} : x \succsim y \text{ for all } y \in A\})$$
$$= \hat{\mu}(\{U_{\succsim} \in \mathbb{R}^X : \succsim \in \mathcal{P} \text{ and } U_{\succsim}(x) = \max_{y \in A} U_{\succsim}(y)\})$$
$$= \hat{\mu}(\{U \in \mathbb{R}^X : U(x) = \max_{y \in A} U(y)\}).$$

(*ii*) $\Rightarrow$ (*iii*): Suppose that ρ is represented by a distribution over utilities $\mu \in \Delta(\mathbb{R}^X)$. Define $\Omega := \mathbb{R}^X$, $\mathcal{F} := \mathcal{B}$ (the Borel σ-algebra), $\mathbb{P} := \mu$, and $\widetilde{U}$ be the identity function, that is, $\widetilde{U}_\omega(x) := \omega(x)$ for all $\omega \in \mathbb{R}^X$. Thus,

$$\rho(x, A) = \mu(\{U \in \mathbb{R}^n : U(x) = \max_{y \in A} U(y)\})$$

$$= \mathbb{P}(\{\omega \in \Omega : \widetilde{U}_\omega(x) = \max_{y \in A} \widetilde{U}_\omega(y)\}).$$

(*iii*) $\Rightarrow$ (*i*): Suppose that ρ is represented by a random utility $(\Omega, \mathcal{F}, \mathbb{P}, \widetilde{U})$. Suppose that with positive probability there is a tie between x and y; then

$$\rho(x, \{x, y\}) + \rho(y, \{x, y\})$$
$$= \mathbb{P}(\{\widetilde{U}_\omega(x) \geq \widetilde{U}_\omega(y)\}) + \mathbb{P}(\{\widetilde{U}_\omega(y) \geq \widetilde{U}_\omega(x)\})$$
$$= \mathbb{P}(\{\widetilde{U}_\omega(x) > \widetilde{U}_\omega(y)\}) + 2\mathbb{P}(\{\widetilde{U}_\omega(x) = \widetilde{U}_\omega(y)\})$$
$$+ \mathbb{P}(\{\widetilde{U}_\omega(y) > \widetilde{U}_\omega(x)\}) > 1,$$

which violates the definition of SCF. So it's without loss of generality to assume that there are no ties. For each strict preference $\succsim \in \mathcal{P}$, define the event $E_\succ := \{\omega \in \Omega : U_\omega$ is represented by $\succsim\}$. Notice that $E_\succ \in \mathcal{F}$ because the set of utility functions $\mathcal{U}_\succ$ that represents $\succsim$ is an open set – an intersection of open sets of the form $\{\widetilde{U} \in \mathbb{R}^X : U(x) > U(y)\}$ – and $E_\succ$ is the inverse image of $\mathcal{U}_\succ$ under a measurable function $\widetilde{U}$.

For any $\succsim \in \mathcal{P}$, define $\mu(\succsim) := \mathbb{P}(E_\succ)$. Since there are no ties, $\mu \in \Delta(\mathcal{P})$. Therefore, we have

$$\rho(x, A) = \mathbb{P}(\{\omega \in \Omega : \widetilde{U}_\omega(x) = \max_{y \in A} \widetilde{U}_\omega(y)\})$$

$$= \mu(\{\succsim \in \mathcal{P} : x \succsim y \text{ for all } y \in A\}). \qquad \square$$

Proposition 1.9 holds for countable X under appropriate definitions (see Cohen (1980)). The equivalence between (ii) and (iii) holds for uncountable X under appropriate technical conditions. For uncountable X, condition (i) is typically modified because preferences are usually assumed to be continuous, which implies that they have nontrivial indifference curves. We will talk more about the infinite case later.

1.6 TIE BREAKING*

Material with an asterisk may be omitted at first reading. If ρ is represented by a distribution over preferences, then ties are ruled out by construction because only strict preferences are realized with positive probability. On the other hand, distribution over utilities and RU in principle allow for ties. But in fact, for choice probabilities to be well-defined, ties must occur with zero probability. To see that, let $T^{xy} := \{\omega \in \Omega : \widetilde{U}_\omega(x) = \widetilde{U}_\omega(y)\}$ be the event in which there is a tie between x and y. As we saw in the proof of Proposition 1.9 if ρ has an RU representation, then it must be that $\mathbb{P}(T^{xy}) = 0$ for all $x \neq y$;

otherwise, $p(x, y) + p(y, x) > 1$ because we are double-counting the event T^{xy}. This means that RU with ties does not lead to a legitimate SCF. I will refer to those RU without ties as as *proper* RU. Formally, $\widetilde{U}$ is *proper* if for any menu $A \in \mathcal{A}$, with probability one $\widetilde{U}$ has a unique maximizer on A.[10]

For various reasons it is sometimes convenient to allow for ties. Let's take a $\widetilde{U}$ that is not proper. One possible way to define p based on $\widetilde{U}$ is to use a tiebreaker. For instance, we could assume that the agent uniformly randomizes over the maximal elements of each menu (*uniform tiebreaking*). This two-stage procedure (maximize $\widetilde{U}$, then break ties uniformly) gives us a well-defined SCF.

A more general notion of tiebreaking was introduced by Gul and Pesendorfer (2006) in the supplement to their paper. A *GP-tiebreaker* is a random utility function $\widetilde{W} : \Omega_W \to \mathbb{R}^X$ that itself is proper. In a random utility representation with a GP tiebreaker, the agent first maximizes $\widetilde{U}$ and then uses $\widetilde{W}$ to break the ties. The state space is now $\Omega \times \Omega_W$ because the tie breaker needs its own state space, as the original one may not be rich enough to allow for a proper W.

Proposition 1.10. *The following are equivalent when X is finite:*

> (i) p has a proper RU representation
> (ii) p has an improper RU representation with uniform tiebreaking
> (iii) p has an improper RU representation with a GP-tiebreaker.

Proof. $(i) \Rightarrow (ii)$: If p has an RU representation, then ties occur with probability zero, so it doesn't matter how we break them.

$(ii) \Rightarrow (iii)$: Uniform tie breaking is equivalent to GP tiebreaking where $\widetilde{W}$ represents a uniform distribution over all strict orders over X.

$(iii) \Rightarrow (i)$: First, rescale $\widetilde{U}$ so that the utility gaps between any two distinct items are larger than one. That is,

$$\widetilde{U}_\omega(x) \neq \widetilde{U}_\omega(y) \Rightarrow |\widetilde{U}_\omega(x) - \widetilde{U}_\omega(y)| \geq 1.$$

Then break any ties according to a rescaled version of $\widetilde{W}$ so that we don't exceed these gaps, that is, for any ω, the maximum difference between two values of $\tilde{U}_\omega$ is strictly less than 1. Finally, note that

$$p(x, A) = \mathbb{P}\left(\{\omega \in \Omega : \tilde{U}_\omega(x) + \tilde{W}_\omega(x) \geq \tilde{U}_\omega(y) + \tilde{W}_\omega(y) \; \forall y \in A\}\right). \quad \square$$

This result makes it sound like it is impossible to know whether randomness in choice reflects the true preference variation or just tiebreaking. In Chapter 8 we will see that it is possible to draw a meaningful distinction between the two in a dynamic model because the two sources of randomness enter differently into the agent's option value calculation (taste variation provides flexibility whereas tiebreaking does not).

---

[10] This property is sometimes called *noncoincidence* (Falmagne, 1983) or *regularity* (Gul and Pesendorfer, 2006).

Instead of using tiebreakers, other papers allow for indifferences by changing the primitive and studying stochastic choice correspondences or capacities: Barberá and Pattanaik (1986); Gul and Pesendorfer (2013); Lu (2016); Lin (2018); Piermont and Teper (2018). To a large extent this approach is "morally equivalent" to assuming tie breakers and I view the choice between them as a matter of convenience.

The issue of ties gets even more subtle when X is "large." Notice that there is another way to define ties: Let $T := \{\omega \in \Omega : \tilde{U}_\omega(x) = \tilde{U}_\omega(y) \text{ for some } x \neq y\}$. This is the event that there is a tie between *some* elements of x. Note that $T = \bigcup_{x \neq y} T^{xy}$ so if X is finite then $\mathbb{P}(T) = 0$ iff $\mathbb{P}(T^{xy}) = 0$ for all $x \neq y$. But with uncountable X, this new definition is too strong. For example, when X is multidimensional and all utilities considered are continuous, then we are forced to have $\mathbb{P}(T) > 0$ because all continuous preferences have well-behaved indifference curves, so for any fixed utility function there will be many points that are indifferent to each other. However, for any two specific points, the probability that they will be indifferent could well still be zero.

1.7 ADDITIVE RANDOM UTILITY

There is an equivalent way of writing random utility, called *additive random utility* (ARU). This involves writing $\tilde{U}(x) = v(x) + \tilde{\epsilon}(x)$, where $v : X \to \mathbb{R}$ is a deterministic utility function, called the "representative utility" or "systematic utility" and $\tilde{\epsilon} : \Omega \to \mathbb{R}^X$ is a "random utility shock," which is private information of the agent.

ARU is the workhorse model in discrete choice econometrics, where the focus is on estimating the function v based on observations of ρ. In game theory, ARU is used as a model of *smoothed best responses* (Fudenberg and Levine, 1998; Hofbauer and Sandholm, 2002).

If X is finite, then I will say that the distribution of $\tilde{\epsilon}$ is *smooth* if it has a density. For infinite X, it is smooth if for any menu $A = \{x_1, \ldots, x_n\}$ the joint distribution of $(\tilde{\epsilon}(x_1), \ldots, \tilde{\epsilon}(x_n))$ has a density. The following definition is based on McFadden (1973).

Definition 1.11. $\rho : \mathcal{A} \to \Delta(X)$ has an *additive random utility* (ARU) representation if it has an RU representation with $\tilde{U}(x) = v(x) + \tilde{\epsilon}(x)$, where $v : X \to \mathbb{R}$ is deterministic and the distribution of $\tilde{\epsilon}$ is smooth.

Note well that the distribution of $\tilde{\epsilon}$ is independent of the menu: For each A we just select the corresponding coordinates.

The smoothness assumption guarantees that we have a proper RU representation, as it implies that ties occur with probability zero. It is worthwhile to notice though that there *are* proper RU representations which are of the form $\tilde{U}(x) = v(x) + \tilde{\epsilon}(x)$ where ϵ has a discrete distribution (take, for example, the one constructed in the proof of (*i*) $\Rightarrow$ (*ii*) in Proposition 1.9). McFadden's (1973) general definition does not require the existence of a density, but as the following result shows, this assumption is without loss of generality. That is, even if we have a discrete distribution over utilities, we can "smoothify" it without affecting the choice probabilities.

Proposition 1.12. *If X is finite then $\rho \sim RU$ if and only if $\rho \sim ARU$.*

The construction used in the following proof shows that it is also without loss of generality to assume that $\tilde{\epsilon}$ has finite moments.

Proof. Let $\rho \sim ARU$, then by definition $\rho \sim RU$. Conversely, assume now that $\rho \sim RU$. By Proposition 1.9, there exists a probability distribution μ over strict preferences $\mathcal{P}$ such that $\rho(x, A) = \mu(N(x, A))$. Let n be the cardinality of X and for any $\succsim \; \in \mathcal{P}$ and $i = 1, \ldots, n$ let $x_{\succsim}(i)$ denote the ith ranked element of X.

Define $v(x) = 0$ for all $x \in X$. We need to find a probability measure $\mathbb{P}$ over $\mathbb{R}^X$ such that $\mathbb{P}(A_{\succsim}) = \mu(\succsim)$ for each event of the type

$$A_{\succsim} = \{\epsilon \in \mathbb{R}^X : \epsilon(x_{\succsim}(1)) > \epsilon(x_{\succsim}(2)) > \cdots > \epsilon(x_{\succsim}(n))\}.$$

To do so, for each $\succsim$ take a probability measure with finite moments and density $\gamma_{\succsim}$ and support equal to the closure of $A_{\succsim}$, for example, a truncated Normal probability distribution. Define our probability measure $\mathbb{P}$ by its density

$$\gamma(\cdot) = \sum_{\succsim \in P} \mu(\succsim)\gamma_{\succsim}(\cdot).$$

This measure has finite moments and a density. $\qquad \square$

ARU representations derive their strength from several powerful parametric special cases where the distribution of ϵ is i.i.d. The most predominant is the extreme value distribution, which leads to *logit*.

Definition 1.13. $\rho : \mathcal{A} \to \Delta(X)$ has a *logit representation* if it has a ARU representation where $\tilde{\epsilon}(x)$ are i.i.d. across x with the Type I Extreme Value (TIEV) distribution, with CDF $G(\epsilon) = \exp(-\exp(-\epsilon))$.[11]

Another well-known model is *probit*, where the distribution of $\tilde{\epsilon}$ is Normal. We will look more at i.i.d. parameterizations in Chapter 3.

Often times it is assumed that the density in an ARU representation not only exists, but is everywhere positive. This ensures that all items are chosen with a positive probability (because arbitrarily large shocks can elevate even dominated alternatives).

Axiom 1.14 (Positivity). $\rho(x, A) > 0$ for any $x \in A$.

This property is important since keeping all probabilities positive leads to a nondegenerate likelihood function, which facilitates estimation of v.

---

[11] TIEV, which is also known as the Gumbel distribution, is actually a whole class of distributions with mean and variance parameters. However, in economics TIEV typically means this particular member of the family.

Moreover, as argued by McFadden (1973), positivity cannot be refuted based on any finite data set.[12]

There are two interpretations of ϵ: (1) preference heterogeneity that is unobserved by the analyst (after conditioning on observable characteristics of the agent), or (2) mistakes/errors on the part of the agent. The difference between the interpretations is that in the first case the preference shocks are embraced by the agent (her tastes do actually change from time to time), while in the second case these shocks lead to choices that the agent disagrees with. While in predictive applications of the static model the two interpretations are largely equivalent, they differ when it comes to normative evaluations and have different predictions for dynamic behavior.

A case that is somewhat in between the two is one of imperfect perception. In the following example the agent sometimes makes mistakes, but they are doing the best they can given their imperfect information. As we will see in Chapter 5 this behavior is Bayes-optimal, so the shocks are embraced by the agent (ex ante) despite sometimes leading to errors.

Example 1.15 (Law of Comparative Judgment). Recall Example 1.5 with weight perception. Thurstone (1927) introduced the probit model to capture such behavior. Suppose that for each weight x the agent forms a subjective, imperfect, and random perception $\gamma(x) + \tilde{\epsilon}(x)$, where γ is a strictly increasing function (typically assumed to be logarithmic) and $\tilde{\epsilon}(x) \sim \mathcal{N}(0, \sigma_\epsilon^2)$ are i.i.d. across x. Faced with items x and y, the agent chooses item x if $\gamma(x) + \epsilon_x \geq \gamma(y) + \epsilon_y$ and chooses y otherwise. A simple calculation reveals that

$$\rho(x, y) = \Phi\left(\frac{\gamma(x) - \gamma(y)}{\sigma_\epsilon \sqrt{2}}\right).$$

Thus, Thurstone's model leads to S-shaped psychometric functions. It is easy to see that by setting $\gamma(x) = \log x$ the model explains diminishing sensitivity. However, it does not explain frequency-dependence because the distribution of ϵ is independent of the distribution of menus $\{x, y\}$.

Finally, the model cannot explain payoff-monotonicity either. This is because $\gamma(x)$ is not the payoff from choosing x, but instead a subjective perception of x. The magnitude of the payoff for guessing correctly does not enter Thurstone's formula. One can view his model as "probit in perceptions" as opposed to "probit in payoffs."[13] $\qquad\triangle$

---

[12] Positivity does not imply that ϵ has positive density (see Example A.1 in the Appendix). Li (2021) shows how to strengthen Positivity to ensure that there exists a ARU representation with positive density.

[13] One could imagine a "probit in payoffs," where it's the payoffs that get distorted. Let $v > 0$ be the payoff of guessing correctly. Then for $x > y$ we have $\tilde{U}(x) = v + \epsilon_x$ and $\tilde{U}(x) = 0 + \epsilon_y$. This leads to payoff-monotonicity, but induces a psychometric function that is a step function (as opposed to S-shaped), so we cannot capture the first two stylized facts. We will need a more fancy model to capture all the stylized facts simultaneously.

While in the most general case RU and ARU coincide, they can lead to very different predictions if the utility is restricted to some specific family. Suppose that our analyst has a theory that the utility function belongs to some class $\mathcal{U}$. RU and ARU suggest different approaches to building a stochastic model. We can either randomize over utilities $u \in \mathcal{U}$ or fix a deterministic utility $v \in \mathcal{U}$ and add stochastic $\tilde{\epsilon}$, where which belongs to some class of distributions $\mathcal{E}$. As we saw before, with $\mathcal{U}$ and $\mathcal{E}$ unrestricted, these two approaches lead to the same class of ρ. But when $\mathcal{U}$ and $\mathcal{E}$ have more structure, often the two induced classes of ρ are disjoint because $v + \epsilon$ does not belong to $\mathcal{U}$. We will see several instances of this: In Chapter 4, we will show that ARU with i.i.d. ϵ leads to "unreasonable" comparative statics in the risk aversion parameter. In Chapter 8, we will show it leads to "unreasonable" option value. In Chapter 10, we will see that it leads to "unreasonable" patterns of substitution.

1.8 SOCIAL SURPLUS

Our analyst often wants to evaluate the agent's welfare. Under RU the natural way to do this is to set

$$V(A) := \mathbb{E}\left[\max_{x \in A} \widetilde{U}(x)\right].$$

This function captures the expected utility from the best item in the menu. McFadden (1973) called it the *social surplus*.[14]

This function is key for dynamic optimization, where the agent evaluates how their current actions impact their own future welfare (Chapters 8 and 12). It also enters into nested logit, where decisions are similarly made in stages (Section 3.4).

Under ARU, we have

$$V(A) := \mathbb{E}\left[\max_{x \in A} v(x) + \tilde{\epsilon}(x)\right].$$

This formula makes sense only if we interpret ϵ as unobservable preference shocks. If we think of them as decision errors of the agent, then there is no reason for them to enter welfare. In this case, it may be more appropriate to treat them as just driving behavior, but evaluate welfare using the undistorted preferences. For example, a formula a la Strotz (1955) would look like:

$$V(A) = \sum_{x \in A} v(x)\rho(x, A).$$

A theory of stochastic choice along these lines has been developed by Ke (2018).

---

[14] This should be called "consumer surplus" because the social surplus also includes the firms.

CHAPTER 2

Basic Properties

2.1 STATISTICAL MODELS

As Proposition 1.12 says, the RU and ARU representations are equivalent in terms of behavior. But these are different *statistical models* because they are parametrized differently. Even distribution over preferences and distribution over utilities are different statistical models because in the first one the parameter is a distribution over strict preferences and in the second one the parameter is the distribution over utility functions. In ARU the parameter is a pair: the deterministic utility function and a distribution over shocks.[1] As we introduce more models, each will be differently parametrized. In general, let Θ be the space of *parameters* and let $(\rho_\theta)_{\theta \in \Theta}$ be the family of SCF's indexed by parameter θ. We hope that the agent's true SCF is a member of this family for some value of θ, otherwise we say that the model is *misspecified*.

To make this concrete, for distribution over preferences $\Theta = \Delta(\mathcal{P})$, for distribution over utilities $\Theta = \Delta(\mathbb{R}^X)$, and for ARU $\Theta = \mathbb{R}^X \times \Delta(\mathbb{R}^X)$, the Cartesian product of the collection of all deterministic utility functions and the collection of all distributions over shocks.

There are three basic questions about (ρ_θ):

(1) *Characterization.* Here we are interested in the image of the mapping $\theta \mapsto \rho_\theta$, that is, the set $\{\rho \in SCF : \rho = \rho_\theta$ for some $\theta \in \Theta\}$. What kinds of distributions over data does the model allow? What things are ruled out? This is where axiomatic decision theory shines: We already saw how Sen's α axiom characterizes deterministic choice and we will see axiomatic characterizations of stochastic choice throughout this book.

(2) *Identification.* Are the parameters pinned down uniquely? If uniqueness fails, then there are some $\theta, \theta' \in \Theta$ such that $\rho_\theta = \rho_{\theta'}$; in that case we can't back out the parameter even if we had infinitely many observations. In econometrics the one-to-one

---

[1] These are infinitely dimensional parameters. In most applications finite-dimensional parameterizations are used.

property of the mapping $\theta \mapsto \rho_\theta$ is called *point-identification*. If this fails, we have *partial identification* and the exercise is to understand the sets of θ that lead to the same ρ (Manski, 2003).

(3) *Comparative statics.* How does ρ_θ change as θ changes? Answering this question helps us understand what the parameter intuitively means. For example, we will see in Chapter 4 that under expected utility, the curvature of the Bernoulli utility function controls the degree of risk aversion.

There are a number of things the analyst can do with her model given a data set.

(4) *Testing the axioms.* Given an axiomatic characterization and a finite amount of data, how much confidence do we have in the fact that our axioms are satisfied? There is some classic literature on this topic and recently there has been is a renewed interest in this question.

(5) *Statistical inference.* Suppose that we have a finite data set. How do we estimate and quantify uncertainty about the parameter θ?

(6) *Counterfactual prediction.* Suppose that you observe choices from menus $A^1, \ldots A^k$ and you want to predict choices from a new menu B. Without a *model* that ties your hands in some way, any probability distribution over B is a legitimate prediction. It is only by assuming a particular model that we can make a connection between behavior across menus. We can trust our prediction only as much as we trust our model (and the data). A frequentist econometrician would estimate the parameter $\hat{\theta}$ on $A^1, \ldots, A^l$ and plug it in to compute $\rho_{\hat{\theta}}(x, B)$. A Bayesian econometrician would look at $\int \rho_\theta(x, B) \hat{\mu}(d\theta)$, where $\hat{\mu}$ is her posterior belief given the data. If the model is not identified, there will be many parameters that match the data, so our predictions will be set-valued (Manski, 2007). On the other hand, if our model is misspecified (i.e., the true ρ does not correspond to ρ_θ for any value of θ), then our prediction may be systematically wrong. We will see this in the blue bus–red bus example (Example 3.11).

We won't talk much about (4), (5), and (6) in this book. These are not trivial topics, but I don't know much about them.

2.2 MAIN AXIOM: REGULARITY

In decision theory we like to characterize a given class of ρ by a list of *axioms*, which are conditions expressed directly in terms of ρ, that is, in the language of observables (agent's choices) and avoid referring to any mathematical representation (e.g., there exists a utility function). This formulation makes axioms directly testable. Because axioms boil down the content of any model to the same language of observables, they can also help us see connections between different models. For example, sometimes models may share an axiom even though their functional forms look very differently.

In Section 1.2 we saw that a deterministic choice function is rationalized by a strict preference if and only if it satisfies Sen's α axiom: For any $x \in A \subseteq B$ if $x = \chi(B)$, then $x = \chi(A)$. The following is a stochastic analogue of Sen's α.

Axiom 2.1 (Regularity). If $x \in A \subseteq B$, then $\rho(x, B) \leq \rho(x, A)$.

This condition is sometimes also called "monotonicity." In the case where ρ is deterministic, it becomes exactly Sen's α (why?). Otherwise, it means that when we add new items to a menu, the choice probability of existing items has to go down to "make room" for new items.[2]

Proposition 2.2 (Block and Marschak, 1960). *If ρ has a random utility representation, then it satisfies Regularity.*

Proof. First note that if x maximizes U on B, then x maximizes U on A (because A is smaller). Thus, for any $x \in A \subseteq B$ we have $N(x, B) \subseteq N(x, A)$. Now, since all probability measures are set-monotone (they attach a bigger probability to bigger sets), we must have $\mu(N(x, B)) \leq \mu(N(x, A))$. □

By analogy to the deterministic case, one would hope that this axiom would be enough to rationalize ρ by random utility. This is true if X has at most three elements, but not more generally.

Proposition 2.3 (Block and Marschak, 1960). *Suppose that $|X| = 3$. If SCF ρ satisfies regularity, then $\rho \sim RU$.*

Proof. Let $X = \{x, y, z\}$. I will write xyz to denote the order $x \succ y \succ z$. With this notation, we have $P = \{xyz, xzy, yxz, yzx, zxy, zyx\}$.

The situation is simple enough that we can define μ "by hand." For example, to define $\mu(xyz)$ note that $N(y, \{y, z\}) = \{xyz, yxz, yzx\}$ and $N(y, X) = \{yxz, yzx\}$. Those two sets differ exactly by what we want, so we can define

$$\mu(xyz) := \rho(y, \{y, z\}) - \rho(y, X).$$

If $\rho \sim RU$, then this is in fact the only way to define μ because $\rho(y, \{y, z\}) = \mu(\{xyz, yxz, yzx\}) = \mu(\{xyz\}) + \mu(\{yxz, yzx\}) = \mu(\{xyz\}) + \rho(y, X)$. We can define μ on the remaining elements of P in the same way.

$$\mu(xzy) := \rho(z, \{y, z\}) - \rho(z, X)$$
$$\mu(yxz) := \rho(x, \{x, z\}) - \rho(x, X)$$
$$\mu(yzx) := \rho(z, \{x, z\}) - \rho(z, X)$$

---

[2] We need a pair of nested sets in our domain for regularity to have bite. For example, we cannot check it when we only observe binary menus. Axioms often lose bite when applied to smaller domains (see De Clippel and Rozen (2021)).

$$\mu(zxy) := \rho(x, \{x, y\}) - \rho(x, X)$$
$$\mu(zyx) := \rho(y, \{x, y\}) - \rho(y, X).$$

Regularity ensures that all six numbers are nonnegative. Moreover, it is easy to see that μ adds up to one.

Finally, to see that μ is a random utility representation of ρ we need to show that $\rho(a, A) = \mu(N(a, A))$ for any $a \in A$. This is also easy to see; for example, $\mu(\{xyz, xzy\}) = \mu(xyz) + \mu(xzy) = [\rho(y, \{y, z\}) - \rho(y, X)] + [\rho(z, \{y, z\}) - \rho(z, X)] = 1 - \rho(y, X) - \rho(z, X) = \rho(x, X)$. Likewise $\mu(\{xyz, xzy, zxy\}) = \mu(xyz) + \mu(xzy) + \mu(zxy) = [\rho(y, \{y, z\}) - \rho(y, X)] + [\rho(z, \{y, z\}) - \rho(z, X)] + [\rho(x, \{x, y\}) - \rho(x, X)] = 1 + \rho(x, \{x, y\}) - 1 = \rho(x, \{x, y\})$. □

There are several well-known violations of Regularity. Each of them is a "paradox" from the point of view of RU: a compelling behavior that cannot be accounted for. Many models have been written to rationalize such paradoxes and we will talk about some of them in future chapters. Regardless of how compelling you find those paradoxes, they are good illustrations of just exactly what the regularity axiom means. This also shows the power of the axiomatic method: To "reject" a model it suffices to show that a very simple condition is violated instead of trying each possible distribution over utilities and establishing that none of them rationalizes the data.

Example 2.4 (Choice overload). Iyengar and Lepper (2000) set up tasting booths in two supermarkets. Customers could taste any number of jams in the tasting booth and were able to eventually buy any variety of jam they wanted. In the first supermarket there were 6 varieties of jam and 30% of the customers purchased some variety. In the second supermarket there were 24 varieties of jam (a superset of those 6) and only 3% of the customers made a purchase. Thus, the probability of choosing the outside option of not buying anything went up as the menu expanded. △

Example 2.5 (Classical Menu Effects). Huber, Payne, and Puto (1982) showed that adding a "decoy" option raises demand for the targeted option. See panel (a) of Figure 2.1, where adding to the menu $\{x, y\}$ any point that is dominated by y but not by x will increase the choice probability of y. Intuitively, adding a decoy makes y shine more by comparison so the agent is more likely to choose it over x. This is known as the *decoy effect* or *asymmetric dominance effect* and is extensively studied in the marketing literature, including situations in which it fails and regularity holds (Huber, Payne, and Puto, 2014). The *compromise effect* is similar to the decoy effect, except like in panel (b) of Figure 2.1 we are now adding an option z that makes y a compromise between x and z so that $\rho(y, \{x, y, z\}) > \rho(y, \{x, y\})$ (Simonson, 1989). △

When there are four or more elements, Regularity is not enough to pin down RU and we need to add other axioms. We will talk about them in the next section, which is optional given that those axioms are more technical. I advise you to skip it on the first reading.

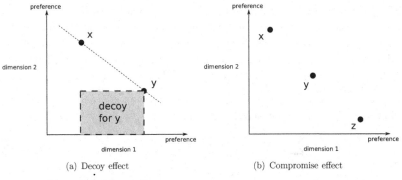

(a) Decoy effect (b) Compromise effect

Figure 2.1 Menu effects.

2.3 MORE AXIOMS*

The axioms that follow are admittedly complicated. Because of this, much of the early work on stochastic choice work was confined the special case of RU called the Luce/logit model, which is characterized by a simple yet restrictive axiom. We will discuss this in Chapter 3. In Chapter 4 we will see that axioms for RU get much simpler in the case where X are lotteries and we assume expected utility.

Recall that $\mathcal{P}$ is the set of strict preferences over X. Note that for each menu A the sets $N(x, A)$ form a partition of $\mathcal{P}$ as x ranges over A (why?). The SCF ρ defines a probability distribution over the cells of this partition. We have as many partitions as there are menus in $\mathcal{A}$. Our axioms on ρ need to ensure that all these probability distributions are consistent with a single $\mu \in \Delta(\mathcal{P})$. This is a lot to ask. Regularity does the job when $|X| = 3$, but is too weak otherwise.

Let's get our hands dirty only a little bit at first. When $|X| = 4$, the additional axiom that we need is still relatively simple.

Axiom 2.6 (Supermodularity). If $x \in A \cap B$, then

$$\rho(x, A) + \rho(x, B) \leq \rho(x, A \cup B) + \rho(x, A \cap B).$$

Supermodularity means that the additional impact on the choice probability of x of adding items to the menu is decreasing in the size of the menu. To see that, let $E := A \setminus B$, $F := A \cap B$, and $G := B \setminus A$ and notice that the condition is equivalent to $\rho(x, E \cup F) - \rho(x, E \cup F \cup G) \leq \rho(x, F) - \rho(x, F \cup G)$.

Proposition 2.7 (Block and Marschak). *Suppose that $|X| = 4$. An SCF ρ satisfies regularity and supermodularity if and only if $\rho \sim RU$.*

The proof is similar to the proof with $|X| = 3$ (see Theorem 5.3 of Block and Marschak (1960)): We want to ensure that the probabilities defined by ρ on the partitions generated by the N-sets extend to a well-defined μ. With more than 3 elements we never get to isolate the probability of a single element in $\mathcal{P}$. This is why we need the additional axiom.

The combinatorial structure of the N-sets gets complicated as the cardinality of X grows. Each time we add an element to X, we need to add another axiom. If we fix x and vary A, then $\rho(x, \cdot)$ defines a function on the collection of all events that contain x. This collection is partially ordered. Regularity says that this function is "decreasing." Supermodularity says that it is "convex." Block and Marschak (1960) proposed an axiom that signs all the "derivatives."

Axiom 2.8 (Block and Marschak). For all $x \in A$

$$q(x, A) := \sum_{B \supseteq A} (-1)^{|B \setminus A|} \rho(x, B) \geq 0.$$

The $q(x, A)$ are called the BM polynomials. Some sources give an equivalent recursive definition: starting from the grand set $q(x, X) := \rho(x, X)$ and

$$q(x, A) := \rho(x, A) - \sum_{B \supsetneq A} q(x, B).$$

Theorem 2.9 (Block and Marschak). *If $\rho \sim RU$, then it satisfies Axiom 2.8.*

As the following proof shows, under RU $q(x, A)$ turns out to be the probability of the event that x is best in A but everything outside of A is better than x. As such, it's probability must be nonnegative.

Proof. This proof is due to Fiorini (2004). We start with a bit of combinatorics. Let $(T, \leq)$ be a finite partially ordered set and suppose a real function $f : T \to \mathbb{R}$ is given. Define the function $F(t) := \sum_{s \geq t} f(s)$, so F is a discrete "integral" of f. Then f is a "derivative" of F and we can recover it by using what is called the *Möbius inversion*: $f(t) = \sum_{s \geq t} m(t, s) F(s)$, where $m : T \times T \to \mathbb{R}$ is the *Möbius function*.

In the case where $(T, \leq)$ is the latice of subsets with $\leq = \subseteq$, the Möbius function equals $m(t, s) = (-1)^{|s| - |t|}$ (see, e.g., Theorem 25.1 and Equation (25.5) of Van Lint and Wilson (2001)).

Now for the actual proof. First, define the sets

$$N^*(x, A) := \{\succsim \in P : z \succ x \succ y \text{ for all } z \in A^c \text{ and } y \in A, y \neq x\}.$$

Observe that $N^*(x, A) \subseteq N(x, A)$ and that $N(x, A) = \bigcup_{B \supseteq A} N^*(x, B)$. Moreover, this union is disjoint. Defining $F(A) := \rho(x, A)$ and $f(B) := \mu(N^*(x, B))$ we get $F(A) = \sum_{B \supseteq A} f(B)$, so by the Möbius inversion we have $f(A) = \sum_{B \supseteq A} (-1)^{|B \setminus A|} F(B)$, that is,

$$\mu(N^*(x, A)) = \sum_{B \supseteq A} (-1)^{|B \setminus A|} \rho(x, B) = q(x, A). \tag{2.1}$$

Given that μ is a probability measure, these sums must be nonnegative. $\quad\square$

In fact, it can be shown (Proposition 7.3 in Chambers and Echenique (2016)) that RU holds if and only if there exists a μ such that (2.1) holds

There are two other axiomatizations of RU. I like them even less, as they explicitly refer to the representation and involve infinite, as opposed to finite, lists of inequalities. In both of them, as the first step you need to compute all the rationalizable deterministic choice functions. The upside is that this approach works on incomplete domains, while the BM approach relies on observing all menus.

The first axiom was developed by McFadden and Richter (1971, 1990); my explanation of it follows Stoye (2019). Take the collection of item-menu pairs $\{(x, A) : x \in X \text{ and } A \in \mathcal{A}\}$; let n be its size. For each preference $\succsim \in \mathcal{P}$ let's form a vector of dimension n equal one if $\succsim$ chooses x from A and zero otherwise; let's denote this vector by $p_{\succsim}$. Now, RU is equivalent to ρ being in the convex hull of those vectors.

Consider any set of points Q in $\mathbb{R}^n$ and another point $r \in \mathbb{R}^n$. It is easy to verify that r is in the convex hull of Q if and only if

$$\langle r, \lambda \rangle \leq \max_{p \in Q} \langle p, \lambda \rangle$$

for all $\lambda \in \mathbb{R}^n$. Now we just need to apply this to $Q = (p_{\succ})_{\succ \in P}$ and $r = \rho$. Actually, it turns out that it suffices to only check $\lambda \in \mathbb{N}^n$, which directly translates to the following axiom.

Axiom 2.10 (Axiom of Revealed Stochastic Preference (ARSP)). For any k and for any sequence $(x_1, A_1), \ldots, (x_k, A_k)$ such that $x_i \in A_i$

$$\sum_{i=1}^{k} \rho(x_i, A_i) \leq \max_{\succsim \in P} \sum_{i=1}^{k} p_{\succ}(x_i, A_i).$$

The second axiom was developed by Clark (1996). This is kind of the flip of the previous exercise. For each $x \in A$ let's now form a long vector with dimension equal to the set of preferences P. Define $p_{(x,A)}$ to be the indicator function of the event $N(x_i, A_i)$.

Axiom 2.11 (Coherency). For any k and any sequence $(x_1, A_1), \ldots, (x_k, A_k)$ such that $x_i \in A_i$, and for any sequence of real numbers $\lambda_1, \ldots, \lambda_k$

$$\sum_{i=1}^{k} \lambda_i p_{(x_i, A_i)} \geq 0 \implies \sum_{i=1}^{k} \lambda_i \rho(x_i, A_i) \geq 0.$$

It's easy to see that Coherency implies the BM axiom, by taking $\lambda_i \in \{-1, 0, 1\}$. The intuition behind Coherency is a no-arbitrage argument. Imagine that $\rho(x_i, A_i)$ is the cost of placing a bet on the event $N(x_i, A_i)$. Suppose that we now have a complex bet on a combination of events that pays off a positive amount in every state of the world. This complex bet must cost a positive amount of money. This axiom is a restatement of de Finetti's coherency condition, which ensures that a set function (here defined over all N-sets) can be extended to a probability measure (over all events) (see, e.g., Pollard (2002)).

Theorem 2.12 (Characterization of RU). *The following conditions are equivalent for an SCF ρ on a finite set X:*

    (i) $\rho \sim RU$
    (ii) ρ *satisfies the BM axiom*
    (iii) ρ *satisfies coherency*
    (iv) ρ *satisfies ARSP.*

Moreover, (iii) and (iv) are equivalent to (i) even if the domain of ρ is arbitrary.

Block and Marschak (1960) showed that their axiom is necessary. Sufficiency was proved by Falmagne (1978) and independently by Barberá and Pattanaik (1986). Other proofs of this theorem can be found in Fiorini (2004) using network flows, Monderer (1992) using cooperative game theory, and Chambers and Echenique (2016) using the Farkas lemma. A version of *(i)–(ii)* for infinite X was discussed by Cohen (1980). The equivalence *(i)–(iii)* was proved by Clark (1996), directly for infinite X. The equivalence *(i)–(iv)* was proved by McFadden and Richter (1990, 1971). A nice and simple proof of this equivalence is in Stoye (2019) and the infinite case was worked out by McFadden (2005) and Gonczarowski, Kominers, and Shorrer (2020).

2.4 UNIQUENESS/IDENTIFICATION

Even though RU and ARU coincide as classes of stochastic choice functions, they differ as statistical models because they are different mappings with different domains. As a result of this, they have different identification properties.

2.4.1 Identification under RU

As we discussed in Chapter 1, since utility is unique only ordinally, we cannot hope to identify its distribution; at best, we can hope to pin down the distribution of ordinal preferences. This is possible when X has only three alternatives.

Proposition 2.13 (Block and Marschak, 1960). *If $|X| \leq 3$, then if μ is a distribution over preferences that represents ρ, then μ is unique.*

Proof. This follows from the proof of Theorem 2.3 because the value of μ on each point of Ω is pinned down uniquely by the choice probabilities, for example, $\mu(xyz) := \rho(y, \{y, z\}) - \rho(y, X)$. $\quad\quad\quad\quad\square$

Unfortunately, with more elements RU is not point-identified. The following example shows two distributions that induce the same SCF.

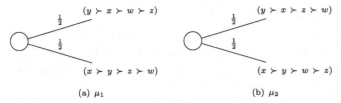

(a) μ_1 (b) μ_2

Figure 2.2 Choice-equivalent, but distinct preference distributions.

Example 2.14 (Fishburn, 1998). Suppose that $X = \{x, y, z, w\}$ and μ_1 and μ_2 are given as in Figure 2.2. Those two probability distributions lead to the same SCF ρ (why?). △

Not only are μ_1 and μ_2 different, but their supports are disjoint. The difficulty here is that although we can determine the probability that x is better than y and the probability that w is better than z, we can't determine the probability of those two events occurring at the same time.[3]

Although the amount of correlation between different rankings is not pinned down, the marginal distributions over the rankings is. In other words, in RU the distribution of preferences is unique *up to* correlations.

Proposition 2.15 (Falmagne 1978). *If μ_1 and μ_2 are two distributions over preferences that represent the same ρ, then for any $x \in X$*

$$\mu_1(x \text{ is kth best in } X) = \mu_2(x \text{ is kth best in } X)$$

for all $k = 1, \ldots, |X|$.

Proof. If μ_1 and μ_2 are RU representations of the same ρ, then they agree on the collection of sets $N(x, A)$. Moreover, as in the proof of Theorem 2.9 we can use the Möbius inversion to show that they agree on the collection of sets $N^*(x, A)$. This yields our desired conclusion because for any $k = 1, \ldots, |X|$

$$\{\succsim \in P : x \text{ is kth best in } X\} = \bigcup_{A \in \mathcal{A}: x \in A, |A| = |X| - k + 1} N^*(x, A). \qquad \square$$

Notice that in fact there is a stronger sense of uniqueness: The probabilities of all N^* sets are identified.

---

[3] McClellon (2015) shows that non-uniqueness occurs in all RU that have a full support distribution. Turansick (2021) characterizes exactly when uniqueness occurs. Moreover, he shows that uniqueness of the distribution occurs if and only if its support is unique.

2.4.2 Identification under ARU

The parametrization of ARU involves a deterministic utility function v and a distribution over $\tilde{\epsilon}$. It turns out that without additional assumptions, the utility is not identified at all (even ordinally). This is perhaps not very surprising because we can just absorb any v into $\tilde{\epsilon}$ by defining

$$\tilde{\epsilon}_2(x) := v_1(x) - v_2(x) + \tilde{\epsilon}_1(x).$$

Remarkably, v is completely nonidentified even if we restrict the mean of ϵ to be a zero vector. This was shown in a binary model by Manski (1988) and in general by Koning and Ridder (2003).[4]

Proposition 2.16. *Suppose that X is finite. If $\rho \sim ARU(v_1, \tilde{\epsilon}_1)$, then for any $v_2 \in \mathbb{R}^X$ there exists $\tilde{\epsilon}_2$ with $\mathbb{E}\tilde{\epsilon}_2 = 0$ such that $\rho \sim ARU(v_2, \tilde{\epsilon}_2)$.*

Moreover, for a fixed v the correlation structure of $\tilde{\epsilon}$ is not pinned down. For example, we can take i.i.d. $\tilde{\epsilon}$ and shift it by a common (same for all x) random variable $\tilde{\eta}$ to make it as correlated as we want.

Proposition 2.17. *If $\rho \sim ARU(v, \tilde{\epsilon})$, then for any random variable $\tilde{\eta} : \Omega \to \mathbb{R}$ we have $\rho \sim ARU(v, \tilde{\epsilon}')$ where $\tilde{\epsilon}'_\omega(x) = \tilde{\epsilon}_\omega(x) + \tilde{\eta}_\omega$.*

Proof. The result follows because

$$v(x) + \tilde{\epsilon}_\omega(x) \geq v(y) + \tilde{\epsilon}_\omega(y) \text{ for all } y \in A, \omega \in \Omega$$

iff

$$v(x) + \tilde{\epsilon}_\omega(x) + \tilde{\eta}_\omega \geq v(y) + \tilde{\epsilon}_\omega(y) + \tilde{\eta}_\omega \text{ for all } y \in A, \omega \in \Omega. \qquad \square$$

The identification result is much improved within the i.i.d. class. I discuss this in the next chapter (Proposition 3.10). Another way to vastly improve identification is to add product attributes (Section 10.3).

---

[4] Their Theorem 1 does not state the restriction $\mathbb{E}\tilde{\epsilon}_2 = 0$ but their proof actually delivers it.

CHAPTER 3

More Models and Properties

3.1 LOGIT OR LUCE MODEL

3.1.1 Logit

Logit is a special case of ARU where $\tilde{\epsilon}(x)$ have an i.i.d. TIEV distribution (Definition 1.13). Logit leads to a very simple specification of choice probabilities.

Theorem 3.1 (Holman and Marley). *If ρ is logit, then*

$$\rho(x, A) = \frac{e^{v(x)}}{\sum_{y \in A} e^{v(y)}}.$$

This makes logit very tractable and is why logit has been a workhorse model for estimation.

3.1.2 Luce

An equivalent model was introduced by Luce (1959). Here $\mathbb{R}_{++}$ is the set of positive real numbers.

Definition 3.2. ρ has a *Luce representation* if there exists a function $w : X \to \mathbb{R}_{++}$ such that for all $A \in \mathcal{A}$

$$\rho(x, A) = \frac{w(x)}{\sum_{z \in A} w(z)}.$$

Here, $w(x)$ is interpreted as the perceived strength of the stimulus x and choice probabilities are proportional to those perceptions.

Notice that the function w is unique up to multiplication by positive numbers. Likewise, the function v in logit is unique up to adding a constant.

Many decision theory models build on the Luce-logit model.[1] One cost of its tractability is that it makes very strong assumptions about the substitution

---

[1] To mention a few, the random consideration model of Manzini and Mariotti (2014), the attribute rule model of Gul, Natenzon, and Pesendorfer (2014), and the additive perturbed utility model of Fudenberg, Iijima, and Strzalecki (2015).

patterns between products. One example is the famous red bus–blue bus problem, which is actually a problem for all i.i.d. ARU models; we will discuss this in Section 3.2.3.

3.1.3   Axioms

Mathematically, the probability distribution on A is the conditional of the probability distribution on the grand set X. This makes it possible to characterize the model by very a simple axiom.

Axiom 3.3 (Luce's IIA). For all $x, y \in A \cap B$ whenever the probabilities are positive

$$\frac{\rho(x, A)}{\rho(y, A)} = \frac{\rho(x, B)}{\rho(y, B)}.$$

This axiom says that the ratio of the choice probabilities of x and y does not depend on what other elements are in the menu. Hausman and McFadden (1984) propose a statistical test of the axiom: If we estimate the model twice, on a full set of alternatives and on a subset, then under IIA the two estimates should not be statistically different.

An equivalent version of this axiom is the following product rule.[2] We will write $\rho(A, B) := \sum_{x \in A} \rho(x, B)$ whenever $A \subseteq B$. This is the probability that something from A gets chosen from the menu B.

Axiom 3.4 (Luce's Choice Axiom). For all $x \in A \subseteq B$

$$\rho(x, B) = \rho(x, A)\rho(A, B).$$

Theorem 3.5. *The following are equivalent for any set X:*

(i) ρ *satisfies Luce's IIA and positivity*
(ii) ρ *satisfies Luce's Choice Axiom and positivity*
(iii) ρ *has a Luce representation w*
(iv) ρ *has a logit representation $v(x) = \log(w(x))$.*

3.1.4   The Noise Parameter

Sometimes we want to scale the variance of the extreme-value shocks $\tilde{\epsilon}$. In *logit with noise parameter* λ we set $\tilde{U}(x) := v(x) + \lambda \tilde{\epsilon}_x$, where $\tilde{\epsilon}_x$ are i.i.d. TIEV. This leads to the choice probabilities:

$$\rho(x, A) = \frac{e^{v(x)/\lambda}}{\sum_{y \in A} e^{v(y)/\lambda}}. \tag{3.1}$$

---

[2] These two axioms are equivalent with or without positivity (Cerreia-Vioglio, Maccheroni, Marinacci, and Rustichini, 2017). Other models that obtain a Luce-like representation without positivity are Echenique and Saito (2019), Ahumada and Ülkü (2018), and Horan (2021).

If we let $\lambda \to 0$, then ρ converges to a deterministic choice function that is the argmax of v (ties are broken uniformly). On the other hand, as $\lambda \to \infty$ choice from any menu becomes uniform. In machine learning, Equation (3.1) is known as the *softmax*.

3.1.5 Social Surplus

Logit has a nice closed-form "log-sum" expression for social surplus (Section 1.8).[3]

Proposition 3.6. *In logit with noise parameter λ the social surplus equals*

$$V_\lambda(A) = \lambda \log \left(\sum_{x \in A} \exp(v(x)/\lambda) \right). \tag{3.2}$$

Note that as we increase the number of goods, the consumer welfare grows without bound.

3.1.6 Another form of IIA*

Luce's IIA has a cardinal feel to it (we require products or ratios of probabilities to be equal to each other). Gul, Natenzon, and Pesendorfer (2014) consider an ordinal axiom that says that the *ranking* of probabilities does not change when adding/taking away other alternatives. This axiom relies only on ordinal information; the exact magnitudes of choice probabilities do not matter.

Axiom 3.7 (GNP's IIA). If $A \cup B$ and $C \cup D$ are disjoint, then

$$\rho(A, A \cup C) \geq \rho(B, B \cup C) \implies \rho(A, A \cup D) \geq \rho(B, B \cup D).$$

The dagger symbol † means I am not stating all technical details. A serious reader will want to consult the original paper.

Theorem[†] 3.8 (Gul, Natenzon, and Pesendorfer, 2014). *In the presence of a richness condition, ρ satisfies GNP's IIA iff $\rho \sim$ Luce.*

3.2 I.I.D. ARU

3.2.1 The Model

Under logit, $\tilde{\epsilon}(x)$ are i.i.d. across $x \in X$, distributed TIEV. Thurstone's model from Example 1.15 had i.i.d. Normal distributions. We will now allow all distributions. Axiomatizing the general class is an open question.

Definition 3.9. $\rho \sim i.i.d.$ *ARU if* $\rho \sim ARU(v, \tilde{\epsilon})$ *where* $\tilde{\epsilon}(x)$ *and* $\tilde{\epsilon}(y)$ *are i.i.d. for every* $x \neq y$.

---

[3] For a history of this expression, see De Jong, Daly, Pieters, and Van der Hoorn (2007).

Recall that $\rho(x,y)$ denotes the probability that x is chosen over y, that is, $\rho(x,\{x,y\})$. If $\tilde{\epsilon}(x)$ are i.i.d. then we have

$$
\begin{aligned}
\rho(x,y) &= \mathbb{P}\big(v(x) + \tilde{\epsilon}(x) \geq v(y) + \tilde{\epsilon}_y\big) \\
&= \mathbb{P}\big(\tilde{\epsilon}(y) - \tilde{\epsilon}(x) \leq v(x) - v(y)\big) = F\big(v(x) - v(y)\big),
\end{aligned} \tag{3.3}
$$

where F is the CDF of the symmetric random variable $\tilde{\eta} := \tilde{\epsilon}(y) - \tilde{\epsilon}(x)$. Models with such a representation for pairwise choices are called *Fechnerian*; we will discuss them later in this chapter.

3.2.2 Identification

The i.i.d. ARU has very clean identification properties.

Proposition 3.10. *Suppose that ρ has two i.i.d. ARU representations with positive density: $(v_1, \tilde{\epsilon}_1)$ and $(v_2, \tilde{\epsilon}_2)$. Let F_i be the CDF of $\tilde{\epsilon}_i(x) - \tilde{\epsilon}_i(y)$. If the range of v_1 is a nontrivial interval, then there exist $\alpha > 0, \beta$ such that $v_2 = \alpha v_1 + \beta$ and $F_2(t) = F_1(\alpha^{-1}t)$ for all $t \in \{v_2(x) - v_2(y) : x, y \in X\}$.*

Proof. See Appendix A.3.2. $\qquad\qquad\qquad\qquad\qquad\qquad\qquad\qquad\square$

The proposition says that if there is enough variation in v, then v is unique up to a positive affine transformation and the distribution of ϵ differences is unique up to a multiplicative factor. Notice that identification occurs only within the i.i.d. ARU class; by Proposition 2.16 $(v, \tilde{\epsilon})$ is not identified within the ARU class.

Does knowing F pin down the distribution of $\tilde{\epsilon}$? Of course, the mean of $\tilde{\epsilon}$ cancels out, so we won't be able to pin it down. How about pinning down the distribution modulo the mean? This is true within some special classes of distributions, such as Normal, but not in general.[4] I do not know what are the exact uniqueness properties of the distribution of $\tilde{\epsilon}$ outside of these classes.

3.2.3 Blue Bus–Red Bus

The following paradox was originally conceived by Debreu (1960) as a critique of Luce's IIA. It actually applies to all i.i.d. ARU models. McFadden adapted his example to transportation choices.

Example 3.11. People can commute by a train or a bus. There are two kinds of buses: a blue bus–red bus. So $X = \{t, bb, rb\}$. Suppose that we observed that $\rho(t, bb) = \rho(t, rb) = \rho(bb, rb) = \frac{1}{2}$. If $\rho \sim$ i.i.d. ARU, then by formula (3.3) we infer that $v(t) = v(bb) = v(rb)$ and predict that $\rho(t, X) = \frac{1}{3}$.

---

[4] This is the subject of *decomposition theory* (see Loève (1978)). Feller (1957) gives an example of two symmetric distributions that lead to the same F, yet differ by more than just the scaling of v (this is number iii of his Curiosities on page 506). I thank Jetlir Duraj for pointing me to this example. These are not full support distributions but perhaps such counterexamples also exist.

But this doesn't make much sense if you think that the main choice is between the modes of transportation (train or bus) and the bus color is just an icing on the cake. In that case we would like to have $\rho(t, X) = \frac{1}{2}$. (If you are still not convinced, imagine that there n colors of buses. Would you insist on $\rho(t, X) \to 0$ as $n \to \infty$? If people behaved this way, a firm could capture the whole market by introducing a bunch of new products that are virtually identical to each other.) $\triangle$

This is a paradox for i.i.d. ARU because in that model all three modes of transportation must be indifferent in terms of v. But really they are not indifferent, and the i.i.d. model just doesn't have enough degrees of freedom to capture this. More generally, i.i.d. ARU with positive density satisfies the following axiom.

Axiom 3.12 (Interchangeability). If $\rho(x, y) = 0.5$, then $\rho(x, z) = \rho(y, z)$ for all $z \neq x, y$.

This is precisely what goes wrong in Example 3.11. From the fact that $\rho(t, bb) = 0.5$ we should not infer that those two are interchangeable. They could be very different objects that have different substitution patterns with a third object rb. However, i.i.d. ARU models squish all of this onto a one-dimensional scale. This might make sense for perception of weight and other physical stimuli, but it is too simplistic to capture economic demand.

Note that this is a paradox only for i.i.d. ARU, not for RU in general. Here is a very simple RU that gives the desired choice probabilities.

Example 3.13. Let $X = \{bb, rb, t\}$. Let μ assign weight $\frac{1}{4}$ to each of the following four orderings:

$$t \succ bb \succ rb$$
$$t \succ rb \succ bb$$
$$bb \succ rb \succ t$$
$$rb \succ bb \succ t$$

Then each pairwise choice is fifty-fifty, but $\rho(bb, X) = \rho(rb, X) = \frac{1}{4}$ and $\rho(t, X) = \frac{1}{2}$.

The above RU implicitly introduces correlation between ϵ. But in fact, these choice probabilities can be explained by ARU with independent but not identical distribution of ϵ. To see that, let $v = 0$ and ϵ_t equal $+10$ or -10 with equal probabilities, ϵ_{bb} equal $+1$ or -1 with equal probability and $\epsilon_{rb} = 0$. (I owe this example to Christopher Turansick.) $\triangle$

3.3 MIXED LOGIT

Mixed logit is an average of logits with different v functions.

Definition 3.14. ρ has a *mixed-logit* representation if there exists a probability measure α over functions $v : X \to \mathbb{R}$ such that

$$\rho(x,A) = \int \frac{e^{v(x)}}{\sum_{y \in A} e^{v(y)}} \alpha(dv).$$

Every ρ with a mixed logit representation must have an RU representation (since every logit has one and a mixed logit is just another randomization over those). Conversely, if ρ has an RU representation, then it can be approximated by a sequence of mixed logits (in other words, mixed-logit is *dense* in RU).

Proposition 3.15. *If $\rho \sim RU$, then there exists a sequence $\rho^n \sim$ mixed logit, such that $\rho^n(x,A) \rightarrow \rho(x,A)$ for all $A \in \mathcal{A}$ and $x \in A$.*

Intuitively, every ρ that has an RU representation is by definition a mixture of deterministic choice functions and each of those deterministic choice functions is a limit of logit choice functions with noise going to zero (Section 3.1.4).

Proof. Suppose that X is finite and let $\mu \in \Delta(\mathcal{P})$ represent ρ. For any $\succsim \in \mathcal{P}$ pick a utility function v that represents it. For any n define the logit $\rho_v^n(x,A) := \frac{\exp(nv(x))}{\sum_{y \in A} \exp(nv(y))}$. Define the mixed logit $\rho^n(x,A) := \sum_v \rho_v^n(x,A)\mu(v)$. Define $\rho_v^*(x,A)$ to be one if x is the argmax of v over A and zero otherwise (this a well defined SCF because v is one-to-one). Note that $\lim_{n \to \infty} \rho_v^n(x,A) = \rho_v^*(x,A)$. Thus,

$$\rho(x,A) = \sum_v \rho_v^*(x,A)\mu(v)$$

$$= \lim_{n \to \infty} \sum_v \rho_v^n(x,A)\mu(v) = \lim_{n \to \infty} \rho^n(x,A).$$

For arbitrary X, see Theorem 3 of Gul, Natenzon, and Pesendorfer (2014). In Chapter 10 we will see a similar result by McFadden and Train (2000).   □

In fact, there is nothing special about logit in the theorem above. The mixed i.i.d. probit is also dense in RU, and so is any other i.i.d. ARU model.

Notice that we could think of mixed-logit as a random v function $\tilde{v} : \Omega \times X \rightarrow \mathbb{R}$ so that $\rho(x,A) = \mathbb{E}\left[\frac{e^{\tilde{v}(x)}}{\sum_{y \in A} e^{\tilde{v}(y)}}\right]$. Even though you could call $\tilde{v}$ a random utility, note that $\tilde{v}$ is *not* an RU representation of this ρ. The RU representation of ρ is $\tilde{U}(x) = \tilde{v}(x) + \tilde{\epsilon}(x)$ where $\tilde{\epsilon}(x)$ is i.i.d. TIEV.

Mixed logit suggests a general class of *mixture models*. Suppose that we have a class $\mathcal{C}$ of ρ's. A mixed-$\mathcal{C}$ model contains all ρ that can be written as $\rho(x,A) = \sum_{i=1}^n \alpha_i\rho_i(x,A)$ such that $\alpha_i \geq 0$, $\sum_{i=1}^n \alpha_i = 1$, and $\rho_i \in \mathcal{C}$ (or an integral more generally). For example, if $\mathcal{C}$ is the class of deterministic choice functions that satisfy Sen's α condition, then the class of mixed $\mathcal{C}$ equals the RU class. We get mixed logit if $\mathcal{C}$ is the logit class. RU is closed under mixtures, whereas logit and i.i.d. ARU are not (Apesteguia and Ballester, 2017a).

3.4 NESTED LOGIT

This is an older solution to the blue bus–red bus paradox. Imagine that instead of a one-shot choice from $\{t, bb, rb\}$ the agent is choosing first from $\{t, b\}$ and then conditional on choosing b the choice is between $\{bb, rb\}$, like in Figure 3.1.

It's clear how to model the second step within the logit framework, but to assign probabilities in the first stage we need to define the value of the menu $\{bb, rb\}$ so that we can compare it with the value of $\{t\}$. The idea is to use expected utility, that is, the social surplus:

$$V_\lambda(A) := \mathbb{E}\left[\max_{x \in A} v(x) + \lambda\epsilon(x)\right] = \lambda \log\left(\sum_{x \in A} \exp(v(x)/\lambda)\right).$$

Intuitively, when evaluating the menu A, the agent does not yet know the realizations of $\epsilon(x)$ for $x \in A$. They think that for each possible realization they will choose the optimal item in the menu and $V(A)$ is the expected value of this optimal strategy. In the context of nested logit, this expression is called the "inclusive value" (McFadden, 1981).

Formally, *rho* is *nested logit* the set of alternatives is partitioned into nests $B_1, \ldots, B_k$. The conditional probability of choosing x from a nest B_i is

$$\frac{\exp(v(x)/\lambda_2)}{\sum_{y \in B_i}(\exp v(y)/\lambda_2)}$$

and the probability of choosing nest i in the initial stage is

$$\frac{\exp(V_{\lambda_2}(B_i)/\lambda_1)}{\sum_{l=1}^{k} \exp(V_{\lambda_2}(B_l)/\lambda_1)},$$

where λ_1, λ_2 are the noise parameters for stage 1 and stage 2 respectively.[5]

Whereas in the basic logit model all ϵ are independent, nested logit can be thought of as allowing for correlation of ϵ within the nest (but not across the nest).

While nesting seems like a nice approach, the analyst has to decide about the nest structure. The advantage of mixed logit is that the correlation structure between utilities of different goods is being estimated instead of being imposed by the analyst upfront. Other approaches include Gul, Natenzon, and

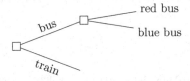

Figure 3.1 A nested decision problem.

[5] Nested logit is consistent with RU iff $\lambda_1 \geq \lambda_2$ (McFadden (1978)).

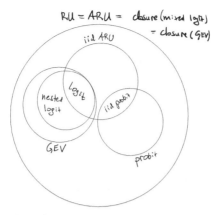

Figure 3.2 A categorization of models with correlated ϵ.

Pesendorfer's (2014) model in which (generalized) nests are revealed from data. Axioms for nested logit are given by Fudenberg, Iijima, and Strzalecki (2014) and Kovach and Tserenjigmid (2022a).

3.5 OTHER MODELS OF CORRELATED ϵ*

Mixed logit and nested logit implicitly allow ϵ to be correlated. There are a few other models that do that. Figure 3.2 illustrates their relationship.

3.5.1 Multivariate Probit

Here $\epsilon \sim \mathcal{N}(0, \Sigma)$ where Σ is the variance-covariance matrix, so we are confronting the correlation issue head-on. Closed forms for choice probabilities are missing, so this literature relies on simulation (see Chapter 5 of Train, 2009).

3.5.2 GEV

Nested logit can be represented as ARU where the $\tilde{\epsilon}$ are correlated. This distribution belongs to the class of generalized extreme value distributions proposed by McFadden (1981), which allows for even more flexible substitution patterns. Like mixed logit, GEV is dense in RU (Dagsvik, 1995). For more, see Appendix A.3.1.

3.6 FECHNERIAN MODELS

Fechnerian models come from the psychometric tradition, where choice randomness is often interpreted as decision error or discrimination error (see Examples 1.5 and 1.15). Whether ρ is Fechnerian or not depends only on its restriction to binary menus.

Definition 3.16. We say that ρ has a *Fechnerian* representation if there exist real functions $v : X \to \mathbb{R}$ and $F : D \to \mathbb{R}$ such that

$$\rho(x, y) = F\big(v(x) - v(y)\big).$$

where $D := \{v(x) - v(y) : x, y \in X\}$, F is strictly increasing and symmetric, that is, $F(-k) = 1 - F(k)$ for all $k \in D$.[6]

In a perception task x is the true stimulus strength and $v(x)$ is the perceived stimulus strength. An S-shaped F leads to an S-shaped psychometric function.

A canonical Fechnerian model is i.i.d. ARU model with positive density. This follows from Equation (3.3) where we take F to be the CDF of the ϵ difference. In fact, when X is finite, all Fechnerian models can be written this way. For infinite X the Fechnerian class is richer because not every F is decomposable as a difference of two i.i.d. random variables.[7] In general, RU is not Fechnerian (Marschak, 1959).

There are a couple of important models that look Fechnerian but where the F function is not strictly increasing and is instead a step-function.

Example 3.17 (Just-noticable Difference). There is a number $\delta > 0$ such that

$$F(t) = \begin{cases} 0 & \text{if } t < -\delta \\ 0.5 & \text{if } -\delta < t < \delta \\ 1 & \text{if } t > \delta, \end{cases}$$

This F is plotted in panel (a) of Figure 3.3. This is the old psychology model of *just-noticable difference*. Here, the agent perfectly distinguishes the objects if they are far enough, but can't distinguish them at all otherwise. These are known as *semiorders* (Luce, 1956). This is the language in wich the orignal Weber Law was formulated (see footnote 8). A weaker class of *interval orders* allows for δ to depend on the alternatives. A recent extension to choice from bigger menus makes δ dependent on the size of the menu (Frick, 2016). $\triangle$

Example 3.18 (The Constant-Error Model). There is a number $0 < \pi < \frac{1}{2}$ such that

$$F(t) = \begin{cases} \pi & \text{if } t < 0 \\ 0.5 & \text{if } t = 0 \\ 1 - \pi & \text{if } t > 0. \end{cases}$$

This F is plotted in panel (b) of Figure 3.3. Here, the agent makes a mistake with a fixed probability p, regardless of how serious this mistake is (Harless and Camerer, 1994). $\triangle$

---

[6] In the early literature this model was sometimes called the *strong utility* model and its special case Luce was called the *strict utility* model.
[7] For example, the uniform distribution is not decomposable (see Example A.2 in the Appendix).

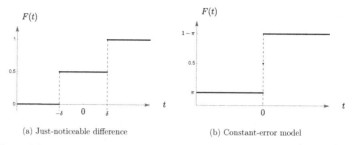

(a) Just-noticeable difference   (b) Constant-error model

Figure 3.3 Examples of F that is not Fechnerian.

Turning back to models that are Fechnerian, the reader can easily check that the following axiom is necessary (Davidson and Marschak, 1959).

Axiom 3.19 (Quadruple Condition).

$\rho(x, y) \geq \rho(w, z)$ if and only if $\rho(x, w) \geq \rho(y, z)$

Debreu (1958) proved that this axiom is also sufficient if a richness condition (sometimes called *solvability* or *stochastic continuity*) is assumed. This condition implies that X is infinite.

Axiom 3.20 (Richness). If $\rho(x, y) \leq \alpha \leq \rho(z, y)$, then there exists $w \in X$ such that $\rho(w, y) = \alpha$.

This theorem uses our convention that $\rho(x, x) = \frac{1}{2}$ for all x.

Theorem 3.21 (Debreu 1958). *Suppose that ρ satisfies Richness. It has a continuous Fechnerian representation if and only if it satisfies the Quadruple condition. Moreover, if (v_1, F_1) and (v_2, F_2) both represent ρ, then there exists $\alpha > 0$ and $\beta \in \mathbb{R}$ such that:*

$$v_2(x) = \alpha v_1(x) + \beta \text{ for all } x \in X,$$
$$F_2(\alpha t) = F_1(t) \text{ for all } t \in D_1,$$

where $D_1 = \{v_1(x) - v_1(y) : x, y, \in X\}$.

Proof. In Appendix A.3.3 I show how this follows from Debreu's theorem. □

Scott (1964) axiomatized the model for finite X.

Axiom 3.22 (Acyclicity). For all n, all sequences $x_1, \ldots, x_n, y_1, \ldots, y_n$ and all bijections $f, g : \{1, \ldots, n\} \rightarrow \{1, \ldots, n\}$

$$\rho(x_k, y_k) \geq \rho(x_{f(k)}, y_{g(k)}) \quad \text{for } 1 \leq k < n$$

implies

$$\rho(x_n, y_n) \leq \rho(x_{f(n)}, y_{g(n)}).$$

The simplest way to understand why the axiom is necessary is to plug it into the representation and see what happens. I invite you to do this right now.

Theorem 3.23 (Scott). *p has a Fechnerian representation if and only if it satisfies the Quadruple condition and Acyclicity.*

Proof. See Appendix A.3.4.   □

3.7 STOCHASTIC TRANSITIVITY*

We say that x is stochastically preferred to y, denoted $x \succsim^* y$, if x is more frequently chosen than y in pairwise choice, that is, $p(x,y) \geq 0.5$. Suppose that $x \succsim^* y$ and $y \succsim^* z$. What can we conclude about the frequency of choices between x and z? Let $p := p(x,y) \geq 0.5$, $q := p(y,z) \geq 0.5$, and $r = p(x,z)$. We have:

- *weak stochastic transitivity* (WST) if $r \geq 0.5$
- *moderate stochastic transitivity* (MST) if $r \geq \min\{p,q\}$
- *strong stochastic transitivity* (SST) if $r \geq \max\{p,q\}$.

WST is the same thing as transitivity of the relation $\succsim^*$. In general, WST does not imply RU and RU can violate WST, as the following example shows.

Example 3.24 (Condorcet Paradox). Let $X = \{x,y,z\}$. Let μ assign weight $\frac{1}{3}$ to each of the following three orderings:

$$x \succ y \succ z$$
$$y \succ z \succ x$$
$$z \succ x \succ y$$

Then we have $p(x,y) = p(y,z) = p(z,x) = \frac{2}{3}$, a violation of WST. If we interpret μ as a population of agents and p as recording their vote fractions in a pairwise election then we have what is called the Condorcet cycle.   △

Another popular example formulates this idea in the language of distribution over utilities.

Example 3.25 (Intransitive Dice). Consider the following three dies:

die x with sides $2, 2, 4, 4, 9, 9$

die y with sides $1, 1, 6, 6, 8, 8$

die z with sides $3, 3, 5, 5, 7, 7$.

Then $p(x,y) = p(y,z) = p(z,x) = \frac{2}{3}$.   △

This may make you relatively uninterested in WST and even stronger properties. But prominent models satisfy them and they are a point of reference in the literature. Notice for instance that WST is satisfied in Fechnerian models because $\rho(x, y) \geq 0.5$ iff $v(x) \geq v(y)$. Fechnerian models not only satisfy WST, but also SST (why?). In fact, SST is satisfied by a wider class.

Definition 3.26. ρ has a *simple scalability* representation if

$$\rho(x, y) = H(v(x), v(y))$$

for some function $v : X \to \mathbb{R}$ and function $H : D \times D \to \mathbb{R}$ such that $D = v(X)$ and H is strictly increasing in the first argument and strictly decreasing in the second argument and symmetric $H(s, t) = 1 - H(t, s)$.

Of course, Fechnerian representations are a special case. Simply scalable ρs are characterized by a slight strengthening of SST.

Axiom 3.27 (SST$^+$). ρ satisfies SST and a strict inequality in both hypotheses implies a strict inequality in the conclusion.

There are two alternative axioms that characterize simple scalability.

Axiom 3.28 (Substitutability).

$$\rho(x, z) \geq \rho(y, z) \text{ iff } \rho(x, y) \geq 0.5.$$

Axiom 3.29 (Tversky's IIA).

$$\rho(x, z) \geq \rho(y, z) \text{ iff } \rho(x, w) \geq \rho(y, w).$$

Note that Tversky's IIA is a singleton version of GNP's IIA (Axiom 3.7).

Proposition 3.30 (Tversky and Russo 1969). *The following are equivalent for any binary ρ that satisfies Positivity:*

    (i) ρ satisfies SST$^+$
    (ii) ρ satisfies Substitutability
    (iii) ρ satisfies Tversky's IIA
    (iv) ρ has a simple scalability representation.

A characterization of a slightly stronger version of MST was recently obtained by He and Natenzon (2024). These are the models that are represented by *moderate utility*, where

$$\rho(x, y) = F\left(\frac{v(x) - v(y)}{d(x, y)}\right)$$

for some $v : X \to \mathbb{R}$, distance metric $d : X \times X \to \mathbb{R}_+$, and $F : \mathbb{R} \to [0, 1]$ strictly increasing transformation, defined on an appropriate domain, that satisfies $F(t) = 1 - F(-t)$.

Axiom 3.31 (MST$^+$). If $\rho(x, y) \geq 0.5$ and $\rho(y, z) \geq 0.5$, then $\rho(x, z) > \min\{\rho(x, y), \rho(y, z)\}$ or $\rho(x, z) = \rho(x, y) = \rho(y, z)$.

Proposition 3.32 (He and Natenzon 2024). *If X is finite, then ρ satisfies MST^+ if and only if it has a Moderate Utility representation.*

He and Natenzon (2024) also obtain a representation for WST similar to Moderate Utility, but where d is a distance semimetric (does not need to satisfy the triangle inequality).

The final axiom that we will consider in this section is known as the triangle axiom.

Axiom 3.33 (Triangle). For any three distinct $x, y, z \in X$

$$\rho(x, y) + \rho(y, z) \geq \rho(x, z).$$

Marschak (1959) thought that Triangle is necessary and sufficient for RU on binary menus but in fact it is only necessary (see Cohen and Falmagne (1990), Gilboa (1990), and Marley (1990)). Sprumont (2020) shows that if ρ satisfies Triangle, then it has an extension to all menus that satisfies Regularity.

Rieskamp, Busemeyer, and Mellers (2006) discuss experimental evidence on stochastic transitivity. From a theoretical point of view, it is reasonable to expect stochastic transitivity in some applications, such as in one-dimensional perception tasks. But in settings with richer substitution patterns, such as the blue bus–red bus example (Example 3.11), we should not be surprised to see violations. Likewise, if we know that ρ represents aggregate behavior, then we should not expect WST to hold because Condorcet cycles might exist (Example 3.24).

3.8 PERTURBED UTILITY*

Definition 3.34. ρ has a *perturbed utility* (PU) representation if for each A the probability $\rho(\cdot, A)$ solves

$$\max_{p \in \Delta(A)} \sum_{x \in A} v(x)p(x) - c(p),$$

where $v \in \mathbb{R}^X$ is a deterministic utility function and $c : \Delta(X) \to (-\infty, \infty]$ is the cost of implementing the probability mixture p.

The leading interpretation is that c is the implementation cost van Damme (1991). The agent implements their choices with an error (trembling hands) that can be controlled at a cost. A commonly used example is where c equals the negative entropy $-H$ (Stahl, 1990; Fudenberg and Levine, 1995).

Definition 3.35. *Entropy* is defined as $H(p) = -\sum_{x \in X} p(x) \log p(x)$ with the condition that $0 \cdot \log 0 = 0$.

The more chaotic is the p, the higher is its entropy $H(p)$. A uniform p has the highest entropy. That's the cheapest thing for our agent to implement, but their utility function v will be pulling them in a specific direction.

Interestingly, if cost equals the negative entropy, then this is observationally equivalent to logit.

Proposition 3.36 (Rockafellar 1970; Anderson, de Palma, and Thisse 1992). *The following are equivalent:*

(i) ρ *has a logit representation with utility* v
(ii) ρ *has a PU representation with utility* v *and cost* $-H$.

A generalization of the entropy model is Additive Perturbed Utility (Fudenberg, Iijima, and Strzalecki, 2015).

Definition 3.37. ρ has an *additive perturbed utility* (APU) representation if it has a perturbed utility representation where

$$c_A(p) = \sum_{x \in A} \phi(p(x))$$

for some $\phi : [0, 1] \to (-\infty, \infty]$ that is strictly convex and C^1 over $(0, 1)$. We say that the cost is *steep* if $\lim_{q \to 0} \phi'(q) = -\infty$.

APU always satisfies Regularity, but APU and ARU are different classes of SCF (logit being in their intersection).

Steep cost implies Positivity. It is satisfied under the negative entropy cost because we know that logit satisfies it. Logarithmic costs $\phi(t) = -\log(t)$ used by Harsanyi (1973b) are also steep.

The quadratic costs $\phi(t) = t^2$ used by Ben-Akiva and Lerman (1985) and Rosenthal (1989) are not steep and choices can violate Positivity. The quadratic cost are known in machine learning as *sparsemax* (as opposed to softmax, which is their name for logit) (Martins and Astudillo, 2016).

In general the solution to APU is characterized by the first-order condition associated with the maximization problem in Definition 3.34: $v(x) + \lambda(A) = \phi'(\rho(x, A))$, where $\lambda(A)$ are the Lagrange multipliers on the constraint that choice probabilities from menu A sum up to one. Imagine a binary relation on menu-item pairs defined by $(x, A) \succsim^* (y, B)$ if $\rho(x, A) \geq \rho(y, B)$. The first-order condition means that ρ satisfies APU with steep costs if and only if ρ^* has an additive representation.

An additive representation is guaranteed by the following axiom, similar to Axiom 3.22 that guarantees a Fechnerian representation.

Axiom 3.38 (Acyclicity). For any n and bijections $f, g : \{1, \ldots, n\} \to \{1, \ldots, n\}$, such that $x_k \in A_k$, and $x_{f(k)} \in A_{g(k)}$ for all $k = 1, \ldots, n$

$$\rho(x_1, A_1) > \rho(x_{f(1)}, A_{g(1)})$$
$$\rho(x_k, A_k) \geq \rho(x_{f(k)}, A_{g(k)}) \quad \text{for } 1 < k < n$$

implies

$$\rho(x_n, A_n) < \rho(x_{f(n)}, A_{g(n)}).$$

One intuition for the axiom is as follows: Suppose you have n xylophones and n Accordions. You have a scale that records the weight of an (x, A) pair. The sum of these weights should not depend on how you pair up the instruments.

Acyclicity implies that $\rho(x, A) \geq \rho(y, A)$ iff $\rho(x, B) \geq \rho(y, B)$, so the agent's choice probabilities do not reverse due to "menu effects" (recall Example 2.5). The ranking that ρ induces on X is represented by the utility function v. Additionally, acyclicity implies that $\rho(x, A) \geq \rho(x, B)$ iff $\rho(y, A) \geq \rho(y, B)$. The ranking that ρ induces over (nested) menus can be interpreted as "competitiveness" of menus and is represented by λ.

Theorem 3.39 (Fudenberg, Iijima, and Strzalecki 2015). *Suppose that X is finite and ρ satisfies Positivity. Then ρ has an APU representation with steep cost if and only if it satisfies Acyclicity.*

Positivity can be dropped by weakening Acyclicity. The finiteness of X can be relaxed by adding continuity and richness. Moreover, on binary menus and under Positivity and technical conditions, Acyclicity holds if and only if there is a Fechnerian representation (see Proposition 1 of Fudenberg, Iijima, and Strzalecki, 2014). The uniqueness properties are inherited from the Fechnerian model. Because of the Fechnerian property, APU is not a good explanation of the blue bus–red bus paradox.

Flynn and Sastry (2023) apply APU to coordination games. Another place where APU shows up are models with attributes. We defer this discussion till Section 10.8.

3.9 SINGLE CROSSING*

In many applications the alternatives are linearly ordered (e.g., levels of effort). We will write $x > y$ to denote that order. Suppose that the admissible preference relations are also ordered (e.g., each reflecting a different level of ability). Formally, let $\succsim_1, \ldots, \succsim_m$ be such that for any $x > y$ if $x \succsim_n y$, then $x \succsim_{n+1} y$. A *SCRU* is any RU model in which the set preferences satisfy this property with probability one.

This can be captured behaviorally by the following axiom.

Axiom 3.40 (Centrality). If $x > y > z$ and $\rho(y, \{x, y, z\}) > 0$, then $\rho(x, \{x, y, z\}) = \rho(x, \{x, y\})$ and $\rho(z, \{x, y, z\}) = \rho(z, \{y, z\})$.

Theorem 3.41 (Apesteguia, Ballester, and Lu 2017). *An SCF ρ has a SCRU representation μ if and only if it satisfies Regularity and Centrality. Moreover, μ is unique.*

Apesteguia, Ballester, and Lu (2017) show that a stronger version of centrality, which does not require the premise $\rho(y, \{x, y, z\}) > 0$ characterizes RU with single-peaked preferences.

PART II

RISK AND LEARNING

CHAPTER 4

Risk

4.1 EXPECTED UTILITY

Our agent will now be choosing between alternatives that involve risk, such as insurance plans, career paths, and so on. We will call them *lotteries*. Formally, let Z be the set of prizes. A *lottery* is a mapping $p : Z \to [0, 1]$ such that $p(z) > 0$ for finitely many $z \in Z$ and $\sum_{z \in Z} p(z) = 1$. The set of such "simple" lotteries is denoted $\Delta^s(Z)$. The assumption here is that the agent knows these probabilities perfectly. Of course this is not realistic; we will relax this assumption in Chapter 5, which allows for subjective probabilities. Lotteries will be denoted $p, q, r \in \Delta^s(Z)$ and elements of Z will be denoted by z, z', and so on. As a prerequisite, this section reviews deterministic choice between lotteries.

Our agent now has preferences over lotteries: $\succsim$ is defined on $X = \Delta^s(Z)$. As usual, we say that U represents $\succsim$ if $U(p) \geq U(q) \iff p \succsim q$.

Definition 4.1. $U : \Delta^s(Z) \to \mathbb{R}$ is an *expected utility* (EU) function if

$$U(p) = \mathbb{E}_p u := \sum_{z \in Z} u(z) p(z)$$

for some function $u : Z \to \mathbb{R}$.

The function $u : Z \to \mathbb{R}$ is called the *Bernoulli utility*. The function $U : \Delta^s(Z) \to \mathbb{R}$ is called the *von Neumann–Morgernstern utility*, or the vNM utility for short.

4.1.1 Mixing Lotteries

The key new thing to play with is the additional structure on X given by the mixing operator. Given any two lotteries, $p, q \in \Delta^s(Z)$ and a number $\alpha \in [0, 1]$, we can define a new lottery

$$\alpha p + (1 - \alpha) q \in \Delta^s(Z).$$

This lottery attaches to each prize z the probability equal to $\alpha p(z) + (1-\alpha)q(z)$, so it's a weighted average of the two lotteries.

One way to achieve this mixed lottery is to first toss a coin that with probability α lands on heads and $1 - \alpha$ on tails. Then give the agent lottery p if heads come up and q if tails come up. Such a two-stage lottery, or compound lottery, is formally an object that lives in a different space $\Delta^s(\Delta^s(Z))$. Our preferences here are defined just on one-shot lotteries $\Delta^s(Z)$, so we need to think of $\alpha p(z) + (1 - \alpha)q(z)$ as the reduced, or flattened lottery, where the probabilities are multiplied out.

4.1.2 The Axioms

A key property of EU is linearity in probabilities:

$$U(\alpha p + (1 - \alpha)q) = \alpha U(p) + (1 - \alpha)U(q). \tag{4.1}$$

The reader should verify that U is an EU function if and only if it is linear in probabilities.

Linearity in probabilities is captured by the following axiom on preferences.

Axiom 4.2 (vNM Independence). For all $\alpha \in (0, 1)$ and $r \in \Delta^s(Z)$

$$p \succsim q \text{ if and only if } \alpha p + (1 - \alpha)r \succsim \alpha q + (1 - \alpha)r.$$

The agent likes p more than q if and only if they like a mixture of p with some lottery r more than a mixture of q with r, as long as the mixtures are of identical proportion.

Since X is now uncountably infinite, it is useful to have some continuity.

Axiom 4.3 (Archimedean Continuity). If $p \succ q \succ r$ there exist $\alpha, \beta \in (0, 1)$ such that

$$\alpha p + (1 - \alpha)r \succ q \succ \beta p + (1 - \beta)r.$$

Another axiom that works is the following.[1]

Axiom 4.4 (Mixture Continuity). For any $p, q, r \in \Delta^s(Z)$ the sets

$$\{\alpha \in [0, 1] : \alpha p + (1-\alpha)q \succsim r\} \text{ and } \{\alpha \in [0, 1] : \alpha p + (1-\alpha)q \precsim r\}$$

are closed in $[0, 1]$.

---

[1] Another notion of continuity is topological. When Z is finite, we equip $\Delta(Z)$ with the Euclidean topology and with the weak* topology (also known as "topology of weak convergence") for Z infinite. In the infinite case the set of lotteries is $\Delta^B(Z)$ – the Borel probability measures and $U(p) = \int u(z)dp(z)$ (see, e.g., Grandmont, 1972). Total nerds will keep in mind that $\Delta^B(Z)$ is a subset of the dual space of the space of bounded and continuous functions from Z to $\mathbb{R}$ hence weak *star*.

Theorem 4.5 (Von Neumann and Morgenstern, 1944). *A preference $\succsim$ on $\Delta^s(Z)$ has an EU representation if and only if it satisfies vNM Independence and Archimedean Continuity (or Mixture Continuity). Moreover, u is cardinally unique, that is, whenever u_1, u_2 represent $\succsim$, there exists a $> 0, b \in \mathbb{R}$ such that $u_2(z) = au_1(z) + b$ for all $z \in Z$.*

Proof. See Theorem 5.5 of Kreps (1988). □

The idea behind cardinal uniqueness is similar to the measurement of temperature: Celsius and Fahrenheit are affine transforms of each other.[2] Cardinal uniqueness makes it meaningful to talk about the curvature of u once we assume that $Z = \mathbb{R}$. As we will soon see, its curvature will control risk aversion.

This theorem combines two of the exercises we talked about in Chapter 2: characterization and identification. The third exercise, comparative statics, is the topic of Section 4.1.3.

4.1.3 Risk Aversion

We say that someone is risk averse if they demand insurance. Suppose that payoffs are monetary, that is, $Z \subseteq \mathbb{R}$, and for any lottery p define $\bar{p}$ to be its expected monetary value. For any prize $z \in Z$ let δ_z denote the lottery that gives z for sure; I will sometimes call it a *point mass* on z.

Definition 4.6. $\succsim$ is *risk averse* if $\delta_{\bar{p}} \succsim p$ for all $p \in \Delta^s(Z)$.

Intuitively, the agent is risk averse if they prefer to get rid of all the risk and get the expected payoff for sure.

Notice that the concept of risk aversion is defined for all risk preferences, not just expected utility. In the EU model there is a particularly nice characterization.

Definition 4.7. $u : Z \to \mathbb{R}$ is *concave* if

$$u(\alpha x + (1 - \alpha)y) \geq \alpha u(x) + (1 - \alpha)u(y)$$

for all $x, y \in Z, \alpha \in (0, 1)$ such that $\alpha x + (1 - \alpha)y \in Z$.

Proposition 4.8. *Suppose that $\succsim$ has an EU representation with Bernoulli utility u. $\succsim$ is risk averse iff u is a concave function.*

Proof. The proof is a restatement of Jensen's inequality. □

Another definition helps us compare risk aversion of two individuals.

---

[2] This implies that U is also cardinally unique. We still have ordinal uniqueness of U from Chapter 1: For any strictly increasing function ϕ the function $\phi \circ U$ represents the preference. However this function will not be of the vNM form unless the function ϕ is affine.

Definition 4.9. $\succsim_1$ is *more risk averse than* $\succsim_2$ if for all $z \in Z$ and $p \in \Delta^s(Z)$

$$\delta_z \succsim_2 p \Longrightarrow \delta_z \succsim_1 p$$

and

$$\delta_z \succ_2 p \Longrightarrow \delta_z \succ_1 p.$$

If agent 2 chooses a sure thing over a lottery, then agent 1 who is more risk averse should also go for the sure thing.

Proposition 4.10. *Suppose that* $\succsim_1, \succsim_2$ *have an EU representation with Bernoulli utilities* u_1, u_2. $\succsim_1$ *is more risk averse than* $\succsim_2$ *iff* $u_1 = \phi \circ u_2$ *for some strictly increasing and concave function* ϕ *whose domain is the range of* u_2.

The price we have to pay for such nice comparative statics is that we restrict attention to a certain subclass (in this case expected utility). This is generally the case: We pay for identification by making assumptions. Ideally, we can test these assumptions by checking whether some axioms hold (in the case of expected utility, it's the vNM axiom).

4.1.4 Stochastic Dominance*

There are three main dominance relations over lotteries with monetary payoffs. They are transitive, but incomplete.

We say that lottery p *first-order stochastically dominates* (FOSD) lottery q if all EU preferences with an increasing u like p more than q, denoted by $p \geq_{FOSD} q$. The relation $\geq_{FOSD}$ can be characterized by comparing the CDFs of the two distributions: $p \geq_{FOSD} q$ iff $F_p(z) \leq F_q(z)$ for all $z \in Z$, where F_p is the CDF of p and F_q the CDF of q, see, for example, expression (1.A.7) of Shaked and Shanthikumar (2007). In other words, p is a definite improvement over q: For any prize z, the probability of getting at least z under p is higher than under q.

We say that lottery p dominates q in the *concave order* if all EU preferences with a concave u like p more than q. This is denoted $p \geq_{cv} q$ and implies that the expectations of those two lotteries are equal (why?). This order is represented as follows: For any p, q with the same mean $p \geq_{cv} q$ iff $\int_{-\infty}^x F_p(z)dz \leq \int_{-\infty}^x F_q(z)dz$ (see, e.g., Theorem 3.A.1 of Shaked and Shanthikumar (2007)).

Finally, lottery p *second-order stochastically dominates* (SOSD) lottery q if all EU preferences with an increasing and concave u like p more than q. This order is represented as follows: For any p, q we have $p \geq_{SOSD} q$ iff $\int_{-\infty}^x F_p(z)dz \leq \int_{-\infty}^x F_q(z)dz$ (see, e.g., Theorem 4.A.2 of Shaked and Shanthikumar (2007)).

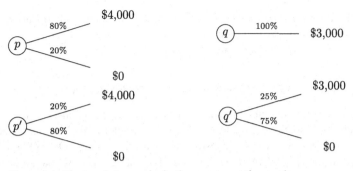

Figure 4.1 The two lottery pairs in the common ratio paradox.

4.1.5 Popular Parameterizations

Two most used families of Bernoulli utility functions are Constant Absolute Risk Aversion (CARA) and Constant Relative Risk Aversion (CRRA). CARA says that risk aversion over incremental wealth stays constant as we make the agent richer (*shift-invariance*). CRRA is a multiplicative version (*scale-invariance*). u is CARA if

$$u(z) = \begin{cases} -\frac{\exp(-\theta z)}{\theta} & \text{if } \theta \neq 0 \\ z & \text{if } \theta = 0 \end{cases}$$

for some parameter $\theta \in \mathbb{R}$. u is CRRA if

$$u(z) = \begin{cases} \frac{z^{1-\theta}-1}{1-\theta} & \text{if } \theta \neq 1 \\ \ln(z) & \text{if } \theta = 1. \end{cases}$$

In either case, higher θ means more risk aversion.

4.1.6 Non-expected Utility

A substantial literature is motivated by the Allais (1953) paradox and the related Common Ratio Paradox.

Example 4.11 (Common Ratio Paradox). Consider the two lottery pairs (p, q) and (p', q') depicted in Figure 4.1:

The Independence axiom implies that $q \succsim p$ if and only if $q' \succsim p'$. This is because $p' = .25p + .75\delta_0$ and $q' = .25q + .75\delta_0$. However in their experiment Kahneman and Tversky (1979) find that among 95 subjects 80 have the preference $q \succ p$ while only 35 have the preference $q' \succ p'$, so preferences of a substantial fraction of subjects are inconsistent with EU.[3]   △

---

[3] This experiment has been replicated a number of times, using both within- and between-subjects designs. Notice that in a between-subject design, we cannot test Axiom 4.2 because we don't observe a preference relation, but instead a SCF $\rho(q,p) = \frac{80}{95}$ and $\rho(q',p') = \frac{35}{95}$.

To accommodate such behavior, non-EU preferences relax linearity in probabilities. A number of classes of nonlinear functions $V : \Delta^s(Z) \to \mathbb{R}$ have been developed and axiomatized.[4]

4.2 STOCHASTIC MODELS FOR EXPECTED UTILITY

It is widely documented that individual choices between lotteries are stochastic (Mosteller and Nogee, 1951). Given a class of deterministic utility functions $\mathcal{U}$ there are two basic ways to construct a stochastic model ρ: One is to randomize over utilities $u \in \mathcal{U}$ and the other is to fix a particular $v \in \mathcal{U}$ and add an error term ϵ. We will now apply these two ideas to $\mathcal{U} =$ "EU preferences."[5]

Our ρ is defined on menus of lotteries: all finite subsets of $\Delta^s(Z)$.

Definition 4.12 (Random Expected Utility). ρ has a *Random Expected Utility* (REU) representation if it has a proper RU representation where with probability one the realized utility satisfies Definition 4.1.

We can think of REU as a probability distribution over EU preferences or alternatively as a distribution over Bernoulli utilities u or a distribution over vNM utilities U. When dealing with a parametric class such as CARA or CRRA, we can think of it as a distribution over the parameter space Θ.

On the other hand, we have a model where shocks are added to the expected utility values.

Definition 4.13 (i.i.d. Additive Random Expected Utility). ρ has an *Additive Random Expected Utility* (i.i.d. AREU) representation if it has a RU representation where $\widetilde{U}(p) = \mathbb{E}_p v + \tilde{\epsilon}(p)$ for some deterministic $v : Z \to \mathbb{R}$ and smooth $\tilde{\epsilon}$ i.i.d. across lotteries.

This is the i.i.d. ARU model adapted to the world of lotteries: The deterministic utility function is expected utility and the error term (known to the agent at the time of choice) is i.i.d. across lotteries.

REU and i.i.d. AREU are both special cases of RU but they are very different animals. By definition, under REU the realized utility $\widetilde{U}$ is with probability one linear. On the other hand, as we will see in Section 4.6, in i.i.d. AREU the

---

[4] Prospect Theory: Kahneman and Tversky (1979); Cumulative Prospect Theory: Tversky and Kahneman (1992); Rank-dependent Expected Utility: Quiggin (1982), Yaari (1987); Betweenness Preferences: Chew (1983), Dekel (1986), and Gul (1991); Quadratic Utility: Chew, Epstein, and Segal (1991); and Cautious Expected Utility: Cerreia-Vioglio, Dillenberger, and Ortoleva (2015). Machina (1982) pioneered a model-free approach by considering the classes of all differentiable and FOSD-monotone or cv-monotone representations.

[5] Sometimes in the literature the first model is called "random parameter" whereas the second "random utility"; we will not use this terminology here. Both kinds of stochastic models were introduced in Block and Marschak (1960) and Becker, DeGroot, and Marschak (1963). By the way, the latter is not the famous paper of the trio. The experimental technique of *random incentive systems* was introduced in Becker, DeGroot, and Marschak (1964).

realized utility $\widetilde{U}$ with probability one represents a preference that violates the vNM Independence axiom.

4.3 AXIOMS FOR RANDOM EXPECTED UTILITY

As we saw in Section 2.3, in the world without lotteries the axioms for random utility are complicated and hard to interpret. Gul and Pesendorfer (2006) showed that the axioms get much simpler in the EU case: We just need Regularity, Continuity, and two versions of Independence. We will also get much better uniqueness properties.

The first version of Independence compares choices from a menu A to choices from a menu A that is mixed with some lottery r. Formally, for any $\alpha \in (0, 1)$ and $r \in \Delta(Z)$ define a new menu

$$\alpha A + (1 - \alpha)r := \{\alpha p + (1 - \alpha)r : p \in A\}.$$

Axiom 4.14 (Linearity). For any $\alpha \in (0, 1)$ any $p \in A$ and $r \in \Delta(Z)$ $\rho(p, A) = \rho(\alpha p + (1 - \alpha)r, \alpha A + (1 - \alpha)r)$.

This axiom is necessary for REU because every vNM utility function is linear in probabilities, so $U(p) \geq U(q)$ iff $U(\alpha p + (1-\alpha)r) \geq U(\alpha q + (1-\alpha)r)$. This implies that

$$N(p, A) = N(\alpha p + (1 - \alpha)r, \alpha A + (1 - \alpha)r),$$

which implies that the choice probabilities are equal. Geometrically, $N(p, A)$ is one of the dashed angles in panel (a) of Figure 4.2, defined as the normal cone of the convex hull of A at point p_1. It equals the other dashed angle because of the "corresponding angles theorem."

In the next axiom the set $\text{ext}(A)$ denotes the set of extreme points of A, that is, lotteries $p \in A$ that cannot be represented as convex combinations of other lotteries in A.

Axiom 4.15 (Extremeness). $\rho(\text{ext}\, A, A) = 1$.

Extremeness is a consequence of linearity of the vNM utility and properness of RU. Any fixed U is maximized on the boundary of A, see panel (b) of Figure 4.2. This may be an extreme point of A, but it may also a nonextreme point (called exposed point, such as p_4 in the figure) if the indifference curve happens to be parallel to the side of A. But since we required REU to be proper, for any fixed A, the probability of finding such a nongeneric utility is zero.

Finally, we need a flavor of continuity. This is a technical axiom, so you can ignore the details. For a fixed menu A we treat $\rho(\cdot, A)$ as a Borel probability measure on $\Delta(Z)$ and equip the set of all Borel measures, $\Delta(\Delta(Z))$, with the weak* topology. We endow the set $M(\Delta(Z))$ with the Hausdorff metric.

Axiom 4.16 (Continuity). The function $\rho : M(\Delta(Z)) \to \Delta(\Delta(Z))$ is continuous.

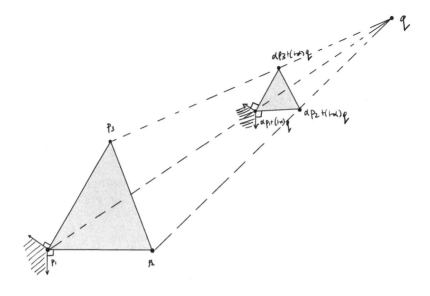

(a) Linearity with $A = \{p_1, p_2, p_3\}$

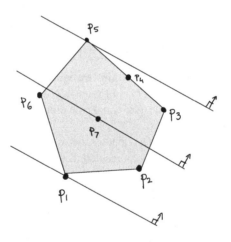

(b) Extremeness with $A = \{p_1, \ldots, p_6\}$

Figure 4.2 Linearity and Extremeness Axioms.

I say that continuity is a technical axiom because to reject it we need to observe an infinite number of menus. On the other hand, to reject the other axioms we just need a small number of menus (especially if we cook them up in a smart way). Of course, to verify that any of those axioms are *satisfied*, we still need infinitely many menus.

Theorem 4.17 (Gul and Pesendorfer, 2006). *Suppose that Z is finite. A SCF ρ satisfies Regularity, Linearity, Extremeness, and Continuity if and only if $\rho \sim REU$. In this case the measure μ is unique over the twice-normalized Bernoulli utilities, that is μ is unique on the Borel σ-algebra of the set $\{u : Z \to \mathbb{R} : u(z_0) = 0, \sum_{z \in Z} u^2(z) = 1\}$, where $z_0 \in Z$ is a fixed prize.*[6]

Recall Example 2.14, which showed that in general we can't determine the probability that p is better than q *and at the same time* p' is better than q'. The reason we are getting stronger uniqueness now is that mixing allows us to determine this probability. We simply need to look at the probability that $\frac{1}{2}p + \frac{1}{2}p'$ gets chosen from the set $\left\{\frac{1}{2}p + \frac{1}{2}p', \frac{1}{2}p + \frac{1}{2}q', \frac{1}{2}q + \frac{1}{2}p', \frac{1}{2}q + \frac{1}{2}q'\right\}$.

More generally, the event $N(\alpha p + (1 - \alpha)q, \alpha A + (1 - \alpha)B)$ equals the intersection of $N(p, A)$ and $N(q, B)$. This is true for any $\alpha \in (0, 1)$ because for any linear $U : \Delta(Z) \to \mathbb{R}$ we have

$$U(\alpha p + (1 - \alpha)q) \geq U(\alpha p' + (1 - \alpha)q') \text{ for all } p' \in A \text{ and } q' \in B$$

iff

$$\alpha U(p) + (1-\alpha)U(q) \geq \alpha U(p') + (1-\alpha)U(q') \text{ for all } p' \in A \text{ and } q' \in B$$

iff

$$U(p) \geq U(p') \text{ for all } p' \in A \text{ and } U(q) \geq U(q') \text{ for all } q' \in B.$$

As you may recall from Chapter 1, in a proper RU representation ties must occur with probability zero. This may be confusing because any fixed EU preference over lotteries must have nontrivial indifference curves (as long as $|Z| \geq 3$). To make this work, in a proper REU representation every single preference has probability zero. This can be done by taking a distribution over preferences that is smooth enough so every particular preference gets zero probability and for any pair x, y the probability of a tie is zero (for example, take a positive density over the set $\mathbb{R}^Z$ of Bernoulli utilities).

4.4 TECHNICAL ASPECTS OF REU*

To work with examples or applications, we might want to have a REU that puts positive probability on finitely many utilities and therefore is *improper*. To do so, Gul and Pesendorfer (2006) introduce tiebreakers, just as we discussed in Section 1.6, with the additional requirement that the tiebreaker a proper REU.[7]

---

[6] Gul and Pesendorfer (2006) have a weaker uniqueness result. The stronger claim asserted here follows from the Caratheodory extension theorem and the construction in Section S3.2 of the supplement of Ahn and Sarver (2013).

[7] This is done in the supplement to their paper. Another way to proceed would be to break ties at random. This was used, for example, by Loomes and Sugden (1995). This leads to a ρ which satisfies Linearity but violates Extremeness (why?).

A technical wrinkle is that for tiebreakers we need to relax the countable additivity assumption and require that they be only finitely additive. This is obtained by relaxing the continuity axiom to mixture continuity.

Axiom 4.18 (Mixture Continuity). For any menus A and B, the function $\alpha \mapsto \rho(\cdot, \alpha A + (1 - \alpha)B)$ is continuous.

Theorem 4.19 (Gul and Pesendorfer, 2006).

    (i)   *ρ has a finitely additive proper REU representation if and only if it satisfies Regularity, Linearity, Extremeness, and Mixture Continuity. In this case the measure μ is unique on the algebra generated by the sets $N(p, A)$.*

    (ii) *ρ has a finitely additive improper REU representation with a GP tiebreaker if and only if it has a finitely additive proper REU representation.*

Ahn and Sarver (2013) study REU representations with finitely many vNM utilities. In the supplement to their paper they present a Finiteness axiom that guarantees that the REU representation is discrete (with a GP tiebreaker). The main idea hinges on their clever construction of a "separating menu." If ρ has a REU representation with finitely many utilities, then for any utility u in the support of μ there is a lottery p_u such that $N(p_u, A) = \{u\}$, where $A = \{p_u : u \in \text{supp}\,\mu\}$. This guarantees that $\rho(p_u, A) = \mu(u)$. By using such constructions it is possible to behaviorally define "menus without ties" and "menus with ties."

Finally, the discussion here assumes that Z is finite. Extensions to infinite Z were obtained by Ma (2018), Frick, Iijima, and Strzalecki (2019), and Lu and Saito (2019).

4.5 AXIOMS FOR ADDITIVE RANDOM EXPECTED UTILITY

An axiomatic characterization of i.i.d. AREU is not known because we don't know axioms for i.i.d. ARU. However, it is easy to see that there are some necessary axioms.

As in Section 3.7, define the stochastic preference $p \succsim^* q$ by $\rho(p, q) \geq \frac{1}{2}$. i.i.d. AREU satisfies a weakening of Linearity.

Axiom 4.20 (Stochastic Independence). $\succsim^*$ satisfies Axiom 4.2.

i.i.d. AREU also satisfies the following continuity axiom.

Axiom 4.21 (Stochastic Continuity). $\succsim^*$ satisfies Axiom 4.3.

A Luce model for choice over lotteries is also sometimes considered.

Definition 4.22 (Luce Expected Utility). ρ has a *Luce Expected Utility* (LEU) representation if it has a Luce representation with $w(p) = h(\mathbb{E}_p v)$ for some deterministic functions $v : Z \to \mathbb{R}$ and $h : \mathbb{R} \to \mathbb{R}_{++}$, where h is strictly increasing on the convex hull of the set $\{v(z) : z \in Z\}$.

There are also Fechnerian versions of EU, see, for example, Becker, DeGroot, and Marschak (1963) and Loomes and Sugden (1995).[8]

LEU is a special case of i.i.d. AREU if h is the exponential function. It is worthwhile to notice that LEU is characterized by the above two axioms (plus Luce's IIA and positivity).

Proposition 4.23 (Dagsvik 2008). *The following are equivalent:*

  (i) $\rho \sim LEU$
  (ii) ρ *satisfies Positivity and Luce's IIA, Stochastic Independence, and Stochastic Continuity.*

Proof. See Appendix A.4.1.   □

4.6 COMPARISON OF REU AND I.I.D. AREU

Table 4.1 summarizes the comparisons between the two models. My take on this is that if we believe in EU, then REU is the more appealing of the two models because i.i.d. AREU leads to non-EU behaviors of a particular form. On the other hand, if we are motivated by departures from EU, then i.i.d. AREU is not the right model either. We may want instead to build the kinds of departures we care about directly into the baseline model, as opposed to generating them as an artifact of the ϵ.

The first row of Table 4.1 says that under REU the realized preference is EU with probability one, while under i.i.d. AREU this happens with probability zero. The first assertion comes directly from Definition 4.12. To see that the second one is true, consider lotteries p, q such $\mathbb{E}_p v = \mathbb{E}_q v$. Fix a realization of $\tilde{\epsilon}$ and suppose w.l.o.g. that $\widetilde{U}(p) \geq \widetilde{U}(q)$. For any $\alpha \in (0, 1)$ and $r \in \Delta(Z)$ we have $\mathbb{E}_{\alpha p + (1-\alpha)r} v = \mathbb{E}_{\alpha q + (1-\alpha)r} v$. Because $\tilde{\epsilon}(\alpha p + (1 - \alpha)r)$ and $\tilde{\epsilon}(\alpha q + (1 - \alpha)r)$ are i.i.d. across $\alpha \in (0, 1)$, by the exact law of large numbers, with probability one there exists α such that $\tilde{\epsilon}(\alpha p + (1 - \alpha)r) < \tilde{\epsilon}(\alpha q + (1 - \alpha)r)$.[9]

Moving to the second row of Table 4.1, i.i.d. AREU violates Extremeness.[10] Likewise, it also violates Linearity (Axiom 4.14).

---

[8] Simple axiomatizations of Fechnerian EU have been obtained, see, for example, Dagsvik (2008) who also shows what additional axioms guarantee the linearity of the function h. Blavatskyy (2008) offers a different axiomatization of the special case of Fechnerian EU with linear h; for a correction see Ryan (2015). Dagsvik (2015) explores the relationship between these axioms.

[9] See, for example, Sun (2006) and Podczeck (2010). If you are uncomfortable with the exact law of large numbers, choose a discrete grid on the interval $[0, 1] \ni \alpha$ and notice that the desired α exists with a probability approaching one as the number of grid points approaches infinity.

[10] Becker, DeGroot, and Marschak (1963) propose to test EU by testing Extremeness. Sopher and Narramore (2000) and Feldman and Rehbeck (2022) show that experimental subjects typically violate Extremeness.

Table 4.1 *Comparison of REU and i.i.d. AREU.*

REU	i.i.d. AREU
$\mathbb{P}(\succsim \in EU) = 1$	$\mathbb{P}(\succsim \in EU) = 0$
Linearity, Extremeness can violate WST	Stochastic Independence, Positivity satisfies SST
FOSD monotone with prob 1	FOSD monotone with prob $\in \left(\frac{1}{2}, 1\right)$
cv-monotone with prob 1	non cv-monotone with prob 1

Example 4.24 (Spurious Common Ratio Paradox). Recall Example 4.11, where

$$.63 = \rho(p', q') > \rho(p, q) = .16.$$

It follows from Linearity that under REU those two choice probabilities are always identical. On the other hand, if we take an i.i.d. AREU model with a deterministic risk-averse EU function v then we get the qualitative preference pattern $\rho(p', q') > \rho(p, q)$. However, both choice probabilities will be on the same side of $\frac{1}{2}$, so i.i.d. AREU cannot really explain the common ratio paradox (Loomes, 2005). $\triangle$

The third row of the table presents another distinguishing feature of i.i.d. AREU and REU: stochastic transitivity. i.i.d. AREU satisfies SST, whereas REU typically violates even WST. Thus, rejections of stochastic transitivity are rejections of i.i.d. AREU, not of Expected Utility in general, see also Mellers and Biagini (1994).

The last two rows of the table refer to the stochastic dominance relations. The idea is easiest to see by implementing both models parametrically. Take, for example, CARA or CRRA preferences, both parametrized by $\theta \in \Theta$. Fix the "average" level risk aversion $\theta \in \Theta$ and let $\tilde{\epsilon}$ be a real-valued random variable that perturbs the risk aversion coefficient. Under REU this leads to the following choice probabilities for $p, q \in \Delta(Z)$:

$$\rho_\theta(p, q) := \mathbb{P}\left(\mathbb{E}_p[u_{\theta + \tilde{\epsilon}}] \geq \mathbb{E}_q[u_{\theta + \tilde{\epsilon}}]\right).$$

In the i.i.d. AREU version of the model there are still $\theta \in \Theta$ and a random variable $\tilde{\epsilon}$. However, ϵ does not perturb the coefficient of risk aversion, but the value of each lottery; that is $\epsilon \in \mathbb{R}^{\Delta(Z)}$. This leads to the following choice probabilities.

$$\rho_\theta(p, q) = \mathbb{P}\left(\mathbb{E}_p[u_\theta] + \epsilon(p) \geq \mathbb{E}_q[u_\theta] + \epsilon(q)\right).$$

Suppose that q strictly FOSD-dominates p. Then under i.i.d. AREU $\rho_\theta(p, q) > 0$. On the other hand, under REU we have $\rho_\theta(p, q) = 0$ because all u are increasing. The difference between the two models becomes starkest when q is just a little bit better than p: Under i.i.d. AREU their choice probabilities will be about equal.[11]

Suppose now that p is a mean-preserving spread of q and that $\tilde{\epsilon}$ has full support. Under REU for any $q \succeq_{cv} p$ the choice probability $\rho_\theta(p, q)$ is decreasing in θ.[12] On the other hand, as shown by Wilcox (2008, 2011) and Apesteguia and Ballester (2017b), under i.i.d. AREU there exists $\bar{\theta}$ above which the function $\theta \mapsto \rho_\theta(p, q)$ is *increasing* in θ.

Given all of this, it sounds like REU is a better model. But perhaps we need a little bit of ϵ to estimate the model, otherwise our likelihood function will be degenerate. This suggests a BLP-style model for choice under lotteries (BLP is discussed in Section 10.6). A model like this is sketched in Section 5.1.2. of Barseghyan, Molinari, O'Donoghue, and Teitelbaum (2018).

Nevertheless, the literature in industrial organization typically uses REU models, where the randomness is purely population heterogeneity (each agent's choices are deterministic), see, for example, Einav, Finkelstein, Ryan, Schrimpf, and Cullen (2013), Handel (2013), and Ho and Lee (2020). The only BLP-style model I'm aware of is Ho and Lee (2017).

4.7 NON-EXPECTED UTILITY*

Machina (1985) noticed that even if the preference is fixed and deterministic, the agent may want to deliberately randomize over alternatives. With a non-linear preference a mixture of lotteries that belong to the menu may be strictly better than any of those lotteries. To implement such a mixture, the agent will toss a "mental coin" and randomly pick a lottery from the menu; thus the choices observed by the analyst will be stochastic.

To see how this works, suppose that the agent's preferences are represented by a quasi-concave function $V : \Delta(Z) \to \mathbb{R}$. Figure 4.3 depicts the indifference curves of V. If the menu is $A = \{p, q\}$ with $V(p) > V(q)$, then the agent will weakly prefer the mixture $r_\alpha = \alpha p + (1 - \alpha)q$ to both of the lotteries in the menu, as long as α is large enough. Let α^* be the value of α that maximizes $V(r_\alpha)$. The agent will implement lottery r_{α^*} by choosing p with probability α^* and q with probability $1 - \alpha^*$, so we have $\rho(p, q) = \alpha^*$.

More generally, let $\bar{\rho}(A)$ be the lottery induced by the stochastic choices of the agent, that is, $\bar{\rho}(A) := \sum_{q \in A} \rho(q, A)q$. For each menu A this lottery corresponds to the "mental mixture" of the agent. We say that ρ has a *Machina representation* if there exists a FOSD-monotone preference $\succsim$ over $\Delta(Z)$ such that $\bar{\rho}(A) \succsim q$ for all $q \in co(A)$, where $co(A)$ is the convex hull of the points (lotteries) in menu A.

---

[11] These patterns were first noticed by Becker, DeGroot, and Marschak (1963) and Loomes and Sugden (1995) in the context of Fechnerian EU models.

[12] This probability can be positive because with some probability $u_{\theta+\epsilon}$ is risk loving. However, as θ increases, this probability goes down.

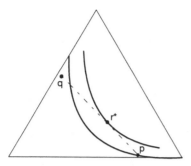

Figure 4.3 Deliberate randomization.

Machina's model was recently axiomatized by Cerreia-Vioglio, Dillenberger, Ortoleva, and Riella (2019) using the following acyclicity-like axiom.[13]

Axiom 4.25. Rational Mixing For any $k \geq 2$ and menus $A_1, \ldots, A_k$ if

$$\bar{\rho}(A_2) \in \text{co}(A_1), \ldots, \bar{\rho}(A_k) \in \text{co}(A_{k-1}),$$

then $q \in \text{co}(A_k)$ implies that $q \not\succ_{FOSD} \bar{\rho}(A_1)$

Proposition 4.26 (Cerreia-Vioglio, Dillenberger, Ortoleva, and Riella 2019). *Suppose that ρ is defined over finite menus of Borel probability measures with prizes in some compact interval. A SCF ρ satisfies Rational Mixing if and only if it has a Machina representation.*

They also show that this class of ρ typically violates Regularity: as long as $\succsim$ has a point of strict convexity. To see that, consider the lotteries p and q as above and the lottery r' that is close to $r^* = \alpha^* p + (1 - \alpha^*)q$, but is FOSD-dominated by it. The choice from menu $\{p, q, r'\}$ is p with probability α^* and q with probability $1 - \alpha^*$; this is because tossing the mental coin implements the lottery r^* which is better than r'. On the other hand, from the menu $\{p, r'\}$ the agent will choose r' with probability close to one because choosing p without being able to mix it with q is not very appealing.

A separate question is what does the agent choose if the optimal mental lottery actually belongs to the menu. Agranov and Ortoleva (2017) show that experimental subjects have a preference for r^* being in the menu, that is, not having to toss the mental coin. Agranov and Ortoleva (in press) provide further evidence of preference for randomization by devising a version of multiple price lists that allows subjects express such a preference. See also Dwenger, Kübler, and Weizsäcker's (2018) field study on university admissions. As far as I understand Machina-style preferences are not a good model of that because in that model all lotteries (mental or not) are treated the same way.

---

[13] As far as I know, nobody has tested those axioms yet. Hey and Carbone (1995) estimate a parametric version of this model (and find that it explains only 10% of subject's choices).

At the level of representation, Machina's model is similar to Perturbed Utility, where the agent maximizes expected utility plus a nonlinear term (Section 3.8, see also Marley (1997)). This is reflected on the level of axioms in the fact that both models are characterized by acyclicity conditions.

There are two other ways deal with non-EU preferences, akin to what we did with REU and i.i.d. AREU: randomize over preferences or add noise to the value of each lottery. The first one was studied by (Lin, 2019a, 2019b), who shows that if the random preferences belong to the betweenness class, stochastic choices still satisfy Regularity and Extremeness. Kashaev and Aguiar (2022) complement these results by studying random Rank-dependent Expected Utility. See also Melkonyan and Safra (2016) who study weak stochastic transitivity of such models. In mathematical psychology, researchers have developed standardized software for testing random non-EU models (Regenwetter, Davis-Stober, Lim, Guo, Popova, Zwilling, Cha, and Messner, 2014; Zwilling, Cavagnaro, Regenwetter, Lim, Fields, and Zhang, 2019).

The second approach was taken by Hey and Orme (1994) who considered i.i.d. ARU implementations of non-EU (without allowing the agent to toss any mental coins). A similar, but different method was introduced by Harless and Camerer (1994) who considered a constant-error choice rule (such as in Example 3.18). Ballinger and Wilcox (1997) derive tests for both implementations. Their experimental data is consistent with the first, but rejects the second. More recently, i.i.d. ARU versions of non-EU models were used by De Palma, Ben-Akiva, Brownstone, Holt, Magnac, McFadden, Moffatt, Picard, Train, and Wakker (2008) and Barseghyan, Molinari, O'Donoghue, and Teitelbaum (2013).[14] See also DellaVigna (2018).

---

[14] Those authors allow for unobservable heterogeneity (i.e., consider models where the parameters of the non-EU risk function vary from person to person), that is, a mixture over i.i.d. ARU models. But importantly, the parameter is fixed within a person, so the stochastic choices of each individual suffer from the same monotonicity violations as those described in Section 4.6.

CHAPTER 5

Passive Learning

5.1 THE BAYESIAN MODEL

Under Random Utility, the agent's observed choices ρ are stochastic because their tastes are randomly fluctuating. Another possible reason for random choices could be that the agent's *beliefs* are fluctuating because the agent is learning new information over time (while tastes stay fixed, for simplicity).

We will start with the simplest model, where the agent gets the same information regardless of the menu they are facing. This is similar to RU (where the distribution over utilities stays the same).

We will then discuss a model where information can depend on the menu. This is similar to making the distribution of utilities menu-dependent. In the extreme case, if dependence is arbitrary, we can explain any ρ.

All of the above are models of *passive learning*, where information arrives whether the agent wants it or not. *Active learning* is when the agent can choose how much and what kind of information to acquire. We will study this in Chapter 6.

5.1.1 Bayes Representations

Let S be the set of *states*: This is what the agent is learning about.[1] The state is initially unknown to the agent as depicted in Figure 5.1.

In economic theory we distinguish three stages: At the *ex ante* stage (before receiving information), the agent's initial belief about the state is represented by a *prior* $p \in \Delta(S)$. From Nature's point of view, the state s is not random: It is fixed and simply unknown to the agent. Their beliefs reflect that subjective uncertainty. At the *iterim* stage (after receiving information) the belief is the *posterior*, that is, the prior updated in light of the new information (according

---

[1] In statistics it is customary to denote states by Θ. In Chapter 2 we used θ for the parameters of the model that our *analyst* is learning about. Since the analyst and the agent are two different people, we need another letter, to denote the states of the *agent*. Note that S is different from Ω in an RU representation. The relationship between S and Ω will become clear as you keep reading along.

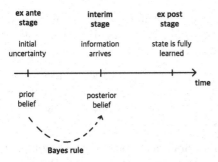

Figure 5.1 Timing in the Bayes model.

to the Bayes rule). Sometimes the *ex post* stage is also considered when the agent fully learns the state. We will not really discuss it here.

Information is modeled as a *message* $m \in M$. In each state s there is a probability distribution over possible messages. The function $\beta : S \to \Delta(M)$ is called an *experiment* (or a *signal structure*, or a *signal*). In statistics this object is known as the *likelihood function*.

For each message $m \in M$ there is a *posterior belief* $q(\cdot|m) \in \Delta(S)$. When S and M are finite, this is given by the *Bayes rule*:

$$q(s|m) = \frac{\beta(m|s)p(s)}{\sum_{s'} \beta(m|s')p(s')} \tag{5.1}$$

as long as the denominator is positive. We will write $q_m \in \Delta(S)$ for the vector $q(\cdot|m)$ and $\beta_s \in \Delta(M)$ for the vector $\beta(\cdot|s)$. If β and p are densities, the density of the posterior is:

$$q(s|m) = \frac{\beta(m|s)p(s)}{\int_{s'} \beta(m|s')p(s')ds'}.^2$$

The agent has a state-dependent utility function $v : X \times S \to \mathbb{R}$, that is, the utility of alternative x can depend on the state s. For any belief $q \in \Delta(S)$ the expected utility of x is denoted by $\mathbb{E}_q v(x) := \sum_{s \in S} q(s)v(x,s)$. Our agent is faced with some menu $A \subseteq X$ and solves $\max_{x \in A} \mathbb{E}_q v(x)$.

We assume that the utility function is deterministic (tastes don't fluctuate), so for any given q the agent's choice is deterministic (modulo ties). In particular, if we observed the agent at the ex ante stage, then the recorded choices would be deterministic.

However, at the interim stage in the eyes of the analyst choices appear to be stochastic because the noisy signals are private to the agent. Modulo ties, the interim choice probability conditional on state s is

$$\rho^s(x,A) = \beta_s\left(\left\{m \in M : \mathbb{E}_{q_m} v(x) = \max_{y \in A} \mathbb{E}_{q_m} v(y)\right\}\right).$$

---

^{2} In the most general case, S is a Borel space, M is a measurable space, and β is a probability kernel from S to M. Then the posterior is the *regular conditional probability*, which is a probability kernel from M to S (see Theorem 6.3 of Kallenberg (2001)).

Note that our primitive is now the collection $(\rho^s)_{s \in S}$, that is, we have a state-dependent SCF. The observed choice probabilities differ in each state because the distribution of messages is different.

Definition 5.1. $(\rho^s) \sim$ Bayes if there exists an experiment $\beta : S \rightarrow \Delta(M)$, a prior $p \in \Delta(S)$, and a utility function $v : X \times S \rightarrow \mathbb{R}$ such that ρ^s has an improper RU representation with a GP-tiebreaker and state space $\Omega = M$, probability $\mathbb{P} = \beta_s$, and utility $\widetilde{U}(x, m) = \mathbb{E}_{q_m} v(x)$.

Even though this is a very natural representation, and one that is widely used, I do not know what the corresponding axioms are. These ρ^s are connected to each other across s because they all come from the same prior and same experiment. This suggests that we need some axiom that ties them together, but I don't know what that axiom is. I will have slightly more to say about this in Section 5.3.3.

5.1.2 HR Example

This is the simplest possible example, with two states, two messages, and two actions. The agent is an HR recruiter who is hiring an applicant based on an interview. Let $S := \{0, 1\}$ be the qualification of the applicant (low or high). The interview can either be a flop or go well: $M = \{m_0, m_1\}$. Suppose that the experiment is symmetric with precision $b := \beta(m_1|s = 1) = \beta(m_0|s = 0)$. Let $p := p(s = 1)$ be the prior belief. Then the recruiter's posterior beliefs are

$$q_{m_1} = \left(\frac{bp}{bp + (1-b)(1-p)}, \frac{(1-b)(1-p)}{bp + (1-b)(1-p)} \right)$$
$$q_{m_0} = \left(\frac{(1-b)p}{(1-b)p + b(1-p)}, \frac{b(1-p)}{(1-b)p + b(1-p)} \right).$$

Consider first how the signal changes as we vary its precision b over the interval $[0.5, 1]$. If $b = 0.5$, then the experiment is completely uninformative so $q_m = p$ for all m. On the other hand, if $b = 1$, then the recruiter learns the true state perfectly: Their belief is a point mass. In general, b measures the "strength" of the evidence.[3]

Notice that M are just "labels." In particular, if we set $b = 0$, we also get a perfectly informative experiment, despite the fact that β tells the "opposite" of the true state. Our Bayesian agent is smart enough to invert the message. Likewise, an uninformative experiment is any constant function β, not just the one that corresponds to $b = 0.5$.

Let $A := \{0, 1\}$ be the HR recruiter's menu of choices (make no hire, or make a hire). The recruiter's utility of hiring a qualified applicant equals 1

---

[3] Starting with Blackwell (1951), there is a tradition of measuring the informational content of β by a partial ordering: We will write $\beta \geq \beta'$ if β is *Blackwell-more informative* than β'. Section A.6.2 in the Appendix provides an overview. In this example, the Blackwell ranking coincides with the ranking of real numbers b on $[0, 0.5]$.

and an unqualified applicant, -1. The utility of not hiring is zero. Thus, for any belief that puts probability bigger than a half on $s = 1$ the HR recruiter will make a hire and will not hire for beliefs below that threshold. Let's pick values of p and b such that the recruiter wants to hire after m_1 but not after m_0. The analyst who observes the qualification of the applicant sees high-skilled applicants hired b percent of the time and low-skilled applicants being hired $1 - b$ percent of the time. In particular, the high-skilled applicants are hired more frequently than low skill applicants. $\triangle$

5.1.3 Distribution over Posteriors

An alternative way to set up the model bypasses the message space M and looks directly at the agent's *ex ante* distribution of posteriors. To see how this works, fix a Bayesian model. In any given state the experiment leads to a distribution over messages, and for each message the agent has a posterior belief. Thus, in each state, there is an induced distribution over posteriors. This is the distribution over posteriors that an outside observer who knows the state would expect the agent to have. In Example 5.1.2 in state $s = 1$ the distribution over posteriors puts probability b on belief q_{m_1} and probability $1 - b$ on belief q_{m_0}. In state $s = 0$ the distribution over posteriors puts probability $1 - b$ on belief q_{m_1} and probability b on q_{m_0}.

The main object of interest in this section is not the state-dependent distribution, but its average according to the prior. This average distribution over posteriors, denoted by $\mu \in \Delta(\Delta(S))$, reflects the expectations of the agent who does not know the state.[4] In the HR example, μ puts probability $pb + (1 - p)(1 - b)$ on belief q_{m_1} and probability $p(1 - b) + (1 - p)b$ on q_{m_0}.

Given any prior p and any experiment β the procedure described above gives us a distribution over posteriors μ. The most important property of μ is that its average equals p; that is, beliefs don't change on average. Formally, $\int q\mu(dq) = p$. This important property is sometimes called the *martingale property of beliefs* or *Bayes plausibility*.

To see that it holds, consider the joint probability measure $P \in \Delta(S \times M)$ induced by p and β. The prior is the marginal of P on S and the posterior is the conditional of P on m. By the law of iterated expectations, the average of the conditionals is equal to the marginal, so Bayes plausibility follows. A more mechanical way to see it is to write the average posterior belief that state s is true as

$$\sum_{s' \in S} \sum_{m \in M} q(s|m)\beta(m|s')p(s'),$$

substitute (5.1) for $q(s|m)$ and reverse the order of the sums.

---

[4] Notice that we already used the symbol μ for the distribution of utilities. Now we are using it for the distribution of posteriors, which is a bit of an abuse of notation, but the two distributions play conceptually the same role.

The marginal property of beliefs holds only unconditionally (i.e., for the average distribution over posteriors μ). Conditional on state s' the distribution over posteriors averages to a belief that is "closer" to s' than p, that is, information brings the agent closer to knowing the truth.

We can go in both directions between these two levels of description. For any μ there exists a prior (uniquely given by Bayes plausibility $p_\mu := \int q\mu(dq)$) and an experiment β_μ such that μ is induced by p and β.[5]

Because of this equivalence, if we want to describe the agent's unconditional choice distribution we can interchangeably use experiments or distributions over posteriors. Modulo ties, we have

$$\rho(x, A) = \mu\left(\left\{q \in \Delta(S) : \mathbb{E}_q v(x) = \max_{y \in A} \mathbb{E}_q v(y)\right\}\right).$$

Definition 5.2. $\rho \sim$ *distribution over posteriors* if there exists $\mu \in \Delta(\Delta(S))$ such that ρ has an improper RU representation with a tiebreaker and $\Omega = \Delta(S)$, $\mathbb{P} = \mu$, and $\widetilde{U}(x, q) = \mathbb{E}_q v(x)$.

Notice, that this ρ does not condition on the state, but rather it should be thought of as the unconditional distribution of choices.

5.1.4 Equivalence

Even though the previous two sections present essentially the same model, they involve different primitives (conditional vs. unconditional SCF).

To complete the connection at the level of the primitive, imagine that the analyst does not observe s but all she can see is the marginal choice distribution: the average of ρ^s over s according to the true probability distribution π that governs s. In principle, this true distribution may or may not be equal to the agent's prior p. We will assume that whenever p assigns probability zero to an event, π also assigns probability zero, and denote this $\pi \ll p$. Under the *rational expectations* assumption, the agent's prior is correct, that is, $p = \pi$.[6]

Definition 5.3. $\rho \sim$ average Bayes if for some (p, β, v) there exists $(\rho^s) \sim$ Bayes(p, β, v) and $\pi \in \Delta(S)$, $\pi \ll p$ such that

$$\rho(x, A) = \int_{s \in S} \rho^s(x, A)\pi(ds).$$

Moreover, we say that $\rho \sim$ average Bayes with rational expectations if $p = \pi$.

Under average Bayes representations the analyst does not observe (ρ^s), nor the frequency π, but just the average SCF ρ.

---

[5] Given μ, the experiment is not necessarily unique. Denti, Marinacci, and Rustichini (2022a) summarize a number of properties of the mapping between β and μ.

[6] This term is used by economists to describe the idea that the agent's beliefs are equal to the true data generating process. In multi-person settings the data generating process includes behavior of "nature" as well as other agents, so rational expectations assumption is an equilibrium requirement. In our one-agent settings the equilibrium part of it is turned off.

As we will now see, looking at average choices is not enough to test the rational expectations assumption. On the other hand, if the analyst has access to the conditional choice probabilities ρ^s, then she presumably also has access to the distribution $\pi \in \Delta(S)$. In this case, one test of rational expectations could involve comparing π to the prior distribution revealed from (ρ^s).

Proposition 5.4. *If X is finite, then the following are equivalent:*

(i) $\rho \sim RU$,
(ii) $\rho \sim$ *average Bayes,*
(iii) $\rho \sim$ *average Bayes with rational expectations,*
(iv) $\rho \sim$ *distribution over posteriors.*

Proof. $(i) \Rightarrow (iii)$: By Proposition 1.9, ρ is represented by a distribution over preferences $\mu \in \Delta(\mathcal{P})$. For each $\succsim \in \mathcal{P}$ let $U_{\succsim}$ be a utility function that represents $\succsim$. Define $S := \mathcal{P}$ (notice that in average Bayes the analyst does not observe s so we can take it to be whatever we want, in contrast with state-dependent Bayes). Define $v(x, \succsim) := U_{\succsim}(x), p = \mu, M := \mathcal{P}, \beta(\cdot \mid \succsim) := \delta_{\succsim}$. This way the agent learns their utility perfectly. For a fixed, $x \in A$ we have

$$\rho(x, A) = \mu(\{\succsim \in \mathcal{P} : x \succsim y \text{ for all } y \in A\})$$
$$= p(s \in S : v(x, s) = \max_{y \in A} v(y, s))$$
$$= \sum_{s \in S} p(s)\beta_s(m \in M : \mathbb{E}_{q_m} v(x) = \max_{y \in A} \mathbb{E}_{q_m} v(y)).$$

$(iii) \Rightarrow (ii)$: The former is a special kind of the latter.
$(ii) \Rightarrow (iv)$ Let $q_m \in \Delta(S)$ be the posterior belief given message m. For any measurable set of beliefs $B \subseteq \Delta(S)$ define the probability that the posterior will land in that set

$$\mu(B) := \int_{s \in S} \beta_s(\{m \in M : q_m \in B\}) \pi(ds).^7$$

By definition of average Bayes, modulo ties, we have

$$\rho(x, A) = \int_{s \in S} \beta_s \left(\left\{ m \in M : \mathbb{E}_{q_m}[v(x)] = \max_{y \in A} \mathbb{E}_{q_m}[v(y)] \right\} \right) \pi(ds)$$

so using the definition of μ

$$\rho(x, A) = \mu \left(\left\{ q \in \Delta(S) : \mathbb{E}_q[v(x)] = \max_{y \in A} \mathbb{E}_q[v(y)] \right\} \right).$$

The new tiebreaker needs to be a π-average of the old tiebreakers over states.
$(iv) \Rightarrow (i)$: By Definition 5.2. $\square$

The equivalence with RU is a bit disappointing. We added all this machinery and don't get anything out. In Section 5.3.1 we will break this equivalence by allowing for a separation of tastes and beliefs.

---

[7] The sets $\{m \in M : q_m \in B\}$ are measurable because by Lemma 1.40 of Kallenberg (2001) the function $q : M \to \Delta(S)$ is measurable.

Another way to break this equivalence is to experimentally vary the prior; for example, give the agent many batches of trials, each batch with a different empirical frequency of state. If $\rho \sim RU$, behavior is independent of the frequency, whereas an average Bayes representation allows such frequency-dependence. We will see this shortly in a series of examples.

5.1.5   Action-Recommendations*

Consider a special kind of experiment, where the message space M is the set of available actions A. It is in some sense without loss of generality to consider such experiments. Intuitively, for any experiment we can "glue together" all the messages that lead to the same action choice. This gives us a new experiment that just suggests which action should be taken. We will call such experiments *action-recommendations*.

Taking this action is the optimal thing to do for the agent as long as the original action choice was optimal conditional on each message because upon hearing the message the agent's posterior is the average of all the posteriors given the messages that got "glued together." For this reason this new experiment leads to the same expected utility and same observed state-dependent choice frequencies as the original experiment.

For a fixed menu A the experiment is given by the stochastic choice function itself, $\beta(x|s) := \rho^s(x, A)$. This can be a useful simplification because we can read off the experiment directly from the observable.

Suppose that the analyst knows the agent's prior p. If $\rho^s(x, A)$ is the agent's experiment, then their posterior upon hearing message x is

$$\hat{q}(s|x) = \frac{\rho^s(x, A)p(s)}{\sum_{s \in S} \rho^{s'}(x, A)p(s')}.$$

This is sometimes called the *revealed posterior*.

The following condition, called Obedience (Myerson, 1982), says that the agent wants to follow the action-recommendation: The expected utility of choosing x upon hearing the action recommendation x is higher than choosing some non-recommended action y. This is basically a restatement of Definition 5.1 by restricting attention to action-recommendations.

Condition 5.5 (Obedience).   For all x such that $\rho(x, A) > 0$ we have

$$\sum_{s \in S} v(x, s)\hat{q}(s|x) = \max_{y \in A} \sum_{s \in S} v(y, s)\hat{q}(s|x).$$

Obedience is used in game theory for defining correlated equilibrium (Bergemann and Morris, 2016). Another name for obedience is *no improving action switches (NIAS)* (Caplin and Martin, 2015).

To check Obedience, the analyst needs to know not only the prior p, but also the utility function v. For the following proposition to hold we need to allow the tie breakers to be message-dependent.

Proposition 5.6. *Suppose that S is finite and that p and v are given to the analyst. For any fixed menu A the choice probabilities $\rho^s(\cdot, A)$ have a Bayes representation if and only if Obedience holds.*

Proof. See Section A.5.1. □

While this equivalence holds for a fixed menu, when the menu varies because Proposition 5.6 only delivers menu-dependent experiments, whereas in a Bayes representation β stays fixed. In this sense, the action-recommendation is "as-if" and may not reflect the true underlying information of the agent. It would seem that to ensure Bayes we need extra axioms that tie choice probabilities across menus.

Another way in which action-recommendations are "as-if" is to consider what happens as we vary the prior of the agent. If we pretend that ρ is the experiment, then it will seem that the agent is choosing a different experiment for each prior. But in the Bayes representation the experiment they are *endowed* with is actually fixed. They just happen to be *producing* a different experiment each time.

The assumption that the analyst knows p and v makes sense in controlled lab experiments, where the analyst can manipulate beliefs and payoffs (under reasonable assumptions about risk preferences). As shown by Denti (2022), if we state the problem in the Anscombe–Aumann setting (Section 5.3.1), then the analyst just needs to know the prior.

5.2 EXAMPLES

5.2.1 HR – continued

So far, we showed that with a binary signal the high-skilled applicants are hired more frequently than low skill applicants.

Axiom 5.7. An SCF ρ is *accurate* if

$$\rho(x = 1 | s = 1) \geq \rho(x = 1 | s = 0).$$

An equivalent way to state this is that conditional on hiring, the workers type is higher in expectation, than conditional on not hiring. Let $p \in \Delta(S)$ be any full support prior and P be the joint distribution over $S \times X$ given by ρ and p, that is, $P(s, x) = \rho(x|s)p(s)$. The reader can easily verify (by using the formula for conditional probability) that Axiom 5.7 is equivalent to

$$P(s = 1 | x = 1) \geq P(s = 1 | x = 0)$$

We will now show that Axiom 5.7 is necessary under any experiment, not just the binary one. They key is that the agent wants to match the state with their action:

$$v(x = 1, s = 1) \geq v(x = 0, s = 1) \text{ and } v(x = 0, s = 0)$$
$$\geq v(x = 1, s = 0). \tag{5.2}$$

Indeed, for any utility function that satisfies (5.2), there will be a threshold t such that if the posterior belief $q(s = 1|m) \geq t$, then the agent chooses $x = 1$ and chooses $x = 0$ otherwise. By the law of iterated expectations, $P(s = 1|x = 1)$ is the expectation of q conditional on $x = 1$, which is larger than t because $x = 1$ implies $q \geq t$. Likewise, $P(s = 1|x = 0)$ is lower than t because $x = 0$ implies $q < t$. Therefore,

$$P(s = 1|x = 1) \geq t > P(s = 1|x = 0), \tag{5.3}$$

which as you verified above implies Axiom 5.7.

In fact, Axiom 5.7 is not only necessary but also sufficient for a Bayes representation with a utility that satisfies (5.2). As you verified above, Axiom 5.7 implies $P(s = 1|x = 1) \geq t > P(s = 1|x = 0)$. If this holds with an equality, then assume that the agent has an uninformative signal and randomly chooses their action. If there is a strict inequality, then there exists t such that condition (5.3) holds. Pick v to be any utility function that leads to that particular threshold t and note that condition (5.3) is equivalent to Obedience with respect to that utility v and the prior p. By Proposition 5.6, p has a Bayes representation with that v and p.

Rambachan (2021) studies an extension of this model where the analyst has access to some regressor ξ, which does not enter the utility function, but does affect the agent's beliefs. In this case, our primitive is a joint distribution P over (x, s, ξ). The axiom now becomes:

Axiom 5.8. An SCF ρ is *strongly accurate* if

$$\min_{\xi} P(s = 1|x = 1, \xi) \geq \max_{\xi} P(s = 1|x = 0, \xi).$$

Proposition 5.9 (Rambachan 2021). *An SCF ρ is strongly accurate if and only if it has a Bayes representation with a utility function that is independent of ξ and satisfies (5.2).*

To prove necessity, observe that for all ξ we will now have

$$P(s = 1|x = 1, \xi) \geq t > P(s = 1|x = 0, \xi).$$

Take the maximum of the first inequality and then the minimum of the second. For sufficiency, repeat the above construction pointwise for each value of ξ.

Rambachan (2021) combines this approach with a potential outcomes model to study a similar decision problem (pretrial release decisions of judges); he uses Axiom 5.8 to determine whether judges make systematic mistakes. △

5.2.2 Character Recognition by Human Subjects

The Bayes representation is the workhorse model in cognitive science (Doya et al., 2007; Ma et al., 2022). It has been known even longer in psychology as *Signal Detection Theory* (Tanner and Swets, 1954; Green and Swets, 1966). Here is a simple example of how this model is applied to a perception task.

In each trial the subject is briefly shown a character c or e and asked to identify it. Formally, $X = \{c, e\}$ and $S = \{c, e\}$ and $v(c, c) = v(e, e) = 1$, $v(c, e) = v(e, c) = 0$. Let p be the subject's prior. Let $M = \mathbb{R}$, so the subject gets a random perception of the sort "the character looks much more like c than e" or "the character only kind of looks like e, but it could be c." Let $\beta(m|s)$ be the experiment with density $b(m|s)$. The Bayes rule says that the posterior is

$$\frac{q(s = c|m)}{q(s = e|m)} = \frac{b(m|s = c)\, p(s = c)}{b(m|s = e)\, p(s = e)}.$$

Let $p := p(s = c)$ and ℓ be the likelihood ratio: $\ell(m) := \frac{b(m|s=c)}{b(m|s=e)}$. Given v, it follows that the agent chooses c conditional on message m if $q(s = c|m) > q(s = e|m)$, which by Bayes rule is equivalent to $\ell(m) > \frac{1-p}{p}$, and chooses e if the opposite inequality holds. Let $L(k) := \{m \in M : \ell(m) > k\}$ and notice that $k > k'$ implies $L(k) \subseteq L(k')$. Thus, if ρ has such a Bayes representation we have $\rho^{p,s}(c) = \beta\left(L\left(\frac{1-p}{p}\right)|s\right)$, an increasing function of p in every state s.

We conclude that the model predicts that the probability that the agent chooses c is an increasing function of the ex ante probability of occurrences of c. This is a key distinction from models like RU which predict no such frequency-dependence. Experiments show that behavior is indeed monotone in the prior (Swets, 1973; Gescheider, 1997). Figure 5.2 shows how data looks like in a typical perceptual experiment. Plots like this are sometimes called ROC (receiver operating characteristic) curves.

A key issue is matching the predictive Bayes model with data from the experiment. Suppose that the true state (character) varies from trial to trial. In a typical experiment trials are batched, so that the frequency of characters π is constant within each batch but varies across batches. Under the rational expectations assumption the agent knows the frequency in each batch, so $p = \pi$.

The simplest justification for this assumption is that the subject habituates to each batch of trials. It's conceivable that by trial 100 out of 250 they adapt to the current batch and believe that the prevalent distribution of s is governed by π. A more detailed model would assume that the agent knows that π changes over time and rationally updates their beliefs about π. In cognitive science

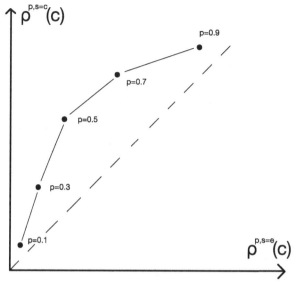

Figure 5.2 An ROC curve. Each point on the curve corresponds to a different prior p for a fixed difficulty of the task. Making the task harder shifts the curve toward the diagonal.

this is sometimes called an "online prior" (Petzschner and Glasauer, 2011; Verstynen and Sabes, 2011; Cicchini, Anobile, and Burr, 2014). △

5.2.3 Law of Comparative Judgment from Bayes Rule

Recall Example 1.15, where we assumed that the agent is facing two objects and is incentivized to pick the one with higher weight. Thurstone's model says that the agent picks the object with a higher perceived weight. In that model the agent is taking their perception at face value. We will now show that this is indeed the optimal thing to do for a Bayesian agent with a symmetric prior.

Suppose that one of the objects is on the left and the other is on the right, so $X = \{l, r\}$. The state consists of the true weights of the two items $s = (s(l), s(r))$. The message space is $M = \mathbb{R}^2$, so the message contains the weight perception of each of the items. In state s the agent gets a message $(\tilde{m}(\ell), \tilde{m}(r))$, where

$$\tilde{m}(x) = \gamma(s(x)) + \tilde{\epsilon}(x), \ x = \ell, r$$

where γ is Thurstone's transformation function and $\tilde{\epsilon}(x) \sim \mathcal{N}(0, \sigma_\epsilon^2)$ are independent across x.

The agent's prior belief is symmetric: $\gamma(s(x)) \sim \mathcal{N}(\mu_0, \sigma_0^2)$ independently across x with the same mean and variance. For example, if γ is log this means that $s(x)$ is distributed log-normally.

The Bayes rule (see, e.g., Lemma 15.7 of Williams (1991)) says that the posterior given message $m(x)$ is $\gamma(s(x)) \sim \mathcal{N}(\mu_1(m(x)), \sigma_1^2)$, where

$$\mu_1(m) = \sigma_1^2 \left(\frac{\mu_0}{\sigma_0^2} + \frac{m}{\sigma_\epsilon^2} \right) \quad \text{and} \quad \sigma_1^2 = \left(\frac{1}{\sigma_0^2} + \frac{1}{\sigma_\epsilon^2} \right)^{-1}.$$

Thus, the agent's posterior is Normal, with a variance that is deterministic (does not depend on the message realization) and mean equal to a weighted average of the prior mean and the message realization. The weights depend on how informative the message is relative to the prior: For a fixed prior sending $\sigma_\epsilon \to \infty$ results in putting zero weight on the message, and sending $\sigma_\epsilon \to 0$ results in putting all the weight on the message.

In the language of distributions over posteriors, μ puts probability one on the collection of Normals with a fixed variance σ_1^2. A calculation reveals that their mean is distributed $\mathcal{N}(\mu_0, \sigma_0^2 - \sigma_1^2)$.

Given the payoff structure it is optimal for the agent to choose l over r if their posterior probability that $s(l) > s(r)$ is bigger than a half. Given the Normality assumption, this holds iff the posterior mean of $\gamma(s(l))$ is greater than the posterior mean of $\gamma(s(r))$, that is, $\gamma(s(l)) + \tilde{\epsilon}(l) > \gamma(s(r)) + \tilde{\epsilon}(r)$. This is exactly Thurstone's probit!

Because of this connection, the model explains the same two of the stylized facts as probit: S-shaped psychometric function and diminishing sensitivity (recall Example 1.15), but cannot give us payoff-monotonicity. We also cannot explain frequency-dependence because the choice probabilities are independent of σ_0. However, we can get another form of frequency-dependence: If the subject is consistently presented with a heavier left item, then as opposed to Thurstone's model, the subject will choose the left item with a higher frequency, much like in the character recognition example (Example 5.2.2).

So far we assumed that m is unobservable to the analyst. Neuroscientists use animal experiments to connect m to neuronal activity, both of single neurons (Hanes and Schall, 1996) and populations of them (e.g., Ratcliff, Cherian, and Segraves, 2003). Kiani and Shadlen (2009) introduce a new kind of experimental task where the subject is offered a third alternative: Opt out and get a sure but lower payoff. The above model predicts that the agent should take the outside option if $|\mu_1(m_l) - \mu_1(m_r)| < t(\sigma_1)$, that is, when their belief is weaker than some threshold $t(\sigma_1)$ that is increasing in posterior variance. Kiani and Shadlen (2009) show that the measured neuronal activity behaves very much in the same way. $\triangle$

Remark 5.10 (Noisy Coding and Efficient Coding). Fechner and Thurstone taught us to think of m as an internal mental representation of the stimulus, a noisy encoding of the truth (Khaw, Li, and Woodford, 2021). Noisy coding does not have to be efficient: In Examples 5.2.2 and 5.2.3 the signals are given exogenously, not optimized over. What is efficient is their usage (the action is Bayes-optimal given the message). In cognitive science *efficient coding* generally means that the signal is fixed but the agent is optimally choosing Thurstone's transformation function γ (e.g., the firing rate of neurons) subject to a metabolic cost (Barlow et al., 1961; Rustichini, Conen, Cai, and Padoa-Schioppa, 2017; Polanía, Woodford, and Ruff, 2019; Bucher and Brandenburger, 2021). This is the territory of active learning (Chapter 6). $\triangle$

5.3   RANDOM TASTES VERSUS RANDOM BELIEFS

Proposition 5.4 shows that random tastes (RU) leads to the same behavior as random beliefs (average Bayes). This is because with state-dependent utility there is no a separation between tastes and beliefs. To see that, suppose that S is finite and we have a (deterministic) preference over X represented by a belief p and a state-dependent utility v, that is, $x \succsim y$ iff $\sum_{s \in S} v(x, s)p(s) \geq \sum_{s \in S} v(y, s)p(s)$. For any other $q \in \Delta(S)$ such that $q(s) > 0$ in all states s, there exists $\hat{v}$ (given by $v(x, s)p(s)/q(s)$) such that $(\hat{v}, q)$ is a state-dependent representation of the same preference. To overcome this problem it is often assumed that v is state-independent. The next section illustrates this approach in the deterministic choice setting.

5.3.1   Deterministic Choice

In this model the agent is choosing between *acts*, which are state-contingent payoffs. Let Z be the set of primitive payoffs, like in Chapter 4. In the Savage (1972) model, an act is a mapping $f : S \rightarrow Z$ that describes which prize the agent gets in every state. Following Anscombe and Aumann (1963), we will study acts $f : S \rightarrow \Delta^s(Z)$. Here, in each state the agent gets a (simple) lottery over prizes. These acts are a bit contrived but they simplify the analysis considerably.[8]

Typical acts are denoted f, g, h and the agent has a preference $\succsim$ over acts. An *Anscombe Aumann (AA) representation* $U(f)$ of $\succsim$ consists of a prior $p \in \Delta(S)$ and a state-independent vNM utility function $v : \Delta^s(Z) \rightarrow \mathbb{R}$, such that

$$U(f) = \mathbb{E}_p v(f) = \sum_{s \in S} v(f(s))p(s).$$

The key assumption is that utility is state-independent, that is, it does not depend on s. State independence is heavily debated (see e.g., Aumann and Savage (1987) and Karni, Schmeidler, and Vind (1983)), but it is an important identifying assumption because it pins down p uniquely and v cardinally.

The representation is characterized by three axioms. The first one relies on the mixing operation for acts. For any fixed $\alpha \in [0, 1]$ an α-mixture of two

---

[8] Actually, Anscombe and Aumann (1963) studied even more contrived acts. The exposition in this section is due to Fishburn (1970).

acts f and g is another act that in each state $s \in S$ gives the lottery $\alpha f(s) + (1 - \alpha)g(s)$. We will denote this act $\alpha f + (1 - \alpha)g$. Formally, $(\alpha f + (1 - \alpha)g)(s) := \alpha f(s) + (1 - \alpha)g(s)$.

Note that U is linear in those mixtures. As a consequence, the main axiom is Independence (Axiom 4.2) written using those mixtures.

Axiom 5.11 (Independence). For all $\alpha \in (0, 1)$ and $f, g, h : S \to \Delta^s(Z)$

$$f \succsim g \text{ if and only if } \alpha f + (1 - \alpha)h \succsim \alpha g + (1 - \alpha)h.$$

Independence only gives us a state-dependent representation. We need another axiom to get state-independence. For each $s \in S$ with a slight abuse of notation we understand $f(s)$ to be a constant act that pays off the same lottery $f(s)$ in every state, that is, the agent gets the lottery $f(s)$ for sure.

Axiom 5.12 (Monotonicity). If $f(s) \succsim g(s)$ for all $s \in S$, then $f \succsim g$.

Intuitively, if for each s you'd prefer to get $f(s)$ for sure rather than $g(s)$ for sure, then you should choose f over g before knowing which state is realized. Finally, we need some form of continuity: the following Mixture Continuity axiom or an Archimedian Continuity axiom similar to Axiom 4.3.

Axiom 5.13 (Mixture Continuity). For any f, g, h the sets

$$\{\alpha \in [0, 1] : \alpha f + (1 - \alpha)g \succsim h\} \text{ and } \{\alpha \in [0, 1] : \alpha f + (1 - \alpha)g \precsim h\}$$

are closed in $[0, 1]$.

Theorem 5.14 (Anscombe–Aumann). *Suppose that S is finite. A preference $\succsim$ satisfies Axioms 5.11, 5.12, and 5.13 if and only if it has an Anscombe–Aumann representation. Moreover, if $\succsim$ is nontrivial, then the probability is unique and utility is cardinally unique.*

5.3.2 Stochastic Choice and Learning

Let's now build a model of stochastic choice based on this approach. Our agent has a deterministic and state-independent utility and a random posterior, which makes their choices look random. In Section 5.1.3 we said this can be modeled by a distribution over posteriors $\mu \in \Delta(\Delta(S))$. Because utility is deterministic, all randomness in choice is driven by learning (variation in information) and not by randomness in tastes.[9] For any posterior q the conditional expected utility of act f is $\mathbb{E}_q v(f)$.

This theory was developed for the average SCF (unconditional on state). Our analyst now observes the agent choosing from finite menus of (Anscombe–Aumann) acts.

---

[9] This distinction is absent in the model without acts. If we assumed that $v(x, s)$ does not depend on s in Section 5.1, this would have given us a model of deterministic choice.

Definition[†] **5.15.** ρ has an *Anscombe–Aumann* representation if there exists a distribution over posteriors $\mu \in \Delta(\Delta(S))$, and a deterministic and state-independent vNM utility function $v : \Delta^s(Z) \to \mathbb{R}$ such that

$$\rho(f,A) = \mu\left(\left\{q \in \Delta(S) : \mathbb{E}_q v(f) = \max_{g \in A} \mathbb{E}_q v(g)\right\}\right).$$

This is not well defined if there are ties. The original paper develops a novel approach to this problem, which I will not discuss but put a dagger † on all the results. A serious reader will want to consult the paper.

If ρ has an Anscombe–Aumann representation, then it satisfies Regularity and the Gul–Pesendorfer axioms (Axioms 4.14, 4.15, and 4.16) written using our new mixture operation over. However, these axioms alone are not enough: They lead to a random linear $\widetilde{U}$ defined over acts, but this doesn't guarantee state-independence. Such a $\widetilde{U}$ can be written as $\widetilde{U}(f) = \sum_{s \in S} \tilde{v}(f(s), s)\tilde{q}$. Lu (2016) showed precisely what other axioms ρ has to satisfy.

The first axiom guarantees state-independence of v. Similarly to the deterministic version, it says that that if there is an act that is best in each state, then this act should be chosen ex ante before the state is known. As you recall, $f(s)$ is understood as a constant lottery that pays off $f(s)$ in every state. Likewise, $A(s)$ is a menu of such lotteries as f varies over A; formally, $A(s) := \{f(s) : f \in A\}$.

Axiom 5.16. If $\rho\big(f(s), A(s)\big) = 1$ for all $s \in S$ then $\rho(f,A) = 1$.

The next axiom guarantees that v is deterministic and thus all the randomness in choice comes from random posteriors, not random tastes.

Axiom 5.17. If A is a menu of constant acts, then $\rho(f,A) = 1$ for some $f \in A$.

Theorem[†] **5.18 (Lu, 2016).** *Suppose that S is finite. ρ has an Anscombe–Aumann representation iff it satisfies Regularity and Axioms 4.14, 4.15, and 4.16 plus 5.16 and 5.17. Moreover, the information structure μ is unique and the utility function v is cardinally-unique.*

This result can be extended in several ways. First, as discussed before, when utility is state-dependent the prior is completely unidentified. However, as Lu (2019) shows, the above methodology can be used to point-identify the prior even under state-dependent utility. The key is to observe the agent's behavior across two information structures. We refer the curious reader to that interesting paper.

Another extension of Theorem 5.18 can used to characterize state-dependent Bayes representations (as opposed to the average SCF)

5.3.3 An Extension to State-Dependent SCF

In Section 5.1.1 we left open the question of characterization of Bayes representations. Here we have developed enough structure that we can take this question up again. Suppose that in each state ρ^s satisfies all the axioms of Theorem 5.18. The question is what other conditions need to be added to guarantee a Bayes representation like in Definition 5.1. Intuitively, the conditions need to link ρ^s across different states s to ensure that they all come from the same experiment β and same utility v.

The first condition ensures that the utility is the same in each state.

Axiom 5.19 (State-Independence of Tastes). For all $s \in S$, when restricted to constant acts, the SCF is the same.

To develop the second condition, assume that the analyst observes the objective frequency of states $\pi \in \Delta(S)$. (Since our analyst observes the choice probabilities in each state, it is conceivable that they can also record the distribution of states.)

Theorem 5.18 implies that in each state $s \in S$ there is a distribution over posteriors μ^s. Suppose for simplicity that each μ^s has finite support. For the moment, let's treat μ^s as the experiment of the agent with message space equal $\Delta(S)$ (Blackwell, 1951, called them standard experiments). For now, let's treat those messages as just labels, that is, let's ignore the fact that they are beliefs. In state s there is probability $\mu^s(q)$ that the agent will get "message" q.

The following condition says that if the agent gets message q and updates their prior π using the Bayes rule, then their posterior belief is precisely equal to q. In other words, the agent can take messages at face value and they are not just "labels."

Condition 5.20 (Bayes Consistency). For all $s \in S$ and for all q that is in the support of at least one μ^s

$$\frac{\pi(s)\mu(q|s)}{\sum_{s' \in S} \pi(s')\mu(q|s')} = q(s).$$

I hesitate to call Bayes Consistency an axiom because it uses derived objects, such as distributions over beliefs.

Proposition[†] 5.21. *Suppose that S is finite and ρ^s satisfies the axioms from Theorem 5.18 in each state and Axiom 5.19 and Condition 5.20 hold. Then there exists an experiment β and a vNM utility $v : \Delta^s(Z) \to \mathbb{R}$ such that in each state modulo ties we have*

$$\rho^s(f, A) = \beta^s(\{m \in M : \mathbb{E}_{q_m} v(f) = \max_{g \in A} \mathbb{E}_{q_m} v(g)\}),$$

where q_m is the Bayesian posterior given the prior π and experiment β.

This result follows by taking $M := \Delta(S)$ and $\beta(q|s) := \mu^s(q)$. By Axiom 5.19, the utility functions are affine transformations of each other; take v to be one of them. Then Condition 5.20 is just (5.1).

Note that this proposition assumes rational expectations. To relax this assumption, we could put an existential quantifier into Condition 5.20. A different approach was taken by Duraj (2018).

5.3.4 Comparative Statics

In this section we will investigate what happens to choices when the experiment becomes more informative. First, let's start with some examples. In Example 5.2.3 we developed the Normal-Normal model of perception. Suppose that the true weights are $s(\ell) > s(r)$, and let γ be the Thurstone transformation function. The parameter σ_ϵ controls the noisiness of the experiment. In this model the agent chooses ℓ with probability $\Phi\left(\frac{\gamma(x\ell) - \gamma(r)}{\sqrt{2}\sigma_\epsilon}\right)$, so as $\sigma_\epsilon \to 0$ the probability of choosing ℓ converges monotonically to 1. Thus, more informative experiments lead to choices that are more deterministic (less stochastic).

Notice that this comparative does not hold in the above example if we only look at unconditional (average) choices. If the analyst does not know which item is heaver, they will observe the agent choosing half-half no matter how informative their signal is. The following example shows a situation in which more information does lead to less randomness in choice unconditional on the state.

Example 5.22. Let $S = \{s_1, s_2, s_3, s_4\}$. There are two acts f and g with payoffs given in Table 5.1. Suppose that $v(x) = x$ and the prior is $(.49, .01, .01, .49)$. Consider two information structures: In the first one, the agent learns perfectly whether the state is in the cell $\{s_1, s_2\}$ or $\{s_3, s_4\}$; the second information structure perfectly reveals the state.

Under the first partition with probability .5 the first cell is realized and leads the agent to deterministically choose f; with probability .5 the second cell is realized and the agent chooses g. Thus, for an analyst who does not observe the state (only has access to the average ρ) the observed choice probabilities are $(.5, .5)$. Under the second partition those choice probabilities are are $(.98, .02)$ – much less random. $\triangle$

While these examples suggest that more information leads to (weakly) less random choices, there is a sense in which the opposite is true. I will now try to explain that. We say that μ is more informative than μ' if μ Blackwell-dominates μ' (Section A.6.2). Intuitively, this means that under μ the posterior is more random than under μ'. Since it's the randomness of the posterior that drives randomness in choice, more information means that choices are more random.

To see how this works, suppose that we are in the Anscombe–Aumann setting. Let $\bar{f}, \underline{f}$ denote the best and worst acts (with state-independent utility we

Table 5.1 *Payoffs in Example 5.22.*

	s_1	s_2	s_3	s_4
f	1	0	0	1
g	0	1	50	0

can choose them to be constant acts). Normalize their utilities to 1 and 0. The utility of act $f^\alpha := \alpha \underline{f} + (1 - \alpha)\bar{f}$ is deterministically equal $1 - \alpha$.

By adding f^α to any menu A we can see what is the probability that the expected utility of some act from the original menu is above $1 - \alpha$. This helps us get a grasp on the distribution μ. The *test function* of A is the mapping $\alpha \mapsto \rho(A, A \cup \{f^\alpha\})$. For each menu this is an increasing function from $[0, 1]$ to itself; in fact (modulo ties) it is a CDF.

We say that ρ is *more random* than ρ' if for any menu A the test function of ρ second-order stochastically dominates the test function of ρ' (Section 4.1.4).

Theorem[†] **5.23 (Lu 2016).** *Suppose that ρ has an AA representation (v, μ) and ρ' has a AA representation (v, μ') such that $p_\mu = p_{\mu'}$. In this case ρ is "more random" than ρ' if and only if μ is more informative than μ'.*

This can be illustrated using the following example.

Example 5.24. The agent is a risk-neutral lender who is faced with a pool of loan applications and has to decide whether to approve or decline each applicant $A = \{a, d\}$. Each applicant has a fixed probability of default. Let $S := \{0, 1\}$ denote whether there is default or not. Approving an applicant results in a payoff of zero for the lender if the applicant defaults and one if they don't default, so it's an AA act $a(1) = \delta_0, a(0) = \delta_1$. The payoff of declining an application is a constant act $d(s) = 1 - \alpha \in [0, 1]$. The lender has utility linear in money and uses a fixed information structure $\mu \in \Delta(\Delta(S))$ to learn about the likelihood of default $\tilde{q}$ before making a decision. This implies that the agent will choose a over d iff $\tilde{q}(0) \geq 1 - \alpha$.

The analyst is a regulator who wants to check whether the lender is following proper antidiscrimination policies, for example, not taking into account demographic information when evaluating loan applications. The regulator cannot condition on the information available to the lender, so the observed approval probability is

$$\rho(a, d) = \mu \left(\{q \in \Delta(S) : q(0) \geq 1 - \alpha\}\right).$$

If the regulator is able to vary α, she can uncover the CDF of μ. Suppose there is another lender ρ' who is known not to condition on demographics. Our regulator can compare the variability of ρ and ρ' and potentially raise a flag.   △

5.4 MENU-DEPENDENT SIGNALS

So far information was independent of the menu. But sometimes new items can provide new information that sheds light on existing items. Consider the following, admittedly silly, example.

Example 5.25. Suppose that our agent is choosing between dishes in a restaurant: steak tartare (st), chicken (c), and fish (f). Their utility is given in Table 5.2.

Table 5.2 *Payoffs in Example 5.25.*

	$\tilde{U}_s$(steak tartare)	$\tilde{U}_s$(chicken)	$\tilde{U}_s$(fish)
$s = good\ chef$	10	7	3
$s = bad\ chef$	0	5	0

Moreover, if a restaurant serves fish, then the moment our agent enters the restaurant this provides an informative experiment about the quality of the chef: If the agent enters the restaurant and the whole restaurant smells like fish, this means that the chef is bad (so our agent chooses c). If the restaurant serves fish but there is no fishy smell in the air, the chef is good (and our agent chooses st). Thus an analyst who observes choice unconditional on the state will record the choice frequencies as $\rho(st, \{st, c, f\}) = \rho(c, \{st, c, f\}) = \frac{1}{2}$ and $\rho(f, \{st, c, f\}) = 0$. On the other hand, in absence of fi on the menu the agent gets no message and has to go by their prior and maximizes ex ante expected utility; this leads to $\rho(st, \{st, c\}) = 0$ and $\rho(c, \{st, c\}) = 1$ (if the prior is uniform). Thus, menu-dependent information behaves very much like menu-dependent utility and can lead to a violation of the Regularity axiom.   △

Definition 5.26. ρ has a *menu-dependent Bayes representation* if there exists a prior $p \in \Delta(S)$, a utility function $v : S \to \mathbb{R}^X$ and for each menu A there exists $\beta^A : S \to \Delta(M)$ such that

$$\rho(x, A) = \sum_{s \in S} \beta_s^A \left(\left\{ m \in M : \mathbb{E}_{q_m^A} v(x) = \max_{y \in A} \mathbb{E}_{q_m^A} v(y) \right\} \right),$$

where q_m^A is the posterior given message m, prior p and experiment β^A.

Theorem 5.27 (Safonov 2017). *Let $x \succsim^* y$ if $\rho(x, A) = 1$ for some $A \ni y$. An SCF ρ has a menu-dependent learning representation iff $\succsim^*$ is acyclic. In particular, this is true when ρ satisfies Positivity (Axiom 1.14).*

One way to add bite to the general model is to add parametric assumptions. Natenzon (2019) develops a *Bayesian probit* model, where the agent observes a Normal signal of the utility of each item in the menu. The prior belief is that each $v(x)$ is Normal with mean $\bar{v}(x)$ and independent across $x \in X$. The message is $m(x) = v(x) + \epsilon(x)$, where ϵ is jointly Normal. The correlation of messages means that adding new items to the menu can shed light on the utilities of existing items and therefore different menus lead to different experiments.

Natenzon (2019) develops a behavioral notion of similarity that captures the ranking of correlation coefficients. In addition he develops identification results, and necessary axioms for the model (versions of moderate stochastic transitivity and the BM axiom). He uses the model to explain decoy effect, compromise effect, and similarity effects. Natenzon (2019) uses the concept of phantom alternatives – ones that are not available for choice, but are seen by the decision maker and therefore convey the message attached to them. This is similar to Safonov's (2017) assumption that information can be varied independently of the menu.

Note that in Bayesian Probit adding an item gives more information about the state. It might be interesting to work out the implications of such a monotonicity assumption in a model without the Normal assumptions.

5.5 OTHER WORK ON LEARNING*

5.5.1 Menu Correlated With the State

So far, the *state* was uncorrelated with the menu. We considered the case where *information* depended on the menu but the true state was uncorrelated with the menu (the distribution of s was the same for each A). What if there is such a correlation? Given Theorem 5.27, it should not be surprising that such a model does not have any bite.

Kamenica (2008) considers a version of such a model where consumers make inferences from menus and firms strategically exploit this. He shows that the model explains choice overload and compromise effect.

5.5.2 Other Related Work

Gabaix and Laibson (2017) use a multiperiod learning model to microfound "as-if" discounting and present bias. Even though the agent's utility is not discounted, their choices appear to reveal impatience because signals about future objects are noisier, so the agent relies more on her prior.

The idea that agents perceive quantities imperfectly can be applied to stochastic choice between lotteries (such as in Chapter 4). Here the agent has a fixed Bernoulli utility function u but perceives the probabilities of each lottery with an error. This model is analyzed in Khaw, Li, and Woodford (2021) and further experiments done by Frydman and Jin (2022); a related idea is Enke and Graeber (2019).[10]

Woodford (2020) overviews the perception literature in much more detail than here. In addition to the two tasks discussed here (Examples 1.5 and 5.2.2), he discusses a reproduction task, directly aimed at measuring the agent's subjective perception of a given stimulus. A Bayesian model can explain a number of stylized facts about this task: The estimate is biased toward the prior (the mean of the batch π), and the variance of the estimate is higher for higher baches (for details, see Jazayeri and Shadlen, 2010).

---

[10] Gabaix and Laibson (2017) and Khaw, Li, and Woodford (2021) are in a sense an application of a similar idea, to the domains of time and risk, respectively.

Finally, there is the classic line of work demonstrating biases in updating and probabilistic reasoning more broadly, such as gambler's fallacy, hot hand fallacy, base rate neglect, confirmation bias, law of small numbers, and non-belief in the law of large numbers. This line of work is very rich in interesting phenomena. There is an ostensible contradiction between using the Bayesian model to explain a number of perceptual phenomena like above, and at the same time noting that it is violated in a number of ways.

CHAPTER 6

Active Learning

6.1 THE MODEL AND MOTIVATING EXAMPLES

In Chapter 5 randomness of choices was generated by the randomness of agent's messages. The experiment generating those messages was exogenous: It was fixed once and for all and could not be affected by the actions of the agent. This is called *passive learning*.

Active learning is when information can be chosen by the agent (at least to some degree). The agent may decide what to learn about and how much. This is sometimes used as a modeling tool for *attention*.

While passive learning satisfies Regularity, active learning can violate it. This can happen because changing the menu changes the incentives to learn about the state and therefore changes the experiment. The following example illustrates this.

Example 6.1. Suppose that the state is determined by the number of red balls on the screen. There are two equally likely states $s_1 = 49$ and $s_2 = 51$. Let $X = \{x, y, z\}$ and the state-dependent utility is given in Table 6.1.

If the menu is $\{x, y\}$ then the payoff from distinguishing the states is low. Provided that the cost of learning the state is higher than 1, the agent chooses y with probability zero in each state. On the other hand, if the menu is $\{x, y, z\}$ then it might make sense to pay attention to the state and choose y in state s_2 and z in state s_1. Thus, there is a violation of Regularity: from the point of view of the analyst who does not observe the state the agent chooses y with probability a half (and z with probability a half). The violation of Regularity also occurs conditional on state s_2, where the probability of choosing y goes up from zero to one. Dean and Neligh (2023) document such violations experimentally. $\triangle$

In this chapter we will study a general model of active learning, where the agent can buy any kind of information they please and there is a cost function defined over information structures. Intuitively, the agent solves:

$$\max_i \left[V^A(i) - \text{cost}(i) \right],$$

Table 6.1 *Payoffs in Example 6.1.*

	s_1	s_2
x	50	50
y	40	52
z	100	0

where i stands for "information" and $V^A(i)$ is the value of information i given by maximizing posterior expected utility over the menu A.

There are two prevailing interpretations of this model:

1. *Costly information acquisition*: The agent can run actual physical experiments, at a cost. For example, hire a geologist to drill in the ground and estimate how much oil there is. This approach has roots in the statistics literature (Wald, 1947; Bohnenblust, Shapley, and Sherman, 1949; Blackwell, 1951; Raiffa and Schlaifer, 1961) and is the basic model in microeconomics (Persico, 2000; Bergemann and Välimäki, 2002).

2. *Costly information processing aka rational inattention*: Information is already out there in front of the agent. The cost represents the mental energy of processing this information (Sims, 2003, 2006, 2010).[1]

The literature on rational inattention traditionally uses a specific cost function from information theory, called mutual information. It leads to a tractable model, but is at odds with some basic stylized facts. For instance, in the weight perception task (Example 1.5) it leads to a psychometric function that is a step function (The error rate is a constant function of the weight difference: It depends only on its sign). This is because, under mutual information, it is equally difficult to distinguish between two "nearby" states (e.g., weight difference of 1g) and between two "far away" states (e.g., a weight difference of 500 g). We will delve more formally into this later in this chapter.

These problems can be fixed by choosing a cost function different than mutual information. Section 6.4 maps out different classes of cost functions and discusses how they relate to each other. Section 6.5 discusses the corresponding axioms on SCF.

Active learning is also present in dynamic models, such as sequential sampling, that will be discussed in Chapter 9. Another example of active learning are *experience goods*, where the agent can learn about their utility through consuming the good (we will discuss them briefly in the Chapter 7).

---

[1] In decision theory this is referred to as *costly contemplation* (see, e.g., Ergin (2003), Ergin and Sarver (2010), De Oliveira, Denti, Mihm, and Ozbek (2016), and de Oliveira (2019)).

In the literature there is sometimes a different formulation of the decision problem, without a cost function but with a constraint. In that alternative formulation the agent solves $\max_{i \in \Gamma} V^A(i)$, where Γ is some set of constraints on i. For example, Γ includes only normal experiments conditional on the state.

For any fixed decision problem the two formulations are equivalent, but across decision problems the cost formulation is more general. To see that cost is more general, set $c(i) = 0$ if $i \in \Gamma$ and infinity otherwise.[2]

One implication of the constraint formulation is that scaling up the payoffs does not change behavior. On the other hand, the cost formulation predicts payoff-monotonicity, that is, the agent makes (weakly) better choices when stakes are raised. Dean and Neligh (2023) show in a perception-style experiment that error rates indeed diminish when payoffs scale up.

6.2 VALUE OF INFORMATION

6.2.1 Expected Payoff

In the introduction above, we had an abstract notion of information i. It is now time to be more specific. Suppose that S is a finite state space. Recall from Chapter 5 that we can define i either as an experiment $\beta : S \to \Delta(M)$ or as a distribution over posteriors $\mu \in \Delta(\Delta(S))$. Moreover, given a prior p and an experiment β we get a distribution over posteriors, which we will denote here by $\mu = p \oplus \beta$. As you may recall, the martingale property of beliefs says that for any β and p if $\mu = p \oplus \beta$, then $\int q\mu(dq) = p$.

Define the *interim utility* of menu A under belief $q \in \Delta(S)$ to be: $v^A(q) := \max_{x \in A} \mathbb{E}_q v(x)$. This is the maximal utility that can be attained given the belief q.

The value of information is computed given a prior $p \in \Delta(S)$. The idea is that given an information structure the agent will arrive at a number of possible posteriors q and each time take the optimal action. The value of information is then the expectation over interim utilities. This can be written in two ways:

$$V_p^A(\beta) = \sum_{s \in S} \int_{m \in M} v^A(q_m)\beta(dm|s)p(s), \qquad (6.1)$$

or alternatively as:

$$V^A(\mu) = \int_{q \in \Delta(S)} v^A(q)\mu(dq). \qquad (6.2)$$

---

[2] This is similar to the literature on ambiguity aversion, where maxmin preferences have a constraint and variational preferences have a cost (Gilboa and Schmeidler, 1989; Maccheroni, Marinacci, and Rustichini, 2006). Likewise, in Hansen and Sargent (2008) there are "constraint preferences" and "multiplier preferences."

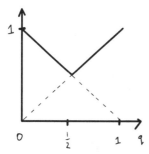

Figure 6.1 The graph of the interim utility function $v^A(q)$ in Example 6.2.

We have $V_p^A(\beta) = V^A(p \oplus \beta)$ for any p and β. The value of information depends on the prior (either explicitly in (6.1) or implicitly in (6.2)) because the value of a piece of information depends on what the agent already knows. Here is a simple example that illustrates that.

Example 6.2. Suppose that $A = \{x, y\}$ and $S = \{s_x, s_y\}$. The agent wants to match the state: $v(x, s_x) = 1 = v(y, s_y)$ and otherwise zero. The reader can easily check that Figure 6.1 plots the interim utility as a function of the posterior. Suppose that β is a binary experiment that is almost uninformative, so that if p is a prior, then the resulting $p \oplus \mu$ puts weight on two posteriors which are very close to p. If $p = \frac{1}{2}$, then we are in the strictly convex part of $v^A(\cdot)$ and therefore the benefit of experiment β is positive: $V_p^A(\beta) - v^A(p) > 0$. On the other hand, if p is close enough to zero or one, then both those posteriors will lie on the linear segment of the function $v^A(\cdot)$ and therefore the net benefit will be zero.[3]   △

6.2.2   Cost

We will denote by h a cost function defined on experiments and by c a cost function defined on distributions over posteriors. Going forward, we will assume that all h and c are Blackwell-monotone, that is, more information is more costly. This is without loss of generality because if a less informative experiment costs more, then nobody would use it.[4] It is also without loss to assume cost is normalized so that uninformative experiments are costless, that is, $c(\delta_p) = 0$ for all $p \in \Delta(S)$ and $h(\beta) = 0$ for any constant experiment β.

---

[3] In general, $v^A(q)$ is a convex and continuous function (why?), so the benefit of any experiment is nonnegative. In general, with finitely many actions $v^A(\cdot)$ will have linear regions where the agent's demand for information is zero (see Radner and Stiglitz (1984) and Chade and Schlee (2002)).

[4] The Blackwell order is introduced in Section A.6.2 in the Appendix. Formally, we can define another cost function where this experiment now costs as much as the more informative one. This will not change behavior because the value function (6.1) and (6.2) is Blackwell-monotone.

The universe of cost functions c is larger than the universe of cost functions h. Recall that for any μ there exists a prior (equal to $p_\mu = \int q\mu(dq)$) and an experiment β_μ such that $\mu = p_\mu \oplus \beta_\mu$. Therefore, given a cost function h we can construct a cost function $c_h(\mu) := h(\beta_\mu)$.[5] Such a cost function is independent of the prior: $c(p \oplus \beta) = c(p' \oplus \beta)$ for all full support p, p'. But not all cost functions c have this property; in general, c can be prior-dependent.

Definition 6.3. A cost function $c : \Delta(\Delta(S)) \to [0, \infty]$ is *prior-independent* if $c(p \oplus \beta) = c(p' \oplus \beta)$ for all β and all full support p, p'. A cost function c is *prior-dependent* if it is not prior-independent.

This distinction doesn't matter if we only observe behavior for a fixed prior. But it does matter if there is experimental variation in prior, or we observe behavior across time (yesterday's posterior is today's prior), or in game theoretic models where the prior is an equilibrium quantity.

I view prior-dependence is a useful working distinction between "costly information acquisition" and "costly information processing." Imagine that you are acquiring information, for example, hiring an expert to perform a geological survey. The expert charges only based on the number of drillings, not on your prior belief, so the cost is prior-independent. On the other hand, the workhorse cost function in the information *processing* literature, the mutual information, depends not only on the experiment but also on the prior, which means that the mental cost of processing the same information β is different for people holding different beliefs.

6.2.3 Optimization

A Bayesian agent maximizes the value of information minus the cost. We can write the maximization problem as choosing an experiment, or equivalently, as choosing a distribution over posteriors.

$$\max_{\beta \in \mathcal{E}} V_p^A(\beta) - c(p \oplus \beta) = \max_{\mu \in \Delta(\Delta(S)) \text{s.t.} p_\mu = p} V^A(\mu) - c(\mu). \quad (6.3)$$

These maxima exist if we assume that c is lower-semicontinuous, S is finite, and M is compact.

Definition 6.4 (Active Learning). (ρ^s) has an *active learning* representation if there exists a prior $p \in \Delta(S)$, utility $v : S \times X \to \mathbb{R}$, and cost $c : \Delta(\Delta(S)) \to [0, \infty]$ such that

$$\rho^s(x, A) = \beta_A^*\left(\left\{m \in M : \mathbb{E}_{q_m} v(x) = \max_{y \in A} \mathbb{E}_{q_m} v(y)\right\} \middle| s\right),$$

where β_A^* solves (6.3) for each A and q_m is the Bayesian posterior given m, β_A^* and p.

---

[5] It doesn't matter which β_μ we choose, as by part (3) of Theorem A.6.4 they are all Blackwell-equivalent, so they have the same cost.

Passive Learning is a special case where cost equals to zero for a given information structure (and all information structures less informative than it) and infinity otherwise.

In Definition 6.4, attention is perfectly tailored to the details of each choice problem (A, v, p). In reality we know little about how fast it adjusts as choice problems change, except in some controlled experiments on perception. Perhaps it is tailored to situations we are facing on average? Maybe agents make systematic mistakes in allocating it?

This optimality assumption should not be taken literally: This is a hard optimization problem. It is a convenient as-if assumption that adds structure to the model and is sensible at least in those cases where we'd expect attention to respond positively to incentives.

For a fixed menu A this maximization problem can be simplified by focusing action-recommendations (where the message space M equals the set of available actions A as in Section 5.1.5). The class of such experiments will be denoted $\mathcal{R}$. If c is Blackwell monotone then without loss the agent can restrict the maximization problem to $\mathcal{R}$.

$$\max_{\beta \in \mathcal{E}} V_p^A(\beta) - c(p \oplus \beta) = \max_{\beta \in \mathcal{R}} V_p^A(\beta) - c(p \oplus \beta).$$

Intuitively, the action recommendation "glues" together all the messages that lead to the same action choice. This new experiment is (weakly) less costly (because gluing messages together makes it less informative) and leads to the same expected utility. Because of this, an optimal experiment is precisely equal to the state-dependent stochastic choice function $\beta_s(x) = \rho_s(x)$. This means that the agent never pays attention to features of the problem that are payoff-irrelevant. This seems like a very strong and likely counterfactual prediction of the model.

6.3 MUTUAL INFORMATION

Rational inattention means solving (6.3) with the mutual information cost. The *mutual information* between the state and the message is given by

$$\sum_s \sum_m P(s, m) \log \frac{P(s, m)}{P(s)(m)}, \tag{6.4}$$

where P is a discrete joint distribution over $S \times M$ (see Cover and Thomas (2006)). This can also be written in terms of the distribution over posteriors.

Definition 6.5. The *mutual information* of μ is defined to be

$$c(\mu) = \lambda \int_{\Delta(S)} [H(p_\mu) - H(q)] \mu(dq),$$

where $\lambda > 0$ and $H(q) = -\sum_{s \in S} q(s) \log_2 q(s)$ is the *entropy* of q.

Intuitively, $H(q)$ measures how much uncertainty is contained in belief q, so $c(\mu)$ is the average reduction in uncertainty in beliefs.

The following lemma gives us a recipe to determine the state-dependent choice probabilities induced by this cost function: Solve problem (6.5) and then then plug it into formula (6.6). The observed choice probability is given by a Luce-like formula, where the Luce choice probabilities are reweighed toward the average choice probabilities.

Lemma 6.6. *Suppose that the cost function is mutual information with parameter λ and the prior is p. Let ρ_*^s be the optimal choice probabilities and $\rho_*(x, A) := \sum_{s \in S} \rho_*^s(x, A) p(s)$ be the average optimal choice probability. Then $\rho_*(\cdot, A)$ is a unique solution to*

$$\max_{\rho \in \Delta(A)} \sum_{s \in S} \log \left(\sum_{y \in A} \rho(y) e^{v(y,s)/\lambda} \right) p(s). \tag{6.5}$$

Moreover, the conditional choice probabilities (and hence the optimal action-recommendation) are

$$\rho_*^s(x, A) = \frac{\rho_*(x, A) e^{v(x,s)/\lambda}}{\sum_{y \in A} \rho_*(y, A) e^{v(y,s)/\lambda}}. \tag{6.6}$$

Finally, if $\rho_*(x, A) > 0$, then the posterior belief in state s given action recommendation x equals

$$\frac{p(s) e^{v(x,s)/\lambda}}{\sum_{y \in A} \rho_*(y, A) e^{v(y,s)/\lambda}}.$$

Proof. See Proposition 2 of Steiner, Stewart, and Matějka (2017) which combines Theorem 1 and Lemma 1 of Matejka and McKay (2015) and Theorem 1 of Caplin and Dean (2013). This result holds also for an infinite state space S, replacing the sum in (6.5) with an integral. $\qquad \Box$

Rather than solving (6.5) directly, in applications the Blahut–Arimoto algorithm is used (Cover and Thomas, 2006, Section 10.8). Another approach using reinforcement learning was given by Lai and Gershman (2021).

Lemma 6.6 makes it possible to axiomatically characterize behavior of an agent with mutual information cost. Matejka and McKay (2015) study an analyst who observes the state-dependent SCF ρ^s defined over Savage acts. Each of their two axioms is a specific weakening of Luce's IIA (Axiom 3.3).

Representing the choice problem as maximizing utility minus entropy cost is superficially similar to the maximization problem under perturbed utility (PU) model of Section 3.8. Proposition 3.36 says that we also have a logit-like formula for choice probabilities. However, in the PU model the agent was maximizing over a different variable and also the interpretation of the model was different, so this analogy is purely formal.

The following example applies Lemma 6.6 to the weight perception task (Example 1.5). We will show that the predicted psychometric function is not S-shaped (as typically observed in experiments), but instead a step function.

Example 6.7 (Weight Perception with Mutual Information Cost). Let $X = \{\ell, r\}$ and $S = \mathbb{R}^X$ like in Example 5.2.3. Suppose that the prior is symmetric, that is, $p(s(\ell) > s(r)) = p(s(\ell) < s(r))$. Let $w > 0$ be the reward for correct answers. The payoff function is $v(\ell, s) = w$ if $s(\ell) > s(r)$ and zero otherwise, $v(r, s) = w$ if $s(r) > s(\ell)$ and zero otherwise.

To solve (6.5), notice that it equals

$$\frac{1}{2} \log \left(\rho(\ell)e^{w/\lambda} + \rho(r)e^0 \right) + \frac{1}{2} \log \left(\rho(\ell)e^0 + \rho(r)e^{w/\lambda} \right),$$

which is symmetric in $\rho(\ell)$ and $\rho(r)$. Given that the objective is concave, the solution must be symmetric, that is, $\rho(\ell, r) = .5$.

By (6.6), we have

$$\rho^s(\ell, r) = \begin{cases} \frac{e^{w/\lambda}}{e^{w/\lambda}+1} & \text{if } s(\ell) > s(r), \\ \frac{1}{2} & \text{if } s(\ell) = s(r), \\ \frac{1}{e^{w/\lambda}+1} & \text{if } s(\ell) < s(r). \end{cases}$$

This is exactly the same step-function as in the constant-error model (Example 3.18). △

Intuitively, this prediction is due to the fact that mutual information "doesn't know" how far states are from each other: The formula for mutual information (6.4) sums uniformly over states without any reference to their distance; the only distinguishing feature is their probability. This motivates the study of other cost functions in the next section.

6.4 OTHER COST FUNCTIONS

First, we define a generalization of mutual information that replaces H with an arbitrary convex and continuous function.

Definition 6.8. A cost function c is *uniformly posterior-separable* (UPS) if

$$c(\mu) = \int_{\Delta(S)} [L(p_\mu) - L(q)]\mu(dq),$$

where $L : \Delta(S) \to \mathbb{R}$ is convex and continuous.

This generalizes the notion of expected uncertainty reduction, allowing for a weaker notion of "uncertainty." This class is referred to as *uniformly posterior-separable* costs (Caplin, Dean, and Leahy, 2022) because the function L is uniformly the same for all priors. An even larger class of *posterior separable* costs allows for such dependence.

Definition 6.9. A cost function c is *posterior-separable* (PS) if

$$c(\mu) = \int_{\Delta(S)} [D(p_\mu, p_\mu) - D(q, p_\mu)]\mu(dq),$$

where $D : \Delta(S) \times \Delta(S) \to \mathbb{R}$ is convex and continuous in the first variable.

The UPS class is characterized by the following condition. Suppose that we have an experiment β' and then conditional on message m we run another experiment β''_m. We could execute it step by step, like a compound lottery, or reduce it and execute it in one shot. We say that a cost function is *indifferent to sequential learning* if for any prior the cost of each execution is the same.

Proposition[†] 6.10. *c is UPS if and only if it is indifferent to sequential learning.*

Proof. See Lemma 1 of Bloedel and Zhong (2021). They assume a slightly smaller domain of the cost function where $\mu = p \oplus \beta$ for some full-support prior and β such that $\beta(s)$ is bounded away from the boundary of the simplex $\Delta(M)$. □

There is something at first sight paradoxical going on with the UPS class. Given that the function L is prior-independent, it is tempting to think that c is prior-independent. But in fact the opposite is true.

Proposition 6.11. *If $c \neq 0$ is bounded and UPS, then it is prior-dependent. In particular, mutual information is prior-dependent.*

Proof. For details, see Appendix A.6.1. This result is Proposition 4 of Mensch (2018), Proposition 1 of Denti, Marinacci, and Rustichini (2022a), and footnote 38 of Bloedel and Zhong (2021). The fact that the mutual information cost is prior-dependent was discussed by Woodford (2012), Gentzkow and Kamenica (2014), and Che and Mierendorff (2019). □

The PS class is larger than UPS and allows for prior-independent costs. The PS class is characterized by the following condition. Suppose that we have two experiments β' and β'' and assume that the set of messages of the two experiments is disjoint so the agent always knows which one was used. Consider another compound experiment that with probability α executes β' and otherwise executes β''. A cost function is *indifferent to randomization* if for any prior the direct cost of the compound experiment equals the expected cost of running the compound experiment. The characterizing condition has the same flavor as linearity in probabilities of EU (4.1) and posterior-separability can be seen as an EU-like representation.

Proposition 6.12. *c is PS if and only if it is indifferent to randomization.*

Proof. See Theorem 1 of Mensch (2018) and p. 354 of Torgersen (1991). □

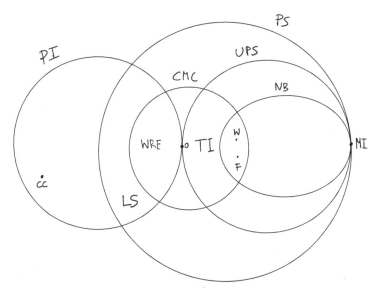

Figure 6.2 A categorization of Blackwell-monotone and bounded cost functions: PI – prior-independent, PS – posterior-separable, UPS – uniformly posterior-separable, CMC – constant marginal cost, WRE – weighted relative entropy, NB – neighborhood based, LS – likelihood-separable, TI–Total Information, W – Wald, F – Fisher Information, MI – Mutual Information, CC – Channel Capacity, 0 – zero cost.

The relationship between UPS, PS, and PI is illustrated in Figure 6.2. The figure also depicts some additional classes, which we discuss in the remainder of this section.

An important class of prior-independent cost functions was studied by Pomatto, Strack, and Tamuz (2023). They assume constant marginal cost (CMC). This consists of *two* axioms: (1) The cost of running the experiment twice (i.i.d. conditional on s) is twice the cost of running it once. (2) Running an experiment with probability a half (and an null experiment with probability half) is equal to half its cost. Notice that the first property is implied by indifference to sequential learning while the second is implied by indifference to randomization. Taken together with prior independence, these conditions plus continuity imply that h has a *weighted relative entropy* (WRE) representation

$$h(\beta) = \sum_{s,s' \in S} \alpha_{s,s'} R(\beta_s || \beta'_s),$$

for some collection weights $(\alpha_{s,s'})_{s,s' \in S}$ in $\mathbb{R}_+$ where for any $\pi, \pi' \in \Delta(M)$ the *relative entropy* or *Kullback–Leibler divergence* is defined by $R(\pi || \pi') :=$ $\sum_{m \in M} \pi(m) \log \frac{\pi(m)}{\pi'(m)}$ if $\pi'(s) > 0 \Rightarrow \pi(s) > 0$ and $R(\pi || \pi') = \infty$ otherwise. Pomatto, Strack, and Tamuz (2023) show that this class is PS with $D(q||p) = \sum_{s,s'} \beta_{s,s'} \frac{q_s}{p_s} \log \frac{q_s}{q'_s}$. This is not UPS because it is prior-independent. They showt that unlike mutual information, WRE leads to reasonable psychometric functions in Example 1.15.

If we take CMC (the two axioms) and instead of PI we insist on UPS, then we get

$$c(p \oplus \beta) = \sum_{s,s' \in S} p(s)\alpha_{s,s'}R(\beta_s||\beta'_s),$$

which was shown independently by Pomatto, Strack, and Tamuz (2023) and Bloedel and Zhong (2021). The latter paper dubs them *total information costs* and studies interesting dynamic stability properties. The UPS representation of total information costs is given by $L(q) = \sum_{s,s'} \beta_{s,s'} q_s \log \frac{q_s}{q_{s'}}$.

A classic prior-independent cost function is *channel capacity*, defined as $h(\beta) := \max_{p \in \Delta(S)} c_{mi}(p \oplus \beta)$, where c_{mi} is mutual information. That is, the cost of a given experiment is the maximal mutual information obtained by choosing over all priors.[6] Woodford (2012) analyzed a series of examples using this cost.

The intersection of prior-independent and posterior-separable costs was characterized by Denti, Marinacci, and Rustichini (2022b). For any prior p and posterior q we can form the vector of likelihood ratios $q(s)/p(s)$; let's denote it by q/p. The function c belongs to the intersection of those two classes if and only if it is *likelihood-separable*: $c(\mu) = \int_{\Delta(S)} \phi(q/p_\mu)\mu(dq)$, where $\phi : \mathbb{R}_+^S \to \mathbb{R}$ is a continuous and sublinear function.

Hébert and Woodford (2021) propose a family of "neighborhood-based" cost functions that allow for the cost of learning about states to be affected by their proximity. This family contains mutual information and is a subset of uniformly posterior-separable class, so by Proposition 6.11 is prior-dependent. Such costs are flexible enough to generate S-shaped psychometric functions.

The intersection of total information costs and neighborhood-based costs includes the Wald costs (Morris and Strack, 2019) and the Fisher Information.

6.5 BEHAVIORAL CHARACTERIZATIONS

Most papers discussed in this section assume that the analyst knows the agent's utility function v and the prior p, similar to Section 5.1.5. In this setting Caplin and Dean (2015) characterize the class of state-dependent SCF (ρ^s) that have an active learning representation (with a general cost function). Their characterization involves obedience (Condition 5.5) and a new acyclicity condition.

To state this new condition we need the concept of *revealed distribution over posteriors*. Suppose the menu is A and the agent faces an action-recommendation that in state $s \in S$ suggests action $x \in A$ with probability

---

[6] According to Shannon's coding theorem, if we think of β as a communication channel, then $h(\beta)$ is the maximal transmission rate achievable with arbitrarily low error probability (Cover and Thomas, 2006).

$\rho^s(x, A)$. Then as discussed in Section 5.1.5, by Bayes rule (5.1) the agent's *revealed posterior* is now

$$\hat{q}(s|x) = \frac{\rho^s(x, A)p(s)}{\sum_{s' \in S} \rho^{s'}(x, A)p(s')}.$$

In every state s there is a distribution over those revealed posteriors with weights given by $\rho^s(x, A)$. Notice that by construction it satisfies Bayes Consistency (Condition 5.20). Unconditionally on the state, the distribution over revealed posteriors $\hat{\mu}_A \in \Delta(\Delta(S))$ is the average of those according to the prior. Formally the probability of any posterior q is given by

$$\hat{\mu}_A(q) := \sum_{s \in S} \sum_{\substack{x \in A \\ \hat{q}(\cdot|x)=q}} \rho^s(x, A)p(s),$$

where the sum over the empty set is zero.

Given any distribution over posteriors μ the agent's net utility is $\int v^A d\mu - c(\mu)$. Consider now two menus A and B and the associated revealed distributions over posteriors $\hat{\mu}_A$ and $\hat{\mu}_B$. It may happen that $\hat{\mu}^B$ is more informative than $\hat{\mu}_A$. In this case the agent's gross utility of using $\hat{\mu}^B$ when choosing from menu A is higher than using $\hat{\mu}^A$, that is $\int v^A d\hat{\mu}^B > \int v^A d\hat{\mu}^A$. However, since $\hat{\mu}_A$ is optimal when choosing from menu A, it must be that $\hat{\mu}_B$ is not worth the extra cost in this situation:

$$\int v^A d\hat{\mu}^A - c(\hat{\mu}_A) \geq \int v^A d\hat{\mu}^B - c(\hat{\mu}_B). \tag{6.7}$$

and likewise when the menu is B and the agent considers using $\hat{\mu}^A$:

$$\int v^B d\hat{\mu}^B - c(\hat{\mu}_B) \geq \int v^B d\hat{\mu}^A - c(\hat{\mu}_A). \tag{6.8}$$

Adding (6.7) and (6.8) we get

$$\int v^A d\hat{\mu}^A + \int v^B d\hat{\mu}^B \geq \int v^A d\hat{\mu}^B + \int v^B d\hat{\mu}^A.$$

The NIAC condition generalizes this to longer cycles. The intuition behind it is similar to other acyclicity conditions that we have seen before (Axioms 3.38, 3.22, and 4.25).

Condition 6.13 (NIAC). ρ satisfies *no improving action cycles* (NIAC) if for any sequence of menus $A_1, \ldots, A_n$ such that $A_1 = A_n$ we have

$$\sum_{i=1}^{n-1} \int v^{A_i} d\hat{\mu}^{A_i} \geq \sum_{i=1}^{n-1} \int v^{A_i} d\hat{\mu}^{A_{i+1}}.$$

Theorem 6.14 (Caplin and Dean, 2015; Caplin, Dean, and Leahy, 2017). *Suppose that S is finite, that p and v are given. (ρ^s) satisfies Obedience and NIAC if and only if it has an active learning representation (Definition 6.4). In addition, the cost function can be chosen to be convex in μ.*

Their original theorem is formulated for Savage acts, but with a known state-dependent utility it is equivalent to Theorem 6.14. The result in Caplin and Dean (2015) assumes that ρ is given on a finite collection of menus and provides partial uniqueness results in the form of bounds on the cost function. Caplin, Dean, and Leahy (2017); Gonczarowski, Kominers, and Shorrer (2020) show that it extends to full domain and under a richness condition the cost function is pinned down uniquely.

Denti (2022) works on the same domain and characterizes the PS class. He also characterizes the UPS class, along with Caplin, Dean, and Leahy (2022). Both papers offer characterizations of the mutual information cost that are different from each other and also from Matejka and McKay (2015). Dean and Neligh (2023) design an experiment that tests these axioms and show that UPS is typically satisfied.

Theorem 6.14 can be used to characterize the prior-independent class. If we impose NIAC for each prior separately (each cycle has its fixed prior), then the theorem delivers a cost function for each prior. But imposing NIAC across priors gives us a prior-independent cost function (Denti, 2023).

Chambers, Liu, and Rehbeck (2020) characterize a general model without the additive separability between the value and cost of information.

The approach taken by the above papers assumes that the analyst knows the prior p and the utility function v. This may seem restrictive, but as shown by Denti (2022), if we state the problem in the Anscombe–Aumann setting (Section 5.3.1), then the analyst just needs to know the prior.

6.5.1 Other Work

Another approach was taken by Lin (2022), who worked with Anscombe–Aumann acts. Here the analyst does not know the utility function nor the prior: They are recovered from the data. The analyst only observes the unconditional SCF ρ. His work builds on Lu's (2016) characterization of passive learning on this domain (Theorem 5.23) and De Oliveira, Denti, Mihm, and Ozbek's (2016) characterization of active learning on the domain of preferences over menus. Lin (2022) characterizes convex and Blackwell-monotone costs, and obtains essential uniqueness of cost. This means that in principle we don't have to observe (ρ^s) but only the average ρ.

Yet another approach was taken by Ellis (2018) who restricts attention to partitional experiments (i.e., in each state of the world the message is deterministic). Conditional on the state the analyst observes the (deterministic) choice function. See also Van Zandt (1996).

For further reviews of this literature, see Caplin (2016) and Mackowiak, Matejka, and Wiederholt (2018).

PART III

DYNAMIC CHOICE

CHAPTER 7

Dynamic Choice

7.1 DYNAMIC RANDOM UTILITY

Dynamic models have important applications to the consumer side of the economy (durable goods purchases, labor supply, education, fertility, and retirement), as well as to the firm side (investment decisions, patent renewals).

Suppose that we are tracking agent's choices over time. In each period t they are choosing x_t from menu A_t. We will now explore the ways in which their choices are connected across periods.

For now, let's set aside the fact that the agent might be forward-looking: incorporating their own future choices into their current decision. We will treat *dynamic optimality* in Chapter 8. For now, we focus on phenomena that exist whether agents are sophisticated or *myopic* (or anything in between). These phenomena are backward-looking in nature and have to do with the fact that observed choices may appear history-dependent, or correlated over time, even if in fact they are not. Consider the following example.

Example 7.1 (History-Dependence). Suppose that r is a habit-forming drug and d is not. We would expect to see *history-dependent* choice probabilities as in Figure 7.1 and the following equation:

$$\rho_{t+1}(r_{t+1}|r_t) > \rho_{t+1}(r_{t+1}|d_t) \tag{7.1}$$

because taking r_t makes the agent crave r more in the future. In terms of the representation, we could capture this by letting U_t depend not only on x_t but also on lagged consumption. This feature of a utility representation is sometimes called *state-dependence* and it covers many more applications than just habit formation.

But history dependence can also occur in a more subtle way. Suppose that you had to predict someone's vote in the presidential election. In forming your prediction it would make sense to condition on how this person's voted previously (if you had access to such data). In this case we would expect (7.1) to hold because political preferences are persistent over time, not because past votes are habit-forming. In other words, we get history-dependence of ρ as a consequence of self-selection: Republican-leaning voters select r_t and to the

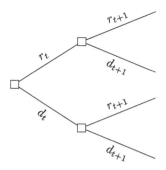

Figure 7.1 Conditioning on past choices.

extent to which their political preferences are persistent, they are more likely to select r_{t+1}. In terms of the representation, we could have

$$\tilde{U}_t(x_t) = \tilde{v}(x_t) + \tilde{\epsilon}_t,$$

where $\tilde{\epsilon}_t$ is a transitory i.i.d. shock and $\tilde{v}$ is a persistent preference, unobservable to the analyst. If someone votes Republican in year t, they reveal that probably $\tilde{v}(r) > \tilde{v}(d)$, so they are more likely to vote republican next period. Crucially, in this case choices appear correlated to the analyst because of asymmetric information (the agent knows their $\tilde{v}$, the analyst does not), and not because x_{t-1} enters $\tilde{U}_t$.

One way to tell apart state-dependence from asymmetric information would be for the analyst to exogenously randomize choices in period 1. In this case, we would expect history-dependence to go away in the voting example (because period t votes are not informative anymore about period $t + 1$ preferences), but not in the drug example (because period t consumption directly affects period $t + 1$ preferences).   △

For now, we will assume away state-dependence and focus on asymmetric information. We will return to it in Section 7.4.

We will also assume that in each period the menu is determined exogenously, that is, drawn independently of past choices. I will call the universe of such choice situations the *simple domain*. This means that the agent's choice in period t does not influence the menu of options available in period $t + 1$. For example, the set of candidates today is unaffected by previous votes of our agent. This assumption is also made by the literature on brand choice dynamics in marketing, where in each period t the agent chooses a brand x_t from some exogenously determined menu A_t. We will relax this assumption later in this chapter.

Assumption 7.2 (Simple Domain). First the menu A_1 is drawn, then the agent learns $\tilde{U}_1$ and chooses $x_1 \in A_1$ to maximize it. The analyst observes that choice. Then the new period begins, the menu A_2 is drawn independently of x_1, the agent learns $\tilde{U}_2$ and chooses $x_2 \in A_2$ to maximize it, and the analyst observes that.

If we take the sample size to infinity, we will get the *joint choice probability*

$$p(x_1, x_2; A_1, A_2).$$

for all menus A_1, A_2.[1] Equivalently, we could record the *marginal choice probability* $p_1(x_1, A_1)$ and the *conditional choice probability*

$$p_2(\cdot | x_1, A_1).$$

The latter formulation is useful in recursive settings. It is sometimes known as a *dynamic SCF*: an SCF in period $t = 1$ and an SCF in period $t = 2$ conditional on each history.

The representation needs to keep track of the distribution of preferences over time. The utility in each period is random $\widetilde{U}_t : \Omega \to \mathbb{R}^{X_t}$ and by definition independent of past choices. Define the event

$$N(x_t, A_t) := \{\widetilde{U}_t(x_t) = \max_{y_t \in A_t} \widetilde{U}_t(y_t)\}.$$

Definition 7.3. p has a *Dynamic Random Utility* (DRU) representation if there exists a probability space $(\Omega, \mathcal{F}, \mathbb{P})$ and utility functions $\widetilde{U}_t : \Omega \to \mathbb{R}^{X_t}$ such that

$$p(x_1, x_2; A_1, A_2) = \mathbb{P}(N(x_1, A_1) \cap N(x_2, A_2)).$$

Alternatively, $p_1(x_1, A_1) = \mathbb{P}(N(x_1, A_1))$ and

$$p_2(x_2, A_2 | x_1, A_1) = \mathbb{P}(N(x_2, A_2) | N(x_1, A_1))$$

for each (x_1, A_1) such that $p_1(x_1, A_1) > 0$. As in the static model, we assume that $\mathbb{P}$ does not depend on the menu pair.

Examples of DRU abound. In panel data econometrics the *random effects* model assumes that $\widetilde{U}_t(x_t) = \tilde{v}(x_t) + \tilde{\epsilon}_t(x)$, where ϵ_t are i.i.d. over time and alternatives; the agent's "type" v is drawn at $t = 1$ and is perfectly persistent. Notice that we could rewrite this representation as $\widetilde{U}_t = v(x_t) + \tilde{\epsilon}_t$ with a deterministic v, but then the ϵ_t would be serially correlated. In practice, this model includes attributes, which we will discuss in Chapter 12; here we focus on models where the source of variation is the menu.

Another example are models of brand choice, where $\widetilde{U}_t$ follows a Markov process and the transition matrix is estimated based on how persistent the choices p_t are.[2]

---

[1] Similar limiting assumptions are made in the literature on panel data, where joint choice probabilities are assumed to be identified from the data. If p represents choices of a single individual, we need many trials for each history and we need to observe many histories. This is asking for a lot, but can be done in some experiments.

[2] For example, Jeuland (1979); Keane (1997); Dubé, Hitsch, and Rossi (2010); Seetharaman (2004); Dew, Ansari, and Li (2020).

A knife-edge case is when $\widetilde{U}_t$ is independent over time. In this case we don't need to condition on histories. Equivalently, this means that the joint is the product of the marginals.

7.2 AXIOMS FOR DRU

Because we ruled out state-dependence, the realization of U_2 does not depend on x_1 as a function. This implies that the marginal choice distribution in period $t = 2$ is independent of the menu in period $t = 1$.

Axiom 7.4 (Marginal Consistency). For any $x_2 \in A_2$ and any A_1

$$\sum_{x_1 \in A_1} \rho_2(x_2, A_2 | x_1, A_1) \rho_1(x_1, A_1).$$

We already implicitly assumed a flavor of Marginal Consistency by writing $\rho_1(x_1, A_1)$ in a way that does not depend on the future menu A_2. Under this notational assumption, Marginal Consistency is equivalent to a Marginality axiom on the joint distribution (Chambers, Masatlioglu, and Turansick, 2021).

Axiom 7.5 (Marginality). For any $x_1 \in A_1$ and any A_2, B_2

$$\sum_{x_2 \in A_2} \rho(x_1, x_2; A_1, A_2) = \sum_{x_2 \in B_2} \rho(x_1, x_2; A_1, B_2).$$

For any $x_2 \in A_2$ and any A_1, B_1

$$\sum_{x_1 \in A_1} \rho(x_1, x_2; A_1, A_2) = \sum_{x_1 \in B_1} \rho(x_1, x_2; B_1, A_2).$$

Another necessary axiom is a dynamic version of Supermodularity (Axiom 2.6). It implies Supermodularity conditional on each history (including the empty history in period $t = 1$).

Axiom 7.6 (Joint Supermodularity). For any $x_t \in A_t \subseteq B_t$.

$$\rho(x_1, x_2; A_1, A_2) + \rho(x_1, x_2; B_1, B_2)$$
$$\geq \rho(x_1, x_2; A_1, B_2) + \rho(x_1, x_2; B_1, A_2).$$

Proposition 7.7 (Li 2021). *When $|X_1| \leq 3$ and $|X_2| \leq 3$, DRU is characterized by Axiom 7.5 and Axiom 7.6.*

Chambers, Masatlioglu, and Turansick (in press) show that when $|X_1| \leq 3$ or $|X_2| \leq 3$, DRU is characterized by Axiom 7.5 and strengthening of Axiom 7.6 based on the BM Axiom 2.8. However, when both of these sets have cardinality larger than 3, there exists a ρ represented by a state-dependent DRU that satisfies Marginality and the dynamic BM-style axiom yet cannot be represented by a state-independent DRU (this is their Example 2).

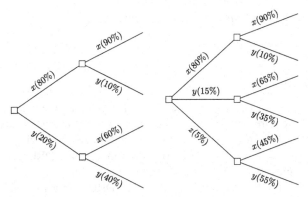

Figure 7.2 History independence.

Chambers, Masatlioglu, and Turansick (in press) show that such cases are ruled out if in at least one of the periods the marginal SCF has a *unique* RU representation. Under this condition, their Theorem 3 implies that Axiom 7.5 and the dynamic BM-style axiom are necessary and sufficient for a state-independent DRU representation.

Chambers, Masatlioglu, and Turansick (in press) also show that regardless of the cardinality of X_t, and regardless of the collection of observable menus, state-independent DRU can be characterized by a joint version of ARSP (Axiom 2.10). Li (2021) shows that the same is true using Coherence (Axiom 2.11).

To understand DRU better, we will introduce another axiom which will be useful going forward. Intuitively, we get history-dependent choices because past choices reveal something to the analyst about the persistent component of agent's utility. If two histories reveal similar information, they should lead to similar choices going forward. To gain more intuition, consider the following example where two histories reveal the exact same amount of information.

Example 7.8. We have $A_1 = \{x, y\}$, $B_1 = \{x, y, z\}$ and $A_2 = \{x, y\}$. The choice probabilities are given in Figure 7.2. Comparing the choice probabilities from menus A_1 and B_1 in Figure 7.2 we can conclude that z does not steal any customers from x, it only steals customers from y. Given this (admittedly extreme) pattern of substitution, period 2 choices of consumers who chose x in $t = 1$ should be the same in each situation. This is because it's exactly the same selection of people who are making this choice. On the other hand, the choices of people who previously chose y are different in the two situations, as these represent different selections of customers. In particular, given that z steals only from y the types that chose y from A_1 are a mixture of the types who chose y from B_1 and those who chose z from B_1. $\triangle$

This example motivates the following axiom.

Axiom 7.9 (α-History Independence). For all $x_1 \in A_1$ if

(i) $A_1 \subseteq B_1$ and
(ii) $\rho_1(x_1, A_1) = \rho_1(x_1, B_1) > 0$,

then $\rho_2(x_2, A_2 | x_1, A_1) = \rho_2(x_2, A_2 | x_1, B_1)$ for all $x_2 \in A_2$.

Both *(i)* and *(ii)* are crucial for the conclusion to hold. In particular, it is not enough to just require *(i)* because in general the analyst learns weakly more after history (x_1, B_1) since x_1 had to beat more alternatives to be chosen.

Axiom 7.9 is silent when *(ii)* fails. However, in this case DRU still makes predictions: Intuitively, ρ_2 should be close after the two histories that are close. Proposition A.7.1 in the Appendix shows that DRU implies the following axiom.

Axiom 7.10 (Bounded History Dependence). If $x_1 \in A_1 \subseteq B_1$, then for all $x_2 \in A_2$

$$\left| \rho_2(x_2, A_2 | x_1, A_1) - \rho_2(x_2, A_2 | x_1, B_1) \right| \leq 1 - \frac{\rho_1(x_1, B_1)}{\rho_1(x_1, A_1)}.$$

7.3 AXIOMS WITH LOTTERIES

Like in the static model, axioms look nicer if we add lotteries and restrict to EU. We will call this model *Dynamic Random Expected Utility*.

In this model the sets $N(p_t, A_t)$ are linar so the REU axioms are satisfied conditional on all observable histories (including $t = 1$). A mirror implication is linearity of ρ in the conditioning event. Choosing p_1 from A_1 reveals the same information as choosing option $\lambda p_1 + (1 - \lambda)q_1$ from menu $\lambda A_1 + (1 - \lambda)\{q_1\}$, so conditioning on either of these observations leads to the same prediction (see also the discussion after Axiom 4.14 and Theorem 4.17). This is captured by the following axiom.

Axiom 7.11 (Linear History Independence).

$$\rho_2(\cdot, \cdot | p_1, A_1) = \rho_2\left(\cdot, \cdot | \lambda p_1 + (1 - \lambda)q_1, \lambda A_1 + (1 - \lambda)\{q_1\}\right)$$

for all $p_1 \in A_1$ such that $\rho_1(p_1, A_1) > 0$, all q_1 and $\lambda \in (0, 1)$.

A stronger version of this is mixing with a menu B_1 instead of a singleton.

Axiom† 7.12 (Strong Linear History Independence).

$$\rho_2(\cdot, \cdot | p_1, A_1) = \rho_2\left(\cdot, \cdot | \lambda p_1 + (1 - \lambda)B_1, \lambda A_1 + (1 - \lambda)B_1\right)$$

for all $p_1 \in A_1$ such that $\rho_1(p_1, A_1) > 0$, all B_1 and $\lambda \in (0, 1)$.

The dagger symbol (†) is here because I am not telling you what it means to mix with a menu. Axiom 7.12 implies Axiom 7.11 and Axiom 7.4.

Below I will present two axiomatizations. In the first axiomatization there are more "conditional" axioms. To avoid conditioning on probability zero events, the distribution of each $\tilde{U}_t$ is discrete and there are tiebreakers $(\tilde{W}_t)_{t=1}^T$

as in Section 4.4. Technically speaking the first theorem is stated on the domain of decision trees (which we will discuss in Section 7.5), but it holds on the simple domain as well.

Theorem[†] 7.13 (Frick, Iijima, and Strzalecki, 2019). ρ *has a Dynamic Random Expected Utility representation with finite support if and only it satisfies*

    (i) α-*History Independence*
    (ii)   *Strong Linear History Independence[†]*
    (iii)   *The GP axioms: Regularity, Linearity, Extremeness, Mixture Continuity, and Finiteness[†] conditional on each history*
    (iv)   *History-Continuity.[†]*

The second axiomatization assumes joint Regularity instead of conditional Regularity. This allows them to weaken the assumptions that discipline history dependence: Strong Linear History Independence and α-History Independence.

Theorem[†] 7.14 (Chambers, Masatlioglu, and Turansick, 2021). ρ *has a Dynamic Random Expected Utility representation if and only it satisfies*

    (i)   *Joint Regularity*
    (ii)   *Linear History Independence[†]*
    (iii)   *The GP axioms: Linearity and Extremeness conditional on each history*
    (iv)   *Joint Mixture Continuity.[†]*

All axioms in the second theorem can be expressed in terms of the joint distribution.

7.4 STATE-DEPENDENCE

So far, we allowed history-dependence of observed choices only to the extent that is implied by self-selection and we ruled out state-dependence of utility, or what Heckman (1981) calls *structural state-dependence*: Period-2 utility $\tilde{U}_2$ depends on the period-1 choices x_1. Heckman's (1981) term for the kinds of history-dependence of observed choice probabilities that come from pure self-selection is *spurious state-dependence*. There is an extensive literature in econometrics that studies state-dependence, including Chamberlain (1993) and Honoré and Kyriazidou (2000). In such models we have

$$\rho_2(x_2, A_2 | x_1, A_2) = \mathbb{P}\left(\tilde{U}_2(x_2; x_1) = \max_{y_2 \in A_2} \tilde{U}_2(y_2; x_1) \Big| N(x_1, A_1) \right).$$

This formulation of utility allows for things such as habit formation and other psychological effects.[3]

---

[3]   See, for example, Becker and Murphy (1988), Constantinides (1990), Campbell and Cochrane (1999), and decision theory papers by Gul and Pesendorfer (2007), Rozen (2010), Gilboa and

A controversial example of what looks like state-dependence comes from psychology. According to the famous *cognitive dissonance* theory, people change their preferences to rationalize past choices: Rejected alternatives are devalued and the chosen ones are bumped up (Brehm, 1956; Harmon-Jones and Mills, 1999). However, as pointed out by Chen (2008) and Chen and Risen (2010), the prevalent method used to test this theory suffers from a spurious state-dependence problem.

Example 7.15 (Cognitive Dissonance). There are three periods. In period 1 the subjects rate n items on a discrete numerical scale. In period 2 the experimental group chooses between two equally rated items (since the numerical scale is discrete, the experimenter can always find such items). Let x be the chosen item and y an unchosen one. The control group makes a choice between items that are rated far from each other or does not make a choice at all. In period 3 the subject is asked to choose between y and z–another item that was initially rated the same as x and y.

The main empirical finding is that in the treatment group subjects are more likely to choose z over y while there is no systematic tendency in the control group. This finding is typically attributed to cognitive dissonance because it looks as if people rationalize their rejection of y by devaluing it. However, Chen (2008) shows that it can be explained purely by spurious state-dependence. To see that, note that even though x, y, z receive the same numerical rating, the rating system is discrete, so the agent may actually have strict preferences over them. In period 2 the analyst observes the event $N(x, \{x, y\}) = \{xyz, xzy, zxy\}$. Assuming a uniform distribution over rankings, conditional on $N(x, \{x, y\})$ the probability that z is above y is $\frac{2}{3}$ (in the control group there is no conditioning so the probability remains at $\frac{1}{2}$).[4]   △

Less controversial examples of state-dependence are models of switching costs (Pakes, Porter, Shepard, and Calder-Wang, 2020) and models of *experimentation* or *experience goods* (see, e.g., Erdem and Keane (1996) and Crawford and Shum (2005)). The following example illustrates the latter concept.

Example 7.16 (Experience Goods). Suppose that there are three products $X = \{x, y, z\}$ and two periods. Each of the goods can either be a "match" for the agent (give utility one) or a "mismatch" (give zero utility). The agent does not know whether a product is a match or not before trying it out. For each product the probability of a match is $\alpha > 0.5$ and the three goods are independent.

Pazgal (2001). Related phenomena include preference for variety McAlister (1982), Rustichini and Siconolfi (2014), and memorable consumption Gilboa, Postlewaite, and Samuelson (2016).

[4] Another, more popular, version of the experiment elicits strict rankings instead of numerical ratings, but a similar argument shows that the observed cognitive dissonance is spurious, provided that subjects make small mistakes when reporting their rankings.

The optimal strategy of the agent is to pick the product at random in the first period and stick with it in the second period if it turns out to be a match and switch to one of the other product if it's a mismatch. This strategy yields the following choice probabilities:

$$p_2(x_2 = x | x_1 = x) = \alpha > \frac{1 - \alpha}{2} = p_2(x_2 = x | x_1 = y). \tag{7.2}$$

Notice that history-dependence in this example occurs due to a different force than the informational asymmetry discussed so far. The example is cooked up so that the period-1 choice of x does not reveal anything about the "type" of the agent: It is purely random. Nevertheless, the observed choices look history-dependent because utility is state-dependent. △

Distinguishing between structural and spurious state-dependence is a key problem. If mere self-selection leads to history-dependent choices, then how much should the analyst attribute to state-dependence? How can we let the data speak on this issue? Heckman (1981) and the literature that follows develop stochastic choice models and econometric techniques that tease apart structural from spurious state-dependence. We will not discuss these techniques here and instead take a different route and assume that there exist lotteries which serve as perfect randomized controlled trials. Consider the following example.

Example 7.17 (Habit Formation). A pharmaceutical researcher wants to determine whether drug x is habit forming. The other drug, y is known not to be habit-forming. If the researcher has only access to the observed choices in the left panel of Figure 7.3, she won't be able to determine how much of the observed serial correlation in choices (i.e., history-dependence) to attribute to selection and how much to habit-formation.

This can be solved if the researcher can randomly assign x and y in the first period. The idea of random assignment is routinely used in econometrics. If the lottery in the first period is independent of everything else, then the population assigned x is the same as those assigned y and therefore if $p_2(x|x) > p_2(x|y)$, we can conclude that the drug is habit forming. This is illustrated in the right panel of the figure. The convention introduced by (Raiffa, 1968) is to denote *decision nodes* by squares and *chance nodes*, that is, lotteries, by circles. △

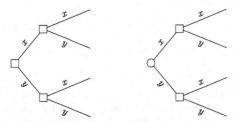

Figure 7.3 Teasing out structural and spurious state-dependence.

Lotteries are an idealized randomizing device, but they do sometimes occur in reality.[5] The next section formulates an axiom based on lotteries that rules out structural state-dependence. In doing so, we will introduce the notion of decision trees which will also prepare us for treating dynamic optimality in the next Chapter.

7.5 DECISION TREES

We have so far worked on the Simple Domain (Assumption 7.2), which assumed away a key feature of dynamics that choices made today shape the menu available tomorrow. This feature is present in the classic consumption-savings problem where the amount consumed in period t influences the income available in period $t + 1$. Classic discrete choice examples include studies of fertility and schooling choices (Todd and Wolpin, 2006), engine replacement (Rust, 1987), patent renewal (Pakes, 1986), or occupational choices (Miller, 1984).

The following example shows the dangers of trying to use a simple domain in such situations.

Example 7.18 (Spurious Violation of Regularity). Consider choices of supermarket customers depicted in Figure 7.4. If we naively define $A :=$ {medium, cheap} and $B :=$ {premium, medium, cheap}, then we code this as a violation of regularity because $\rho(\text{medium}, A) < \rho(\text{medium}, B)$. This happens because the distribution of preferences is different between menus A and B as a result of *self-selection*: Agents of different types select differently into the two supermarkets.   △

To avoid such problems, we will enhance the description of each alternative and define $x_t = (z_t, A_{t+1})$, where z_t is an immediate consumption (or payoff) and A_{t+1} is a menu of choices available in the next period.

In order to also incorporate lotteries, we will define what are known as *decision trees*. This is a canonical domain in dynamic decision theory (Kreps and Porteus, 1978). Now x is a lottery over pairs such as (z_t, A_{t+1}).[6] Formally, there are finitely many time periods $t = 1, \ldots, T$ and let Z be a finite set of instantaneous consumptions. Each period-t menu is a finite set of lotteries over the period-t outcome space X_t; formally, the set of period-t menus is $\mathcal{A}_t := \mathcal{A}(\Delta(X_t))$, where for any set Y the collection of finite subsets of Y is

---

[5] For example, schools ration their seats via lotteries, a fact that is widely exploited in the empirical literature on school choice to generate quasi-experimental variation (Abdulkadiroglu, Angrist, Narita, and Pathak (2017); Angrist, Hull, Pathak, and Walters (2017); Deming, Hastings, Kane, and Staiger (2014); Deming (2011)).

[6] A small technical difference is that Kreps and Porteus (1978) look at Borel instead of simple lotteries, and compact instead of finite menus. Their paper is often remembered for *temporal lotteries*: the important special case of decision trees where all the decision nodes are singletons. However, general decision tress are also defined and analyzed in Sections 1–3 of that classic paper.

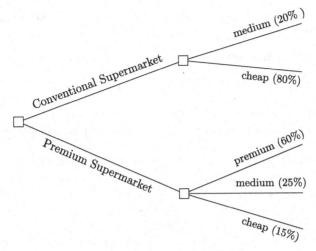

Figure 7.4 A spurious violation of Regularity.

denoted by $\mathcal{A}(Y)$. The spaces X_t are defined recursively: In all periods $t < T$ the outcome space $X_t := Z \times \mathcal{A}_{t+1}$ consists of pairs of current-period consumption and next-period continuation menus. To close this construction, the outcome space in the final period T is just $X_T = Z$, as there is no continuation menu in the terminal period.[7]

As opposed to the simple domain (Assumption 7.2) here only A_1 is exogenous. All subsequent menus are chosen by the agent (and possibly randomized). More precisely, the chronology works as follows: Each trial is defined by a menu A_1 of lotteries p_1. In period 1 the agent chooses a lottery p_1, which subsequently resolves giving the agent immediate consumption z_1 and menu A_2. The new period begins with history (A_1, p_1, z_1) and the agent chooses p_2 from A_2, then (z_2, A_3) is realized according to p_2, and the cycle continues. Like on the simple domain, we could be sampling from a population of individuals or sampling the same agent over and over again in a stationary environment.

Our simple domain is a subset of decision trees where the agent cannot choose future menus. Formally, there is a fixed lottery π_{t+1} over menus A_{t+1} and each $p_t \in A_t$ is a product measure of a lottery over Z and the lottery π_{t+1}.

The choices that occur with positive probability under ρ_1 define the set of all period-1 *choice histories*: pairs (p_1, A_1) such that $\rho_1(p_1, A_1) > 0$. Conditioning on choice histories will allow our analyst to take care of self-selection. As discussed in Example 7.17, the analyst might also want to keep track of *consumption histories*: triples (z_1, p_1, A_1) such that $\rho_1(p_1, A_1) > 0$ and $p_1(z_1) > 0$.

---

[7] Thus, in a sense, the sets X_t are getting "smaller" as time goes by. This construction can be extended to an infinite time horizon (see, e.g., Gul and Pesendorfer (2004)), where X_t is constant over time.

Conditioning on consumption histories allows for a simple axiom that rules out state-dependence.

Axiom 7.19 (State Independence). For all $p_1 \in A_1$ with $p_1(z_1), p_1(z_1') > 0$

$$p_2(\cdot, A_2 | z_1, p_1, A_1) = p_2(\cdot, A_2 | z_1', p_1, A_1).$$

Frick, Iijima, and Strzalecki (2019) showed that under Axiom 7.19 Theorem 7.13 offers a characterization of (state-independent) DRU on decision trees

If we go outside of the simple domain, we will have a *limited observability problem*. In Example 7.18, if the agent chooses to go to supermarket A, we only observe their choices from menu A. We do not have access to the choices they would make from the menu B. We cannot extrapolate from choices of those who go to B because they are a different population with different preferences. In the extreme case, if we do not know anything about the selection mechanism, then we do not learn anything from those choices.

When lotteries are absent, there is only one observable menu after each history, so limited observability is very severe. The following example shows that by adding lotteries we can overcome the limited observability problem and extrapolate across histories.

Example 7.20 (School Choice). In period 1, parents decide to enroll their child in one of two schools, which differ along many decision-relevant dimensions. Upon enrolling, in period 2, parents must choose between a number of after-school care options: H (home); Q (high quality after-school); or B (basic after-school program offered *only* by school 1). Thus, choosing school 1 leads to period-2 menu $\{H, Q, B\}$, whereas school 2 leads to menu $\{H, Q\}$.

This situation is illustrated by the decision tree in the left panel of Figure 7.5. There is limited observability, similar to Example 7.18: We don't know how parents who select to school 1 would choose from the menu $\{H, Q\}$. We need to overcome this problem if we want to make policy recommendations about eliminating option B in school 1.

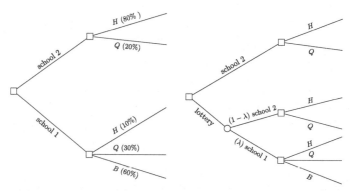

Figure 7.5 Limited observability.

The inclusion of lotteries allows us to do so. Consider the decision tree in the right panel of Figure 7.5. Here seats to school 1 are allocated by a lottery and the student gets admitted with probability λ, while with probability $1 - \lambda$ they must go to school 2. If preferences in period 1 are EU, then the event in which the agent chooses school 1 in the decision tree on the left is precisely the same as the event in which the agent chooses the lottery in the decision tree on the right, that is, we get the same selection of people. Another way to see this is to notice that Linear History Independence ensures that choice probabilities from $\{H, Q, B\}$ are the same in the left and right panels of Figure 7.5. $\triangle$

CHAPTER 8

Dynamic Optimality

8.1 THE BELLMAN EQUATION

In Chapter 7 we defined dynamic random utility (DRU), where the agent in each period t maximizes a random utility function $\tilde{U}_t$. This is a very general model that does not take a stance on whether the agent thinks about the future: It allows for both myopic and forward-looking agents. Typically, economists assume that $\tilde{U}_t$ additionally satisfies the *Bellman equation*, which implies that agents are forward-looking and have correct expectations. We will now explore this in detail.

Assume that $\Omega = \Omega_1 \times \Omega_2 \times \cdots$, where in period t the agent observes $\omega_t \in \Omega_t$. The vector $\omega^t = (\omega_1, \ldots, \omega_t)$ describes information known by the agent at time t.[1] The utility function is $U_t : \Omega^t \to \mathbb{R}^{X_t}$. Each alternative is $x_t = (z_t, A_{t+1})$, i.e., it involves a payoff today and a continuation menu for tomorrow. In other words, the domain of choice are the deterministic decision trees (Section 7.5).

Definition 8.1. $(\tilde{U}_t)$ satisfies the *Bellman equation* if

$$U_t(z_t, A_{t+1}, \omega^t) = u_t(z_t, \omega^t) + \delta \mathbb{E}\left[\max_{x_{t+1} \in A_{t+1}} \tilde{U}_{t+1}(x_{t+1}, \omega^{t+1}) \,\middle|\, \omega^t\right]$$
(8.1)

where $u_t : \Omega^t \to \mathbb{R}^{Z_t}$ is a random *flow utility* (also called felicity) and $\delta \in [0, 1]$ is the *discount factor*.[2]

---

[1] The analyst does not have access to this information. Her information is much coarser: She knows only as much as she can infer from agent's past choices via the events $N(h_t)$. A similar situation occurs in dynamic mechanism design (see, e.g., Pavan, Segal, and Toikka (2014)), where the mechanism designer gradually learns information about the agent's type by looking at their choices.

[2] In general, δ is not identified because u_t can depend on t in an arbitrary way, so it could absorb δ. However, δ is identified for some important special cases, for example under stationarity, where $u_t(z_t, \omega^t) = u(z_t, \omega_t)$ for some time-invariant function u.

112

This means that preferences are additively separable over flow utility, and *continuation value*, which is the expectation of future (maximized) utility

$$\widetilde{V}_t(A_{t+1}) := \mathbb{E}\left[\max_{x_{t+1} \in A_{t+1}} \tilde{U}_{t+1}(x_{t+1})|\omega^t\right],$$

which captures the fact that the agent is forward looking (unless $\delta = 0$). The formula for $\widetilde{V}$ is a generalization of the social surplus formula (Section 1.8). A Bellman agent is using that formula to evaluate their own future welfare (conditional on their current information). By applying the equation recursively it follows that the agent is looking into all the future periods. Notice that $(\tilde{U}_t)$ satisfies the Bellman equation vacuously on what we called the simple domain (Assumption 7.2) because the agent was forbidden from affecting the future (the continuation menu was fixed).

This specific form of V_t makes two important assumptions. First, the agent foresees that they will learn something between periods t and $t + 1$ and adapt their action optimally to this new information. This implies that, adding more options to the menu is always weakly better because they may be useful in some situations and they cannot hurt in any situation. This implication is often called *preference for flexibility*. The following example illustrates.

Example 8.2 (Sun glasses and rain coat). Suppose that on Saturday you are going on a trip and on Friday you are packing your bag. You can bring: your sun glasses $\{g\}$, your rain coat $\{c\}$, or both items $\{g, c\}$. By packing $\{g, c\}$ you de facto delay the choice between g and c until Saturday. If you don't choose that menu, then you are de facto choosing between g and c on Friday. Of course, it's better to make an informed choice, so you bring both items.[3]

Suppose that $t = 1$ is Friday and $t = 2$ is Saturday. In period $t = 2$ you will learn the weather and pick the most appropriate item from your bag. You have some weather-dependent utility function $\tilde{u}_2$. There are no more periods after $t = 2$, so we just set $\tilde{U}_2 := \tilde{u}_2$. Since we are not interested in what you are consuming while you are packing your bag, we set $\tilde{u}_1 := 0$. For simplicity set $\delta := 1$.

The Bellman equation says that:

$$\tilde{U}_1(\{g\}) = \mathbb{E}[\tilde{u}_2(g)|\omega_1],$$
$$\tilde{U}_1(\{c\}) = \mathbb{E}[\tilde{u}_2(c)|\omega_1],$$
$$\tilde{U}_1(\{g, c\}) = \mathbb{E}[\max\{\tilde{u}_2(g), \tilde{u}_2(c)\}|\omega_1].$$

There are two ways to see that the last expression dominates. The first one is to notice that the component-wise maximum always has a higher expectation, i.e., $\max\{\tilde{u}_2(g), \tilde{u}_2(c)\} \geq \tilde{u}_2(g)$ in each state of the world (ω_1, ω_2) and taking conditional expectations preserves this inequality (likewise for $\tilde{u}_{(c)}$).

---

[3] If delay is costly, then there is a tradeoff between the option value and the delay cost. This typically generates a probability distribution over the choice to delay. We will discuss such models in Chapter 9.

Another way to see this is to notice that max : $\mathbb{R}^n \to \mathbb{R}$ is a convex function, so by conditional Jensen's inequality we have $\mathbb{E}[\max\{\tilde{u}_2(g), \tilde{u}_2(c)\}|\omega_1] \geq \max\{\mathbb{E}[\tilde{u}_2(g)|\omega_1], \mathbb{E}[\tilde{u}_2(c)|\omega_1]\}$. $\triangle$

The second assumption behind the Bellman equation is that the agent's belief over future states is correct, i.e., it corresponds to the true data generating process $\mathbb{P}$. In general, there could be one distribution that governs the true variability of preferences (say in our example, the true probability of rain) and another that represents the agent's subjective belief (say the weather forecast). (8.1) says that those two are the same; this is often called *rational expectations*. This assumption seems innocuous in the weather forecast example. It seems strong in other settings: consumers predicting their future income streams, firms predicting profitability of new products, and so on.

Notice a formal difference between preference for flexibility and rational expectations: The latter imposes a consistency condition between ρ_t and ρ_{t+1}. On the other hand, the former is purely a condition on the structure of $\widetilde{U}_t$, so it will manifest itself by axioms imposed on ρ_t alone.

Models used in the dynamic discrete choice literature in econometrics and industrial organization specify the Bellman equation somewhat differently. While similar in spirit, those models are not equivalent: many specifications, such as dynamic logit, violate preference for flexibility, and associated notions. We discuss this in Chapter 12.

8.2 PREFERENCE FOR FLEXIBILITY

It's good to keep our options open, as long as it is costless. If the agent is directly choosing between a menu and its superset, they will always take the superset, except if the added items are so bad that they are dominated in each state of the world by something already in the menu (in that case there is a tie between the two menus).

Like in Example 8.2, we will make the following simplifications: There are two periods and consumption in period $t = 1$ is suppressed, so in that period we observe choices over menus of $t = 2$ consumptions. Moreover, suppose that there is no private information in period $t = 1$ so that choices between menus are deterministic in the eyes of the analyst. This allows us to capture observed choices by a preference relation $\succsim_1$ instead of an SCF ρ_1.[4]

As a further simplification, let's forget about ρ_2 for now and just focus on choices made in period $t = 1$. This allows us to drop the subscripts and write things like $A \succsim B$ instead of $A_2 \succsim_1 B_2$.

8.2.1 Preferences over Menus

Our primitive is $\succsim$ defined over $\mathcal{A}(X)$. On this domain, the Bellman equation boils down to the following.

---

[4] This is more generally true under a weaker assumption that $\omega_2 \perp \omega_1$.

Definition 8.3. $\succsim$ has a *Koopmans representation* if there exists a random utility $\tilde{U} : \Omega \to \mathbb{R}^X$ such that

$$V(A) = \mathbb{E}\left[\max_{x \in A} \tilde{U}(x)\right]$$

represents $\succsim$.

Koopmans (1964) asks what axioms on $\succsim$ pin down this representation. The key axiom says that bigger menus are better.

Axiom 8.4 (Preference for Flexibility). If $A \supseteq B$, then $A \succsim B$.

This is almost all that we need: We just need to add another axiom that disciplines the ties.

Axiom 8.5 (Modularity). If $A \sim A \cup B$, then $A \cup C \sim A \cup B \cup C$.

Intuitively, if adding B to A doesn't create any value, this must be because items in B are statewise dominated by items in A. Adding C to both sides does not change that.

Theorem 8.6 (Kreps 1979). *Suppose that Z is a finite set. A preference $\succsim$ satisfies Preference for Flexibility and Modularity if and only if it has a Koopmans representation.*

Preference for flexibility makes sense in an idealized model. But in real life, it can be violated in many ways. For example, if there is *choice overload*, then going through the options in the menu and making a decision is costly to the agent. If they anticipate this cost, they may prefer to rule out options right away (presumably at some cost too, but suppose that such cost is sunk).

Other situations involve temptation, where preferences at t and $t + 1$ (about x_{t+1}) disagree with each other. There are several ways to resolve this conflict. The agent could be *sophisticated* and perfectly foresee their future preferences (Strotz, 1955). Or they could try to resist temptation by exerting *costly self-control* (Gul and Pesendorfer, 2001). Or they could be *naive* and think there is no conflict whatsoever. Agents who are sophisticated or have costly self-control will violate the preference for flexibility axiom because they may want to commit to exclude options from the menu that are tempting and harmful. Naive agents will satisfy it. They think they think they satisfy the Bellman equation, but they do not actually satisfy it: They violate rational expectations. The large axiomatic literature on temptation is summarized in Lipman and Pesendorfer (2013).

8.2.2 Preferences over Menus of Lotteries

Kreps's theorem is very elegant, but has very weak uniqueness properties. Perhaps this should not come as a surprise, given the weak uniqueness properties of RU we discussed in Section 2.4: The distribution of $\tilde{U}$ is not identified, nor is the set of preferences they represent.

Adding lotteries helped with RU, and it does here as well. Following Dekel, Lipman, and Rustichini (2001), henceforth DLR, let $X = \Delta(Z)$ and assume that preferences $\succsim$ are defined on all nonempty and compact subsets of X.

Definition 8.7. $\succsim$ has a *DLR representation* if there exists a random expected utility $\widetilde{U} : \Omega \to \mathbb{R}^{\Delta(Z)}$, such that

$$V(A) = \mathbb{E}\left[\max_{p \in A} \widetilde{U}(p)\right]$$

represents $\succsim$.

Instead of Modularity, we will now have axioms that rely on the lottery structure, which allows us to mix menus in the following way:

$$\alpha A + (1 - \alpha)B := \{\alpha p + (1 - \alpha)q : p \in A \text{ and } q \in B\}.$$

Axiom 8.8 (Menu Independence). If $A \succ B$, then for all C and all $\alpha \in (0, 1]$ we have $\alpha A + (1 - \alpha)C \succ \alpha B + (1 - \alpha)C$.

This is just the menu version of the vNM axiom (Axiom 4.2). We also need a form of continuity.

Axiom 8.9 (Archimedean Continuity). If $A \succ B \succ C$, then there exist $\alpha, \lambda \in (0, 1)$ such that $\alpha A + (1 - \alpha)C \succ B \succ \lambda A + (1 - \lambda)C$.

Theorem 8.10 (DLR). *A preference $\succsim$ has a DLR representation if and only if it satisfies Preference for Flexibility, Menu Independence, and Archimedean Continuity.*

Proof. See Theorem S.2 in the supplement to Dekel, Lipman, Rustichini, and Sarver (2007). $\qquad\square$

Adding lotteries to the domain helps with uniqueness in the following sense. In each state $\omega \in \Omega$ the agent has a preference over lotteries $\succsim_\omega$ represented by $\widetilde{U}(\cdot, \omega)$. Let $P(\widetilde{U}) := \{\succsim_\omega : \omega \in \Omega\}$. In other words, $P(\widetilde{U})$ is the support of the distribution over preferences induced by $\widetilde{U}$.

Theorem[†] 8.11 (DLR). *If there is a representation with a finite state space, then the sets $P(\widetilde{U})$ coincide for all representations.*

Proof. See Theorem 1, parts B and C of Dekel, Lipman, and Rustichini (2001). This result holds under the additional assumption that all states are relevant. In the infinite case, the closures of those spaces coincide. $\qquad\square$

This sort of uniqueness is weaker than the one we have for REU representations, where the probability distribution over $P(\widetilde{U})$ was pinned down uniquely (Theorem 4.17). Here we can only pin down its suport. In the next section we will discuss how to get a stronger form of uniqueness by coupling preferences over menus in period $t = 1$ with choices from menus in period $t = 2$.[5]

8.3 RATIONAL EXPECTATIONS

Another assumption behind the Bellman Equation is that the agent has rational expectations. In the weather example (Example 8.2) this means that the weather forecast is correct on average. Whenever the states are objective, rational expectations impose consistency between the objective frequency of states and the agent's beliefs revealed by ρ (as in Chapter 5). In this chapter states are subjective to the agent and unobservable to the analyst. In this case, rational expectations imposes a connection between ρ_t and ρ_{t+1}.

The simplest case is when the only meaningful private information is in period $t = 2$, so the analyst observes a deterministic preference $\succsim_1$ on menus and an SCF ρ_2. Formally, ρ_2 is defined on $X_2 = \Delta(Z_2)$ and $\succsim_1$ on $X_1 = \mathcal{A}(X_2)$.

Suppose that we have a DLR preference $\succsim_1$ and a REU SCF ρ_2.

Definition 8.12. We say that $(\succsim_1, \rho_2)$ is a *Ahn–Sarver pair* if $\succsim_1$ has a DLR representation $(\Omega, \mathcal{F}, \mathbb{P}_1, \widetilde{U}_2)$ and that ρ_2 has a REU representation with $(\Omega, \mathcal{F}, \mathbb{P}_2, \widetilde{U}_2)$ and $\widetilde{U}_2$ has finitely many possible realizations.

Here $\mathbb{P}_1$ is the belief that the agent holds in period $t = 1$ and $\mathbb{P}_2$ is the true data generating process that drives random variation in agent's period $t = 2$ choices.[6] These two probability measures can be very different for an arbitrary pair $(\succsim_1, \rho_2)$. For example, the agent may be over-optimistic about option value, or over-pessimistic. Rational expectations is when the agent's expectations are exactly right.

Definition 8.13. We say that a Ahn–Sarver pair $(\succsim_1, \rho_2)$ has *Rational Expectations* if the distribution of $\widetilde{U}_2$ under $\mathbb{P}_1$ is the same as under $\mathbb{P}_2$.[7]

Ahn and Sarver (2013) found a sharp axiom that captures this property.

Axiom[†] 8.14 (Sophistication). For any menu without ties[†] $A_2 \cup \{p_2\}$

$$A_2 \cup \{p_2\} \succ_1 A_2 \iff \rho_2(p_2, A_2 \cup \{p_2\}) > 0$$

This axiom says that the agent wants to include additional options into the menu if and only if they actually choose them at least some of the time.

---

[5] An alternate route (Dillenberger, Lleras, Sadowski, and Takeoka, 2014) involves adding an objective state space (observable by the analyst) and studying choices between menus of Anscombe–Aumann acts.

[6] It is without loss of generality to assume that they share the measurable space $(\Omega, \mathcal{F})$ and period-2 utility function $\widetilde{U}_2$.

[7] In other words, $\mathbb{P}_1$ and $\mathbb{P}_2$ are equal except for payoff-irrelevant events.

Theorem[†] 8.15. *(Ahn and Sarver, 2013).* $(\succsim_1, \rho_2)$ *has Rational Expectations iff it satisfies Sophistication.*

To understand Sophistication better, assume that it holds only in one direction. First imagine that

$$A_2 \cup \{p_2\} \succ_1 A_2 \implies \rho_2(p_2, A_2 \cup \{p_2\}) > 0.$$

Whenever the agent wants to include a new option in period 1, they then choose it at least some of the time in period 2. But there could be options the agent is sometimes choosing in period 2 that they do not value in period 1. This is because of *unforeseen contingencies*: Scenarios that the agent does not imagine happening and does not not value flexibility along these dimensions. In other words, the agent does not perceive all the option value there actually is in a menu.

Now imagine the opposite:

$$A_2 \cup \{p_2\} \succ_1 A_2 \impliedby \rho_2(p_2, A_2 \cup \{p_2\}) > 0.$$

Whenever it's sometimes worth choosing an option in period 2, the agent wants to include it in period 1. Yet the agent may want to include some options that never end up getting used. This may be because some scenarios that they are imagining are completely impossible. In other words, the agent perceives too much option value in a menu.[8]

The Rational Expectations assumption helps with identification. As discussed in Section 8.2, looking at $\succsim_1$ alone identifies just the support of the distribution over ordinal risk preferences. Theorem 4.17 says that just looking at ρ_2 identifies that distribution. This still means that in each state we can multiply the utility by a positive constant α and add a constant β to it, where both constants can depend on the state. Remarkably, Ahn and Sarver (2013) show that putting $\succsim_1$ and ρ_2 together the constant α has to be state-independent.

The reason for this stronger uniqueness result is that the probability $\mathbb{P}_1 = \mathbb{P}_2$ is identified, so although changing the scale of utility in some states does not change period $t = 2$ choices, it does impact the option value and therefore changes preferences because changes in utility cannot be absorbed by rescaling the probability.

Finally, the rational expectations assumption becomes much weaker if we don't observe a preference $\succsim_1$ over menus, but instead just a preference over lotteries (singleton menus). Suppose that our primitive is an EU preference $\succsim_1$ over lotteries and a REU SCF ρ_2. Given that there are finitely many possible realizations of $\widetilde{U}_2$, we have finitely many possible EU preferences in period 2: $\succsim_2^1, \ldots, \succsim_2^n$.

---

[8] Another explanation is that the agent enjoys a *pure freedom of choice*.

Definition 8.16. We say that there is a *preference reversal* if there exist $p, q \in \Delta(Z)$ such that $p \succsim_1 q$ and $q \succsim_2^i p$ for all i with at least one of the preferences $\succsim_1, \succsim_2^1, \ldots, \succsim_2^n$ strict.

Theorem 8.17. *(Strack and Taubinsky, 2021).* $(\succsim_1, \rho_2)$ *has Rational Expectations iff there are no preference reversals.*

8.4 RECENT AXIOMATIC WORK*

So far we allowed for private information only in period $t = 2$. Frick, Iijima, and Strzalecki (2019) allow for intermediate payoffs and more importantly for private information in all periods, so their primitive is the collection (ρ_t). They define the stochastic versions of DLR axioms and Sophistication and prove that they are equivalent to Definition 8.1. They also axiomatize a multiperiod learning model where tastes are not allowed to vary over time, but only beliefs.

Lu and Saito (2019) unpack the simple domain Assumption 7.2. As discussed above, the simple domain makes sense under the time-separability assumption that is built into the Bellman equation. Lu and Saito (2019) study a model where time-separability is violated, as in Kreps and Porteus (1978) and Epstein and Zin (1989). In such models the (fixed) continuation menu will affect the current risk attitudes. They show that the analyst's estimates of the function u may be biased if they are contaminated by the nonlinear continuation utility.

Lu and Saito (2018) study static choices between consumption streams. In their model the randomness in choices is driven by preference shocks to discounting attitudes: The felicity function is deterministic, but the discount factor is stochastic. They provide an axiomatic characterization of this model. They also look at an extension where the analyst observes the average of ρ_t in each period t, that is the unconditional choice probabilities.

Following Ahn and Sarver (2013), the two papers by Ahn, Iijima, Sarver, and Yaouanq (2019); Ahn, Iijima, and Sarver (2020) study a pair $(\succsim, \rho)$, where $\succsim$ is a preference over menus and ρ is a stochastic choice function from menus. These papers look at models where the rational expectations assumption is violated, and in particular focus on naivete for time-inconsistent preferences.

CHAPTER 9

Response Times

9.1 NEW VARIABLE AND NEW QUESTIONS

So far we looked at what the agent choses. In this chapter we will turn our attention to a new variable: How much time it takes them to make a choice.

In psychology these are known as *response times*. They are routinely collected for perceptual tasks such as those discussed in Section 1.3.[1] The increased availability of data about online and in-app behavior makes response times a potentially fruitful object to study in economics.

One stylized fact that can be formulated using this primitive is that difficult problems take more time than easy ones. For example, in the weight perception task (Example 1.5) reaction times are longer if the two items are closer in weight. The models that we study in this chapter predict this stylized fact.

Another stylized fact is that fast decisions are better (or more accurate) than slow ones.[2] That is, conditioning on trials in which the agent makes their decision quickly, the quality of this decision is better than conditioning on trials in which the agent takes longer. The situation here is more complicated because there are two effects that push in opposite direction. First, spending more time making the decision presumably has some benefits, for example, the agent receives more information about the alternatives. This is known as the *speed-accuracy trade-off*: The agent can make quick but inaccurate decisions, or take more time to improve accuracy. Based on this effect alone, we would expect that the more time the agent spends on the decision, the better this

---

[1] See, for example, Luce (1986), Gold and Shadlen (2007), and Ratcliff and McKoon (2008). Response times are also used in other contexts: A historic example is Jung's (1910) word association test used for revealing subject's emotional states. An example from contemporary psychology is the implicit association test (see, Greenwald, McGhee, and Schwartz (1998)).

[2] For perceptual tasks, see, for example, Swensson (1972), Luce (1986), Ratcliff and McKoon (2008), and Shadlen, Hanks, Churchland, Kiani, and Yang (2006). A similar patterns appears for economic choices (see, e.g., Reutskaja, Nagel, Camerer, and Rangel (2011), Fehr and Rangel (2011), Krajbich, Armel, and Rangel (2010)).

decision is. In other words, if we *forced* the agent to stop at time t, accuracy would be increasing in t.

However, our agent's decision when to stop is *endogenous*. If the agent made a fast decision, they may have had a reason for doing so and likewise for a slow decision. In particular, taking more time typically has some opportunity costs, so the decision to stop depends on how much the agent expects to learn (the option value of waiting). If they get an informative signal, they may want to stop early, but they will continue if the signal is noisy. If the informativeness of the signal required to trigger stopping (i.e., the stopping boundary) is decreasing over time, then the observed choice accuracy is decreasing.

To study these effects formally, we will set up a model of *optimal stopping* or *sequential sampling*, where the agent is optimally choosing when to stop (and what to choose in the event of stopping). This is a model of active learning because by choosing when to stop the agent de facto decides how much to learn. In Wald's model (binary prior) the optimal stopping boundary is constant in time, so fast choices are equally good as slow ones. But this is an exception: With other priors the optimal boundary is time-dependent.

Papers in psychology and cognitive science often use a "reduced-form" model where the boundary is not optimally chosen by the agent, but instead exogenously specified by the analyst. The most popular Drift-Diffusion Model (DDM) uses a constant boundary. We will relate such models to models of optimal stopping.

Remark 9.1 (The dual system hypothesis). There are situations in which fast decisions are impulsive, instinctive, and often wrong, while slow decisions are deliberate, cognitive, and often right (Kahneman, 2011). The evidence behind this focuses mostly on choices where to arrive at the correct answer, the agent needs to solve a puzzle of some sort, or "think about the problem the correct way" (Rubinstein, 2007; Caplin and Martin, 2016). In contrast, in simple perception experiments, the gut feeling is often correct and if we start doubting ourselves, there is a good chance we are off base. Of course, economic choices involve a combination of both kinds of processes. $\triangle$

Remark 9.2 (Bandits). In another popular model of dynamic learning the agent continually experiments with each alternative and potentially flips back and forth each period. This is a different dynamic optimization problem, known as multiarmed bandit (Gittins, 1979; Gittins, Glazebrook, and Weber, 2011; Weitzman, 1979; Keller, Rady, and Cripps, 2005; Doval, 2018). Example 7.16 was a very simple illustration in the context of experience goods. The primitive here is different because the analyst observes choices in each period. Little is known about stochastic choices induced by optimal choice rules in this environment. The deterministic decision theory literature includes Piermont and Teper (2019), Hyogo (2007), and Cooke (2017). $\triangle$

9.2 OPTIMAL STOPPING

9.2.1 Primitive

The set of time indices is $\mathcal{T} = [0, \infty)$ or $\mathcal{T} = \{0, 1, 2, \ldots\}$. To simplify the exposition, I will favor the discrete time formulation as much as possible. In an idealized situation with a lot of data the analyst has access to the joint distribution $\rho \in \Delta(A \times \mathcal{T})$, for some collection of (typically binary) menus $A \in \mathcal{A}$.[3] For any menu A we can decompose the joint distribution ρ into the distribution of response times and the conditional choice probability $\rho_t \in \Delta(A)$ for each $t \in \mathcal{T}$. For simplicity, assume that the response times distribution has full support, so the conditional choice probabilities ρ_t can be computed for each t. Typically ρ_t will depend on t, that is, there will be some correlation between time and choice.

It is useful to think of our agent as solving the stopping problem depicted in Figure 9.1, with the binary menu $A = \{\ell, r\}$. In each period, the agent can pick one of the items immediately, or they can delay, ponder the decision a bit more and make their decision later, or delay even more, and so on.

9.2.2 Dynamic Learning

Let S be the state space, as in Chapters 5 and 6. At each time t the agent receives a message $M_t \in \mathcal{M}_t$ and $M^t := (M_1, \ldots, M_t)$ denotes the history of messages up to time t.[4] The agent is endowed with a prior on S and a dynamic experiment: The distribution of M^t depends on $s \in S$ (typically

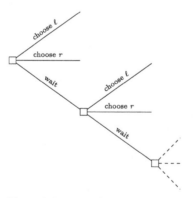

Figure 9.1 A stopping tree.

---

[3] This data can be obtained in one of two ways: either by sampling one individual many times, or by sampling each individual a limited number of times (maybe even once) and using a mixture model that accounts for heterogeneity in tastes and/or stopping dynamics.

[4] In this chapter we will use upper case M for messages and $\mathcal{M}$ for the set in which they live.

messages are i.i.d. conditional on s). It is useful to consider the probability space $\Omega = S \times \left(\times_{t \in \mathcal{T}} \mathcal{M}_t \right)$, so that the message and the stopping times are random variables carried by Ω.

The message process can be interpreted in various ways: recognition of objects in a lab experiment or some form of introspection, for example, retrieving pleasant or unpleasant memories. In perceptual tasks it is assumed that the signal strength depends on the difficulty of the task; for decision tasks it depends on the true underlying utility. Consistently with Chapters 5 and 6, we will treat messages as unobserved by the analyst.

The agent has a state-dependent utility $v : S \to \mathbb{R}^X$. In period t their conditional expected utility of choosing x is $U_t(x) := \mathbb{E}[v(x)|M^t]$. The agent's optimal choice from menu A is given by the *choice function* $\chi_t = x$ iff $U_t(x) > U_t(y)$ for all $y \in A$.[5] Given that M^t is private, observed choices are stochastic.

9.2.3 Stopping Times

Let τ be the time at which the agent stops and makes a choice. We say that stopping is *exogenous* if the agent is forced to make a decision precisely at a time that is controlled by the analyst. In this case, τ is a random variable that is independent of M^t. We say that stopping is *endogenous* when the agent can decide themself when to stop; in this case, τ typically depends on M^t.

To model this formally, we will use the notion of a stopping time from probability theory. The main idea is that the event "the agent stops at time t" is fully determined by the message history up to time t and does not depend on future messages. Let Σ^t denote the collection of message histories after which the agent stops at time t.

Definition 9.3. A *stopping time* τ is a mapping $\tau : \Omega \to \mathcal{T}$ such that for each t we have $\tau(\omega) = t$ iff $M^t \in \Sigma^t$.[6]

Given a stopping time τ, the agent's choices are χ_τ and their ex ante expected utility is $\mathbb{E}[U_\tau(\chi_\tau)]$. The analyst observes ρ^s, which is the distribution of (χ_τ, τ) in state s. ρ^s_t is the distribution of χ_t *conditional* on state s and the event that the agent stopped at time t, that is, $\{\tau = t\}$.

9.2.4 Optimal Stopping/Sequential Sampling

So far, we described an arbitrary stopping time. But in this model the stopping time is chosen optimally: There is a deterministic cost of waiting, a nondecreasing function $c : \mathcal{T} \to \mathbb{R}$. The optimal stopping time τ^* solves:

---

[5] For expositional purposes we assume away ties; in parametric models discussed below they will happen with probability zero.

[6] Formally, for τ to be well defined, we need the following condition: $\Sigma^{t+1} \subseteq (\Gamma^t)^c \times \mathcal{M}_{t+1}$.

$$\max_\tau \mathbb{E}[U_\tau(\chi_\tau) - c(\tau)]. \tag{9.1}$$

In statistics, this is known as sequential sampling: The analyst can buy additional data (experiments) at a cost. The special case of *linear* time cost is often used where $c(t) = \gamma t$ for some $\gamma > 0$.[7]

Even though the stopping time is optimal, the experiment (M_t) is fixed and cannot be chosen by the agent. Yet, there is still an element of active learning, in the sense of Chapter 6, because waiting longer gives the agent more information (at a cost). However, the scope for attention allocation is limited here: Our agent cannot pay more attention to one item than the others, just get more information overall. Section 9.8 discusses papers where the agent optimizes over (M_t).

9.2.5 Accuracy

Accuracy is the probability of making the correct choice conditional on stopping at time t.

Definition 9.4. Let $x^s := \arg\max_{x \in A} v(x, s)$ be the correct choice in state s. *Accuracy* is defined as $\alpha^s(t) := \rho_t^s(x^s, A)$.

Here "correct" means "ex post correct," that is, correct conditional on the state. Since the agent does not know the state, they will sometimes make expost errors, even though their decisions are correct from a dynamic point of view, that is, they are dynamically optimal by solving (9.1).

Definition 9.4 applies in situations when the analyst knows the true state of the world. This makes sense in the domain of perceptual tasks, where the analyst knows which choice is objectively correct in each trial (e.g., which weight is heavier). In choice tasks, where preferences are subjective, even if the analyst is conditioning choices on some fixed state s, she may not know whether $v(x, s) > v(y, s)$ or the opposite holds in that fixed state. Typically in choice experiments an additional elicitation of preferences is made as a proxy for the true v.[8] Alternatively, with a lot of data, the correct choice is revealed by the modal choice (the sign of the utility difference is revealed by which item is chosen with the higher probability).

---

[7] Another flavor of this model, which we will not discuss here, involves *discounting*: There is $\delta \in (0, 1)$ such that τ^* solves $\max_\tau \mathbb{E}[\delta^\tau U_\tau(\chi_\tau)]$.

[8] For example, Krajbich, Armel, and Rangel (2010) for each subject elicit a rating of each $x \in X$ on the scale $-10, \ldots, 10$ and equate "accurate" with "higher ranked." Likewise, Oud, Krajbich, Miller, Cheong, Botvinick, and Fehr (2016) elicit willingness to pay for each item. Of course, the subject's rating may itself be stochastic, so this approach should be treated only as the first step. In addition, this approach is probably not well suited in situations where preference reversals are present (Tversky and Thaler, 1990). See also a discussion in Khaw, Li, and Woodford (2021).

9.3 WALD MODEL

In the *Wald model* the agent is choosing from a binary menu $A = \{\ell, r\}$. There are two states $S = \{s_\ell, s_r\}$. We have $v(x, s) = \mathbb{1}_{\{s = s_x\}}$, that is, the agent wants to match the state, and cost is linear, $c(t) = \gamma t$ for $\gamma > 0$. Conditional on the state s, messages are i.i.d. $M_t \sim \mathcal{N}(\delta(s), \sigma^2)$, where $\delta(s_\ell) = \eta$ and $\delta(s_r) = -\eta$ for some $\eta, \sigma > 0$. Because of the Normality assumption, it is sufficient for the agent to keep track of the running sum $\hat{M}^t := M_1 + \cdots + M_t$, instead of the whole vector M^t.

From the point of view of the agent, the process $\hat{M}^t$ is a random walk with unknown drift (η or $-\eta$). The agent is learning about the drift by observing realizations of $\hat{M}^t$. By Bayes rule, the posterior log-likelihood ratio is

$$L_t(\hat{M}) := \log \frac{\mathbb{P}(s_\ell | \hat{M}^t)}{\mathbb{P}(s_r | \hat{M}^t)} = \log \frac{\mathbb{P}(s_\ell)}{\mathbb{P}(s_r)} + \hat{M}^t \frac{2\eta}{\sigma^2}. \tag{9.2}$$

Given v, the agent chooses ℓ over r whenever $\mathbb{P}(s_\ell | \hat{M}^t) > \mathbb{P}(s_r | \hat{M}^t)$, which by formula (9.2) holds whenever $\hat{M}^t > \frac{\sigma^2}{2\eta} \log \frac{\mathbb{P}(s_r)}{\mathbb{P}(s_\ell)} =: w$. Thus, in state s_ℓ, if we force the agent to choose at time t they will choose ℓ with probability $\mathbb{P}^{s_\ell}(\hat{M}^t > w) = 1 - \Phi\left(\frac{w - t\eta}{\sqrt{2t}\sigma}\right)$, where Φ is the CDF of the standard Normal distribution. If the prior is symmetric, then $w = 0$ and this function is increasing in t, which formalizes the intuitive reasoning behind the speed-accuracy trade-off.[9]

The following theorem describes the optimal stopping time in the Wald model.

Theorem 9.5. *In the Wald model there exists $k > 0$ such that*

$$\tau^* = \min\{t \geq 0 : |L_t| \geq k\}, \tag{9.3}$$

where (L_t) is given by (9.2). Moreover, if the prior is symmetric, τ^* can also be written as

$$\tau^* = \min\{t \geq 0 : |\hat{M}^t| \geq b\} \tag{9.4}$$

for some $b > 0$.

Proof. See Arrow, Blackwell, and Girshick (1949). □

Thus, under τ^*, the agent stops the first time the posterior hits a time-invariant boundary (9.3). The constancy of the boundary in the space of beliefs does not depend on the assumption that signals are Normally distributed.

---

[9] Notice a subtlety: A nonmonotonicity occurs the agent initially believes that ℓ is more likely. For small values of t they mostly go by their prior and correctly choose ℓ. For large values of t, their posterior will correctly put a high weight on ℓ, so they will choose correctly as well. But for intermediate values of t, there will be signal realizations that make the agent change their mind and incorrectly choose r.

It holds for any distribution of M_t as long as they are i.i.d. and the cost is linear.[10]

When the prior is symmetric, then the boundary in the signal space (9.4) is also constant in time. This again has to do with the fact that there are two states. To see that, suppose that $\hat{M}^t$ is close to zero after a long t. With two states, the agent is certain that the drift is either η or $-\eta$, so this signal is interpreted as pure noise (and the agent continues). On the other hand, if there are more states, for example, the agent is learning about the difficulty of the task, or about the stakes, then there are many possible values of the drift, so $\hat{M}^t \approx 0$ is now interpreted as carrying some information (e.g., that the task is difficult, or that the stakes are low) and the agent may want to stop. We will see this later on in more detail.

Equation (9.4) has no reference to the belief process. The agent follows a simple heuristic: Stop the first time the signal process $\hat{M}^t$ hits $b > 0$ and choose ℓ if it hits the upper boundary and r if it hits the lower boundary. This makes it tempting to forget about optimization altogether and think of (9.4) as a "reduced-form" model of reaction times. The continuous time version of such a model is known as the Drift-Diffusion Model (DDM).

9.4 THE DRIFT-DIFFUSION MODEL

DDM was brought to psychology by Stone (1960) and Edwards (1965) to study perception and by Ratcliff (1978) to study memory retrieval. It is now a well established benchmark in psychology and neuroscience. In this model the cumulative signal is a *diffusion* with drift δ and noise σ: Time is continuous $\mathcal{T} = [0, \infty)$ and

$$\hat{M}^t = t\delta + \sigma B_t, \tag{9.5}$$

where B_t is a standard Brownian motion[11] This ensures that $\hat{M}^t \sim \mathcal{N}(t\delta, t\sigma^2)$, just like in the discrete-time version.

Definition 9.6. Fix $A = \{\ell, r\}$. The SCF $\rho \in \Delta(A \times \mathcal{T})$ has a *DDM representation* if there exists $\delta \in \mathbb{R}$ and $\sigma, b > 0$ such that (9.5) holds and ρ is induced by χ and τ where

$$\chi_t = \ell \text{ if } \hat{M}^t = b,$$
$$\chi_t = r \text{ if } \hat{M}^t = -b,$$
$$\tau = \inf\{t \geq 0 : |\hat{M}^t| \geq b\}.$$

In this case we write $\rho \sim DDM(\delta, \sigma, b)$.

---

[10] If the current belief equals $p \in [0, 1]$, then it doesn't make any difference how much time has elapsed so far: It's as if the agent is starting with a prior equal to p, as long as the marginal cost is constant over time.

[11] A standard Brownian motion starts at zero, has continuous sample paths, and independent normally distributed increments, meaning that for $t' > t$ the value of $B_{t'} - B_t$ is distributed $\mathcal{N}(0, t' - t)$ independently of the past.

To see how this fits with the previous section, note that in the (continuous time version of the) Wald model we have $\rho^{s_l} \sim DDM(\eta, \sigma, b)$ and $\rho^{s_r} \sim DDM(-\eta, \sigma, b)$.

The assumption that M_t is a diffusion is key. For a general process M_t, Definition 9.6 is vacuous (see, e.g., Jones and Dzhafarov (2014) and Fudenberg, Strack, and Strzalecki (2015)).

The DDM is a very tractable model thanks to the following result from probability theory.

Theorem 9.7 (Gambler's Ruin Problem). *If $\rho \sim DDM(\delta, \sigma, b)$, then the parameters are unique up to a common positive scalar multiple. Moreover, ρ is a product measure, that is, ρ_t is a constant function of t. Furthermore, for any $t \in \mathcal{T}$*

$$\rho_t(\ell, r) = \frac{e^{\delta b/\sigma^2}}{e^{\delta b/\sigma^2} + e^{-\delta b/\sigma^2}}$$

and

$$\mathbb{E}[\tau] = \frac{b}{\delta} \tanh\left(\frac{b\delta}{\sigma^2}\right),$$

where $\tanh$ *is the hyperbolic tangent function;* $\tanh(x) = \frac{e^x - e^{-x}}{e^x + e^{-x}}$.

Since ρ_t is independent of t, to describe ρ we can just look at the marginals on A and $\mathcal{T}$. We are already familiar with the marginal on A: It's the psychometric function. The theorem above says it is of a Luce/logit variety. The new object is the *chronometric function*: the mapping $\delta \mapsto \mathbb{E}[\tau]$.[12] A comparison of these two functions (Figure 9.2) illustrates the usefulness of including response times in estimation. The psychometric function is flat where the chronometric function is steep and vice versa (see, e.g., Clithero and Rangel (2013)).

The chronometric function is decreasing in $|\delta|$, which means that difficult trials ($|\delta|$ small) take longer than easy trials ($|\delta|$ large). This is consistent with the first stylized fact from Section 9.1. However, DDM is inconsistent with the second stylized fact because ρ_t is independent of t, that is, the model predicts constant accuracy. This was recognized in the psychology literature from the beginning and many extensions off DDM have been proposed to address this issue. We will discuss them later in this chapter.

DDM is a good description of some perceptual tasks, where the drift of $\hat{M}_t$ can take one of two possible values. However, it doesn't not really make sense in situations where there are more than two possible states because the Wald model does not apply to such situations. For example, in a weight perception

---

[12] Just to clarify, the psychometric function and the chronometric function are functions of δ and other parameters. In contrast, accuracy is a function of t. Theorem 9.7 does not uniquely pin down the distribution of τ. There are Fourier series expressions for the CDF of τ (see Chapter 10, Section 4 of Feller (1957) and Smith (1990)).

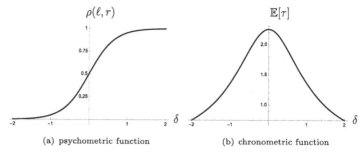

(a) psychometric function   (b) chronometric function

Figure 9.2 Psychometric and chronometric functions in DDM, as a function of $\delta \in [-2, 2]$. Fixed parameters are $b = 1.5$, and $\sigma = 1$.

task (Example 1.5) there are many possible values of the drift (many possible values of the weight difference between the two objects). This makes the state space larger than two points and, as we will see later in this chapter, makes a constant boundary suboptimal. Thus, an application of DDM to such tasks is inconsistent with the rational expectations assumption (that the agent's prior equals the data generating process).

DDM has recently been used to study choice tasks.[13] Let $\mathcal{A}$ be the collection of all binary menus. The analyst observes the family $\rho^A \in \Delta(A \times \mathcal{T})$ such that $\rho^A \sim DDM(v(x) - v(y), \sigma, b)$ for $A \in \mathcal{A}$, where $v : X \to \mathbb{R}$ is the utility function of the agent. Like in perception tasks, the application of DDM to choice tasks is inconsistent with the rational expectations assumption. The agent who faces a randomly chosen pair of items from X should have a prior belief given by the distribution of utilities of all items in X, which is *not* a binary prior.

9.5 TIME-DEPENDENT DDM

One of the extensions of DDM proposed to address the constant accuracy prediction relaxes the constant boundary assumption of DDM.

Definition 9.8. Fix $A = \{\ell, r\}$. The SCF $\rho \in \Delta(A \times \mathcal{T})$ has a *time-dependent DDM representation* if there exists $\delta \in \mathbb{R}$ and a boundary $b : \mathcal{T} \to \mathbb{R}_+$ such that ρ is induced by χ and τ

$$\chi_t = \ell \text{ if } \hat{M}^t = b(t),$$
$$\chi_t = r \text{ if } \hat{M}^t = -b(t),$$
$$\tau = \inf\{t \geq 0 : |\hat{M}^t| \geq b(t)\},$$
$$\hat{M}^t = \delta t + \sigma B_t,$$

---

[13] Roe, Busemeyer, and Townsend (2001); Krajbich, Armel, and Rangel (2010); Krajbich, Lu, Camerer, and Rangel (2012); Milosavljevic, Malmaud, Huth, Koch, and Rangel (2010); Reutskaja, Nagel, Camerer, and Rangel (2011).

where B_t is a standard Brownian motion. In this case we write $\rho \sim DDM^+(\delta, \sigma, b)$.

Similarly to DDM, here the chronometric function is decreasing in $|\delta|$, so the model explains the first stylized fact. Moreover, in DDM$^+$, the choice probabilities have a logit-like closed-form expression that generalizes the gambler's ruin formula.

Theorem 9.9 (Fudenberg, Strack, and Strzalecki, 2018). *Suppose that* $\rho \sim DDM^+(\delta, \sigma, b)$. *Then*

$$\rho_t(\ell, r) = \frac{e^{\delta b(t)/\sigma^2}}{e^{\delta b(t)/\sigma^2} + e^{-\delta b(t)/\sigma^2}}.$$

Thus, DDM$^+$ can explain our second stylized fact if the boundary is a decreasing function. To see the intuition behind this result, suppose that b is a decreasing function. This means that there is a higher bar to clear for smaller t than for larger t. So, if the agent stopped early, $|\hat{M}^t|$ must have been high and therefore the chance of making the correct choice is higer than if the agent stopped late, where $|\hat{M}^t|$ was low.[14]

While DDM$^+$ can explain both stylized facts, it has the same "reduced-form" status as DDM because the boundary is exogenously specified and not tied to the optimization problem of the agent. The next section microfounds a special case of DDM$^+$.

9.6 CHERNOFF MODEL

In this section we will study a model similar to Wald's, except that the prior of the agent is Normal, as opposed to binary.

The agent is facing a menu $A = \{\ell, r\}$. The state space is $S = \mathbb{R}^A$ and we assume that the prior is such that $s(x) \sim \mathcal{N}(\mu_0^x, \sigma_0^2)$ independently across $x \in A$. For each dimension x of s the agent gets a cumulative signal $\hat{M}_x^t$, which is a diffusion with drift $s(x)$ and noise σ

$$\hat{M}_x^t = ts(x) + \sigma B_t^x,$$

where the Brownian motions B_t^x are independent across x.

The payoff of choosing x is $v(x, s) = s(x)$, the true utility of good x, which is unknown to the agent. The posterior is in the same family as the prior: $s(x) \sim \mathcal{N}(\mu_t^x, \sigma_t^2)$, where

$$\mu_t^x := \mu_0^x \frac{\sigma_t^2}{\sigma_0^2} + \hat{M}_x^t \frac{\sigma_t^2}{\sigma^2} \quad \text{and} \quad \sigma_t^{-2} := \sigma_0^{-2} + t\sigma^{-2}. \tag{9.6}$$

---

[14] There is a complication, as we need to condition on the event that the boundary has not been crossed before. However, because of the symmetry of the boundary, the same "number" of paths cross the upper and the lower boundary, so the conditioning event does not matter.

This is a continuous-time version of the Normal updating formula in Example 5.2.3. The posterior mean is combination of the prior mean and the cumulative signal. The posterior precision evolves deterministically and linearly in time.

To sum up, the *Chernoff model* is an optimal stopping model with a Normal prior, diffusion signal, payoff $v(x, s) = s(x)$, and linear time cost.[15]

Proposition 9.10 (Fudenberg, Strack, and Strzalecki, 2018). *In the Chernoff model there exists a decreasing function $k : \mathcal{T} \to \mathbb{R}$ such that*

$$\tau^* = \inf\{t \geq 0 : |\mu_t| \geq k(t)\},$$

where $\mu_t := \mu_t^\ell - \mu_t^r$ is the posterior mean difference process given by (9.6). Moreover, if $\mu_0 = 0$, then there exists $b : \mathcal{T} \to \mathbb{R}$ such that

$$\tau^* = \inf\{t \geq 0 : |\hat{M}^t| \geq b(t)\},$$

where $\hat{M}^t = \hat{M}_\ell^t - \hat{M}_r^t$.

The net signal $\hat{M}^t$ is a sufficient statistic for our agent's decision because of the diffusion assumption and the additive cost assumption; it is not sufficient in models with discounting, where the absolute level of the signals matters as well as their difference.

The key intuition for this result is non-stationarity: With a Normal prior the option value of waiting is decreasing. Suppose that the agent observes $\hat{M}_l^t \approx \hat{M}_r^t$ after a long t. With a Normal prior, the agent will conclude that the two items are nearly indifferent and they will decide to stop, given that there is not much left to learn. This is different from the Wald model, where there is no room for such an interpretation of the signal and the posterior given $\hat{M}_l^t \approx \hat{M}_r^t$ is nearly uniform over the two states (and uniform belief actually maximizes the option value of waiting in the Wald model). Hence the agent behaves as if M_t is pure noise and starts from scratch.

The theorem is silent on the monotonicity properties of b. For some parameter values it is decreasing, but for some it is hump-shaped. However, Fudenberg, Strack, and Strzalecki (2018) show that accuracy is always decreasing in expectation (according to agent's prior).

A similar model can be used for perception tasks. The only difference is that $v(x, s) = \mathbb{1}_{\{s_x > s_{-x}\}}$, that is, the agent is rewarded for guessing correctly but the payoff is independent of the difficulty of the task. Drugowitsch, Moreno-Bote, Churchland, Shadlen, and Pouget (2012) numerically estimate such a model. Tajima, Drugowitsch, Patel, and Pouget (2019) extend their computational framework beyond binary menus. These papers also allow for the marginal cost to be nonconstant.

The following result shows that any boundary can be rationalized by an appropriately chosen nonlinear cost function.

---

[15] Chernoff's (1961) original formulation involved regret-minimization. It can be shown that this formulation is equivalent (Fudenberg, Strack, and Strzalecki, 2018).

Theorem[†] **9.11 (Fudenberg, Strack, and Strzalecki, 2018).** *Consider either the binary or Normal prior. For any b there exists a (potentially nonlinear) cost function c such that b is the optimal solution to the stopping problem.*

Remark 9.12. A common stylized fact in behavioral economics is that people "overthink" decision problems that don't matter and "underthink" those that are important. Whether this intuition is consistent with our models depends how we define "problems that don't matter" and those that are "important."

Let's focus on choice tasks where the drift equals the difference in utilities. Here problems that don't matter are those where $|v(\ell) - v(r)|$ is small and problems that are important are those where the utility difference is large. As mentioned before, in DDM and DDM$^+$ the expected reaction time is decreasing in $|\delta|$. Thus, it is *optimal* to spend more time on problems that (ex post) don't matter than on those that are important (because important problems are easier, under the assumption about drift being equal to the utility difference) Of course, in many situations important decisions are actually difficult (e.g., choosing a retirement plan), so this assumption is violated.

Oud, Krajbich, Miller, Cheong, Botvinick, and Fehr (2016) designed experiments where subjects are sometimes forced to make decisions after a set amount of time elapsed. This de facto implements a new boundary that collapses at zero at some point in time. On trials with such an intervention subjects perform better than on trials when the response time is freely chosen by them. This shows that the orignal boundary couldn't have been optimal. This pattern is true for value-based choices as well as perceptual choices where subjects are incentivized more on easy trials and less on hard trials.   △

9.7 OTHER MODELS FROM PSYCHOLOGY

9.7.1 Full DDM

Full DDM or *extended DDM* is a mixture of constant-boundary DDMs where mixing occurs over three parameters: the drift δ, the starting point M_0, and the initial latency T_0 (inaction period, so that the analyst observes the realizations of $T_0 + \tau$).[16] We have encountered mixture models in static domain (e.g., the mixed logit model in Section 3.3). We interpreted this as pooling over subjects. Here, the randomization is done for a fixed experimental subject.

The full DDM model is extremely popular in applications, as it introduces more parameters that can be estimated and in particular allows for time-varying accuracy.

The example below introduces a related model where the randomness of the initial starting point M_0 has a nice interpretation.

---

[16] See, for example, Ratcliff (1978), Ratcliff and McKoon (2008), Ratcliff and Smith (2004), and Bogacz, Brown, Moehlis, Holmes, and Cohen (2006).

Example 9.13 (Ads). Imagine that there is a non-skippable advertisement in agent's phone app. This advertisement adds an initial latency (of a deterministic length) and endows the agent with a signal, thus randomly moving the agent's belief at the beginning of the decision phase.

Let T_0 be the length of the advertisement. If the drift of the signal during the advertisement is $\kappa(v(\ell) - v(r))$, then

$$M_0 \sim \mathcal{N}(T_0\kappa(v(\ell) - v(r)), T_0).$$

Chiong, Shum, Webb, and Chen (2018) estimate a DDM with M_0 distributed as above and simulate what would happen in a counterfactual, where the marketing company allows for skippable ads. This approach is somewhat different from the way the full DDM is typically used because in full DDM, the distribution of M_0 is independent of T_0. $\triangle$

9.7.2   Attentional DDM

In lab experiments we can record additional data, such as eye movements (Krajbich, Armel, and Rangel, 2010; Krajbich and Rangel, 2011; Krajbich, Lu, Camerer, and Rangel, 2012; Gaia Lombardi, 2020; Callaway, Rangel, and Griffiths, 2020). That literature uses the Attentional DDM model, which is an extension of DDM that incorporates eye movement data. In those models "attention" is an exogenous process that does not condition on the signal $\hat{M}_t$. Evidence is accumulated only for the item that is currently paid attention to. This assumption makes the model easy to estimate, but makes it difficult to think of good microfoundations akin to the Wald or Chernoff models.

9.7.3   Race Models or Accumulator Models

Race models, otherwise known as *accumulator models* assume a separate signal $\hat{M}_x^t$ and a separate boundary for each $x \in X$. The agent stops the first time one of those signals hits the corresponding boundary. Here the evidence can be accumulated at different speeds and there can be correlation between the signals (see, e.g., Vickers (1970)). Pike (1966) studies finite Markov models. The following example assumes a Poisson process (Audley, 1960).

Example 9.14 (Eureka Moment). There is a utility function $v : X \to \mathbb{R}$ and each $\hat{M}_x^t$ is an independent Poisson process with intensity $e^{v(x)}$. The agent stops the first time one of these processes hits the value 1 and picks the corresponding x. It is easy to show (see Appendix A.9.1) that such defined $\rho \in \Delta(A \times \mathcal{T})$ is a product measure, where the marginal on choices is of the logit form

$$\rho_t(x, A) = \frac{e^{v(x)}}{\sum_{y \in A} e^{v(y)}}$$

and the marginal distribution of τ is exponential with parameter $\sum_{x \in A} e^{v(x)}$.[17]

---

[17] The constant accuracy prediction depends on the assumption that the boundary equals one. For $b > 1$ accuracy is decreasing (Lensman, 2023). A peculiar feature of this model is that

Given the closed forms, this model is equally easy to fit as the DDM and it extends beyond binary menus. However, a constant boundary is not optimal for a model where $\hat{M}_t^x$ is a Poisson process with intensity proportional to the utility of x. △

Smith and Vickers (1988) derive the stopping probabilities for a general class of accumulator models. An even more general model was proposed by Marley (1989). Here, each item x is associated with a random time T_x and the agent chooses the item whose time comes first.

A special kind of accumulator models are Linear Ballistic Accumulator (LBA) models (see Brown and Heathcote (2008) and Terry, Marley, Barnwal, Wagenmakers, Heathcote, and Brown (2015)). In those models the paths of $\hat{M}_t^x$ are linear and randomization is over the starting point and the angle of the path (uniform and Normal, respectively).

As shown by Jones and Dzhafarov (2014) without those parametric assumptions LBA has no predictive content (see also Marley and Colonius (1992)). Webb (2019) shows that for accumulator models, the marginal choice probability is governed by a static ARU model with attributes such as in Definition 10.3 but where the distribution of ϵ is allowed to depend on v.

9.7.4 Mean Reverting Stimulus or Leaky Models

Busemeyer and Townsend (1993) study an accumulator model where instead of $\hat{M}_t$ being a diffusion with a constant drift, it is a mean-reverting (Ornstein–Uhlenbeck) process:

$$d\hat{M}^t = (\delta - \gamma \hat{M}^t)dt + \sigma \, dB_t.$$

Such a mean-reverting accumulator model is sometimes called a "leaky accumulator" or "Decision-Field Theory." A nice exposition of these and other models is given by Bogacz, Brown, Moehlis, Holmes, and Cohen (2006).

9.7.5 Recent Papers in Economics

Alós-Ferrer, Fehr, and Netzer (2021) take as a primitive the marginal over choices $\rho \in \Delta(A)$ together with a distribution over stopping times. They look at a generalization of ARU where the distribution of ϵ is menu-dependent.

Epstein and Ji (2020) study learning in a diffusion setting where there is prior ambiguity. Auster, Che, and Mierendorff (2022) look at a similar setting with Poisson signals.

Branco, Sun, and Villas-Boas (2012) look at decisions derived from optimal stopping rules where the gains from sampling are exogenously specified as

---

adding options reduces the reaction time. This may seem counterintuitive, given what we know about choice overload. In perceptual tasks there is the "Hick–Hyman Law" which says that the average decision time *increases* logarithmically in the menu size (Luce, 1986).

opposed to being derived from Bayesian updating. Ke, Shen, and Villas-Boas (2016) apply this model to consumers searching for products.

Duraj and Lin (2019) and Duraj and Lin (2021) provide a decision-theoretic analysis of versions of the general model presented in Section 9.2. Baldassi, Cerreia-Vioglio, Maccheroni, Marinacci, and Pirazzini (2020) give a partial axiomatization of DDM with a constant boundary. Fudenberg, Newey, Strack, and Strzalecki (2020) give necessary and sufficient conditions for an arbitrary boundary.

9.8　DYNAMIC ATTENTION

This is a very active area of research and it should be its own chapter, but the literature is moving faster than I can catch up, so this is just a brief introduction. We can distinguish three types of problems.

- Pure stopping (choose τ given (M^t))
- Pure attention (choose (M^t) given τ)
- Joint optimization (choose both τ and (M^t)).

9.8.1　Pure Stopping

In the pure stopping problem, the agent cannot direct their attention. But they can decide how much overall information to get. Notice that by choosing τ we are facto choosing a distribution over posteriors μ. Morris and Strack (2019) show that with a diffusion signal and binary state space any μ can be obtained by an appropriate choice of τ. They define the induced cost of μ to be $\mathbb{E} \int_0^\tau c(q_t)dt$, where q_t is agent's posterior and $c(q_t)$ is the (potentially posterior-dependent) flow cost of waiting. This induced cost function is prior-dependent because it depends on the expectation of τ under the prior. Morris and Strack (2019) show that the induced cost function is posterior separable and moreover all PS cost functions can be written this way.[18] An interesting special case is posterior-independent flow cost, which leads to a special case of total information cost. Another special case is mutual information, which corresponds to the case where the flow cost is posterior-dependent and equals the variance of the posterior.

9.8.2　Pure Attention

Woodford (2014) solves an optimal attention problem (with a constant boundary and the mutual information cost, or more precisely constraint) and shows that optimal behavior leads to decreasing accuracy. Steiner, Stewart, and Matějka (2017) study optimal attention with mutual information

---

[18] With more than two states not all μ are achievable, but the cost for any τ is still PS. Hébert and Woodford (2017) show a similar reduction to a static separable problem in the joint optimization problem.

and evolving state. They apply their general solution to the study of time-varying accuracy. Miao and Xing (2023) generalize these results to uniformly posterior-separable cost functions.

9.8.3 Joint Optimization

Fudenberg, Strack, and Strzalecki (2018) study joint optimization with Normal signals and show that it is always optimal to pay equal attention to alternatives (or switch between them infinitely often), under a parametric assumption on the trade-off between the informativeness of each signal. Liang, Mu, and Syrgkanis (2022) generalize this by allowing the prior to have an arbitrary covariance matrix. Liang and Mu (2020) find conditions under which the dynamically optimal strategy is close to the myopic strategy. Ke and Villas-Boas (2016) study joint optimization with two states per alternative.

Che and Mierendorff (2019) study the joint optimization problem with two states by restricting the class of signals to be Poisson. They find that coexistence of two strategies is optimal: a contradictory strategy that seeks to challenge the prior and a confirmatory strategy that seeks to confirm the prior. Zhong (2022) shows that Poisson signals are optimal under discounting.

PART IV

DISCRETE CHOICE

CHAPTER 10

Discrete Choice

10.1 ATTRIBUTES

So far, our alternatives were some abstract items $x \in X$. In *discrete choice* theory the alternatives are described by their *attributes*. We already saw something like that. In the weight perception task (Example 1.5), each item was identified with its weight (one-dimensional attribute). In Chapter 4, a lottery was a vector of probabilities of each prize (a vector of attributes).

In general, for each alternative x let ξ_x be a vector of its attributes. These are also called *characteristics* or *hedonics* (see, e.g., Griliches (1961) and Lancaster (1966)). Sometimes ξ can be controlled by the researcher (in a lab experiment), but sometimes it cannot (market prices are endogenous).

A version of ARU is typically assumed where $\tilde{U}(x) = v(\xi_x) + \tilde{\epsilon}_x$. The TIEV parameterization is the *conditional logit* (McFadden, 1973).

The literature typically assumes that the menu is fixed and equal to X and focuses on attribute-variation.[1]

The primitive is a stochastic choice function that maps the profile of attributes of all items to their choice probabilities. Formally, let $\xi := (\xi_x)_{x \in X}$ be the profile of characteristics of all the items. Let $\mathcal{E}$ be the space of attributes; assume that $\mathcal{E} \subseteq \mathbb{R}^n$ for some n. Let $\mathcal{E}^X$ be the set of all attribute profiles of members of X.

Definition 10.1. An *SCF with attributes* is a function $\rho : \mathcal{E}^X \to \Delta(X)$. We will write $\rho(x, \xi)$ to mean the probability of choosing x when the vector of attributes is ξ.

For example, in applications to consumer demand, the analyst observes a number of markets. In each market k she records the attributes of all goods $(\xi^k) \in \mathcal{E}^X$ and the market shares $s^k \in \Delta(X)$. We assume here that each market is large enough so that $s^k = \rho(\cdot, \xi^k)$ for all k. By observing enough markets with different ξ^k, we can trace out the function ρ pretty well. If price is one of the attributes, then we can study price elasticities and substitution patterns

---

[1] There are some exceptions, such as Hausman and McFadden (1984) and Buchholz, Doval, Kastl, Matějka, and Salz (2020).

between various goods. In demand applications it is quite important to explicitly include an outside good. This makes it possible to model market size and it makes price elasticities more realistic (Berry, 1994).

Though there is no explicit menu variation in this model, if an attribute of x changes, this in fact does change the menu because now the new "version" of x is included and the old one is absent. For this reason, any SCF with attributes can be represented by our usual SCF with menu variation defined on a restricted set of menus with a fixed size.

Because of this close association, I denote those two by the same letter ρ. However, I will keep distinguishing them as functions, $\rho : \mathcal{A} \to \Delta(X)$ and $\rho : \mathcal{E}^X \to \Delta(X)$, because the two have a different mathematical structure and different results have been proved about them.

Sometimes an additional assumption is made that all relevant information about alternatives is encoded in their characteristics, so x are just labels that do not affect choice (Manski, 1977; McFadden, 1981).[2] Taken literally this is very restrictive. For example, consumers can prefer brand x over generic brand y even if they have identical physical attributes $\xi_x = \xi_y$. This problem goes away if we include brands as characteristics.

A different, but related model in consumer theory allows agents to continuously choose the quantities of each good. This is the classical setting of GARP (Afriat, 1967). The analyst observes the population frequency of each chosen consumption bundle. McFadden (2005) shows how to transform this continuous problem to a discrete RU problem.[3]

10.2   INDEPENDENT ADDITIVE RANDOM UTILITY

10.2.1   IARU

In this model the utility of item x depends on the vector $\xi_x \in \mathcal{E}$ of observable attributes of x, but not on attributes of other items. (Utility can potentially also depend on the attributes of the consumer, but we will abstract from that here).

Definition 10.2. Let X be a finite set. $\rho : \mathcal{E}^X \to \Delta(X)$ is represented by *Independent Additive Random Utility (IARU)* if

$$\rho(x,\xi) = \mathbb{P}\left(\left\{\omega \in \Omega : \widetilde{U}(x,\xi_x)(\omega) = \max_{y \in X} \widetilde{U}(y,\xi_y)(\omega)\right\}\right),$$

where the agent's random utility equals

$$\widetilde{U}(x,\xi_x) = v_x(\xi_x) + \tilde{\epsilon}(x),$$

---

[2] Formally, for any permutation π of X and any ξ define ξ^π by $\xi_x^\pi := \xi_{\pi(x)}$. McFadden's (1981) assumption PC5.2 says that $\rho(x,\xi) = \rho(\pi(x),\xi^\pi)$.

[3] Kitamura and Stoye (2018) take this insight further and construct a test of this model. Smeulders, Cherchye, and Rock (2021) show that implementing this test is NP-hard.

where for each $x \in X$ the utility function $v_x : \mathcal{E} \to \mathbb{R}$ is deterministic and $\tilde{\epsilon}$ is a random vector independent of ζ with a smooth distribution.

Here $\tilde{\epsilon}(x)$ does not have to be independent across $x \in X$, but the vector $\tilde{\epsilon}$ is assumed to be independent of ζ. The independence of ϵ and ζ is the analog of the independence assumption from the model with menu variation, where ϵ was independent of the menu (Sections 1.5.1 and 1.7).[4]

In applications independence often fails. For example, firms endogenously adjust prices in response to demand shocks, which are driven by utility shocks of consumers, which makes prices correlated with ϵ. We will discuss endogeneity in Section 10.7; for now we will assume that the econometrician has solved this problem for us and handed us the ρ that satisfies independence.

10.2.2 Simple IARU

In applications, the distribution of ϵ is often fixed and not estimated. The econometrician focuses on estimating the functions v. This is done as follows: For each possible v we can compute the choice probabilities ρ. We then check how far those are from the observed data and choose another v that gets us closer (iterate till we converge). A key object here is the mapping between v and ρ, we will write this as $\rho(x, v)$.

Definition 10.3. $\rho : \mathbb{R}^X \to \Delta(X)$ has a *simple IARU* representation if there exists a random variable $\tilde{\epsilon}$ with values in $\mathbb{R}^X$ distributed smoothly and independently of v, such that

$$\rho(x, v) = \mathbb{P}\left(v(x) + \tilde{\epsilon}(x) = \max_{y \in X} v(y) + \tilde{\epsilon}(y)\right).$$

Simple IARU can be thought of as a special case of IARU, where the utilities are "magically" observed by the analyst, but in reality it's more of an intermediate object of analysis. A situation where the analyst gets close to observing v occurs when utility is quasilinear in prices.[5]

10.2.3 Conditional Logit

With attributes, the logit model (Section 3.1) is called *conditional logit* (McFadden, 1973). This means that $\tilde{\epsilon}_x$ are i.i.d. TIEV and v is a linear function given by the inner product

$$v_x(\xi) = \langle \beta, \xi_x \rangle$$

---

[4] Notice that while with menu-variation the independence assumption can be expressed both for RU and ARU, with attribute-variation this notion only makes sense for ARU. In RU, the distribution of utilities must depend on ζ, otherwise ρ will be constant in ζ.

[5] For example, see Koning and Ridder (2003). Such models are a special case of IARU where $\mathcal{E} = \mathbb{R}$ and $v(x, \xi) = w(x) - \xi_x$ for some deterministic function w, where ξ_x is the price of good x. More generally, $\mathcal{E}$ could also include observable attributes other than price. Interestingly, despite its seeming generality, such a model cannot generate a linear demand schedule (Jaffe and Weyl, 2010).

for some vector of parameters β, to be estimated. To capture fixed effects, we add the intercept

$$v_x(\xi) = \beta_x^0 + \sum_{i=1}^{n} \beta^i \xi_x^i.$$

We will still write this as the inner product $\langle \cdot, \cdot \rangle$ with an extra entry equal 1 added to ξ.

A curiosity: The early literature (McFadden, 1975; Train, 1986) discussed something called the *mother logit*. Here, we have $\tilde{U}(x, \xi) = v_x(\xi) + \tilde{\epsilon}_x$, where the function v_x can depend on the characteristics of not only good x but also other goods. It is easy to see any SCF with attributes that satisfies Positivity has a mother-logit representation.

10.3   IDENTIFICATION

If $\rho \sim IARU$, then the utility function v and the distribution of ϵ are identified up to a normalization, provided that there is enough variation in attributes (see Theorems 2, 3, and 4 of Matzkin (1993); see also Manski, 1988; Matzkin, 1992; Khan, Ouyang, and Tamer, 2021). Theorem 1 of Matzkin (1993) relaxes the assumption that ϵ is independent of ξ, but imposes the assumption that conditional on ξ it is i.i.d. across members of X. For a review of this area, see Matzkin (2013).

There are also results on partial identification using moment inequalities. Here it is assumed that the analyst has at her disposal a parametric function that approximates v, or some additively separable component of v, such as transportation cost (Pakes, 2010; Pakes, Porter, Ho, and Ishii, 2015).

For simple IARU, point identification means that the mapping $\rho : \mathbb{R}^X \to \Delta(X)$ is invertible (upon normalizing the utility of one item). Such inversion plays an important role in dynamic models (Hotz and Miller, 1993) and when correcting for endogeneity (Berry, 1994; Berry, Levinsohn, and Pakes, 1995). See also Chiong, Galichon, and Shum (2016) and Soerensen and Fosgerau (2020).

10.4   THE WDZ LEMMA

The Williams–Daly–Zachary (WDZ) Lemma says that in the simple IARU model, the choice probability ρ is the gradient of the social surplus function (Williams, 1977; Daly and Zachary, 1979; McFadden, 1981). The WDZ lemma allows us to compute welfare by integrating the choice probabilities (if we can observe a sufficiently rich variation in v). Formally, the social surplus is

$$V(v) := \mathbb{E}\left[\max_{x \in X} v(x) + \tilde{\epsilon}(x) \right].$$

Lemma 10.4 (WDZ). *Suppose that X is finite. If $\rho \sim$ simple IARU and $\tilde{\epsilon}$ has finite first moments, then:*

> (i) *For any $v \in \mathbb{R}^X$ the associated social surplus $V(v)$ is finite.*
> (ii) *The function $V : \mathbb{R}^X \to \mathbb{R}$ is differentiable and convex.*
> (iii) $\rho = \nabla V$.

Equation (iii) can be directly verified in case of logit. By the log-sum expression (3.2), we have $V(v) = \log \sum_{x \in X} e^{v(x)}$, so taking the partial derivative of V with respect to the utility of good y, we get $\frac{\partial V(v)}{\partial v(y)} = \frac{e^{v(y)}}{\sum_{x \in X} e^{v(x)}} = \rho(x; v)$.

For a formal proof, see Shi, Shum, and Song (2018). Intuitively, part (iii) is the envelope theorem. Its analog in production theory is Hotelling's (1932) lemma, which says that the quantity produced equals the derivative of the profit function. The analog in classical demand theory is Roy's (1947) identity.

10.5   THE WDZ THEOREM

The WDZ theorem is basically an axiomatization of simple IARU.

10.5.1   The Theorem

For the purpose of this section, let $\frac{\partial \rho_x}{\partial v_y}(v)$ denote the derivative of $\rho(x, v)$ with respect to the yth coordinate of v (computed at v). For any v and $k \in \mathbb{R}$ the function $v + k$ assigns utility $v(x) + k$ to item x.

Theorem 10.5 (WDZ). *Suppose that $\rho : \mathbb{R}^X \to \Delta(X)$ is $|X|$-times continuously differentiable. Then $\rho \sim$ simple IARU iff it satisfies:*

> (i) **Translation invariance:** $\rho(v) = \rho(v + k)$ *for all $v \in \mathbb{R}^X$, $k \in \mathbb{R}$*
> (ii) **Zero limit demand:** $\lim_{v_x \to -\infty} \rho(x, v) = 0$ *for all $v_{-x} \in \mathbb{R}^{X \setminus \{x\}}$*
> (iii) **Symmetric partials:**
>
> $$\frac{\partial \rho_x}{\partial v_y}(v) = \frac{\partial \rho_y}{\partial v_x}(v) \text{ for all } v \in \mathbb{R}^n \text{ and } x \neq y$$
>
> (iv) **Gross substitutes:**
>
> $$\frac{\partial \rho_x}{\partial v_y}(v) < 0 \text{ for } x \neq y \text{ and all } v \in \mathbb{R}^X$$
>
> (v) **Alternating signs of partials:**
>
> $$(-1)^k \frac{\partial^k \rho_{x_0}}{\partial v_{x_1} \cdots \partial v_{x_k}}(v) > 0$$
>
> *for all $v \in \mathbb{R}^X$ and for each $k = 2, \ldots, |X| - 1$ and each set of $k + 1$ distinct elements $\{x_0, \ldots, x_k\} \subset X$.*

For more about this theorem, see Appendix A.10.1.

10.5.2 Intuition Behind These Conditions

Translation invariance means that shifting all utilities by a constant does not change the choice. This is because what matters are utility differences, not absolute levels.

Zero limit demand says that by sufficiently lowering the utility of x we can reduce demand for x as much as we want (holding the utilities of $y \neq x$ constant). This is because the distribution of $\tilde{\epsilon}$ is fixed so for x to be chosen $\tilde{\epsilon}_x$ must clear a higher and higher bar, and the probability of such a tail event goes to zero.

Symmetric partials is similar to the symmetry of the Slutsky matrix in the classical demand theory.[6] It is equivalent to $\rho = \nabla V$ for some differentiable function V.

Gross substitutes means that demand for good x decreases if the utility of good $y \neq x$ increases.

Alternating signs is a stronger version of gross substitutes, similar to the exclusion-inclusion formula in Axiom 2.8.

10.5.3 Relationship Between These Conditions

Symmetric partials together with gross substitutes imply that the Jacobian of ρ is symmetric and positive semi-definite (see Hofbauer and Sandholm (2002)).

We have symmetric partials and positive semi-definiteness if and only if ρ is the gradient of a convex function.[7]

As we know from the WDZ Lemma, that function will turn out to be the social surplus function.[8]

Another way to capture both symmetric partials and positive semi-definiteness is *cyclic monotonicity* (see Theorem A.10.1 in the Appendix).

Definition 10.6. ρ satisfies *cyclic monotonicity* if for any k and any sequence of values $v_1, \ldots, v_k \in \mathbb{R}^X$ where $v_{k+1} = v_1$

$$\sum_{i=1}^{k} \langle \rho(v_i), v_i - v_{i+1} \rangle \geq 0.$$

Note that cyclic monotonicity is discrete in nature and thus it may be easier to test on a finite data set, as it does not rely on small variations in v.

---

[6] See a discussion in McFadden (1981) in whose model the agent is also consuming some perfectly divisible commodities and has a Gorman-style utility, which guarantees that the indirect utility is quasilinear in prices.

[7] This follows from Theorem 10.9 of Apostol (1969) and Theorem 35 of Fenchel (1953).

[8] Actually, the WDZ Lemma assumes finite moments of $\tilde{\epsilon}$ but this assumption does not automatically follow from Theorem 10.5. While this assumption was w.l.o.g. with menu-variation, it is not with attribute-variation. In this case, if moments are infinite, ρ is a gradient of another function, which is defined even in that case. For more on the issue of finite moments (see Fosgerau, McFadden, and Bierlaire (2013)).

Related conditions were used to axiomatize the GEV model (Smith, 1984). In Section 10.8 we'll see that *perturbed utility* satisfies (i), (ii), (iii), and positive definiteness, but not the stronger conditions (iv) and (v).

10.5.4 Tests of These Conditions

Of course we can't test these conditions directly, as we do not observe v. However, if utility is quasilinear in prices, then prices play the same role as utilities and the conditions below can be tested.[9]

In such a setting, Koning and Ridder (2003) test gross substitutes, Shi, Shum, and Song (2018) test cyclic monotonicity, and Abaluck and Adams-Prassl (2021) test translation invariance and symmetric partials.

In economic applications prices are often correlated with unobserved taste shocks, so care needs to be taken when directly testing conditions (i)–(v) and cyclic monotonicity, as they rely on independence.

10.6 PATTERNS OF SUBSTITUTION

Suppose that we are in a market setting where each good x has a price p_x. Let p be the vector $(p_x)_{x \in X}$. There may be other attributes but for simplicity we will abstract from them. Suppose that utility is quasilinear in prices so that $v(x, p_x) = w(x) - p_x$, where $w \in \mathbb{R}^X$ is a fixed and deterministic utility function and p_x is the price of good x. We know from the WDZ theorem (Theorem 10.5) that goods are gross substitutes: If the price of good x increases, the demand for all other $y \neq x$ goes up (and the demand for x decreases).

A particularly stark example is the logit model, which has *proportional substitution*: for any $x \neq z$

$$\frac{\partial \rho_x}{\partial p_z} = \rho(x, p)\rho(z, p).$$

This is a very strong prediction, which is obviously counterfactual. For example, a full-size car x and a midsize car y, must have the same elasticity with respect to the price of a compact car z. This inflexibility of the model is another manifestation of the blue bus–red bus problem (Example 3.11). This is not a consequence of the TIEV assumption but rather of the i.i.d. assumption.

Proposition 10.7. *If* $\rho \sim IARU$ *with quasilinear prices like above and i.i.d.* $\tilde{\epsilon}$, *then* $\rho(x, p) = \rho(y, p)$ *implies that* x *and* y *have the same elasticity with respect to the price of a third good* z.

Proof. See Appendix A.10.2.   □

As Berry and Haile (2021) stress, "this is a bug, not a feature." The conclusion can be escaped by relaxing the i.i.d. assumption and introducing some

---

[9] Since in the quasilinear model prices enter with a negative sign, the signs in conditions (ii), (iv), and (v) need to be adapted; in particular the term $(-1)^k$ drops from condition (v).

correlation into ϵ. This can be done directly, by estimating the covariance matrix of $\tilde{\epsilon}$, which can be hard when there are many alternatives. Nested models, as in Section 3.4, are another route. Yet another route are mixed models, which we will discuss next. They are more tractable and intuitive because they can be interpreted as heterogenous tastes for product characteristics and they generate more intuitive substitution patterns.

10.6.1   Random Coefficient Models

Under logit, we have

$$\tilde{U}(x,\xi) = \langle \beta, \xi_x \rangle + \tilde{\epsilon}_x,$$

where the coefficients β are deterministic (Section 10.2.3).

In *random coefficients models* the coefficients β are random to reflect the heterogeneity of unobserved individual characteristics:

$$\tilde{U}(x,\xi) = \langle \tilde{\beta}, \xi_x \rangle + \tilde{\epsilon}_x.$$

You can think of this as a special case of mixed logit (Section 3.3), where the randomization over the coefficients implements a mixture over linear utility functions v. Here the preference heterogeneity is explicitly modeled by the mixing distribution and the shocks $\tilde{\epsilon}$ are i.i.d. Early papers include Daly and Zachary (1975), Boyd and Mellman (1980), and Cardell and Dunbar (1980). Fox, il Kim, Ryan, and Bajari (2012) show that the distribution over $\tilde{\beta}$ is identified nonparametrically. Fox, Kim, Ryan, and Bajari (2011) and Fox, il Kim, and Yang (2016) develop finite-mixture estimators (such estimators are nonparametric and often rely on tuning parameters that can be sometimes hard to select in practice). There is also mixed polynomial logit.

Definition 10.8. ρ has a *mixed polynomial logit* representation if it has a mixed logit representation where all functions v are polynomials of ξ.

Saito (2018) offers an axiomatization of mixed polynomial logits, where the polynomials are of degree at most d.

McFadden and Train (2000) show that if $\mathcal{E}$ is a compact set, then any ρ with an RU representation is a limit of ρ's with mixed polynomial logit representation. The additional difficulty here (as compared with Proposition 3.15) is approximating the v function by polynomials. Under the assumption that $\mathcal{E}$ is finite, Chang, Narita, and Saito (2022) show that the convergence result of McFadden and Train (2000) may not hold if we insist that there exists a uniform bound on the order of all the polynomials.

Random coefficient models were also studied for mixed probit (Hausman and Wise, 1978). Brownstone and Train (1998) only add random intercepts (the multiplicative coefficients are deterministic). When the mixture over the intercepts is normal, this mixed probit is simply a probit.

10.6.2 Pure Characteristics and Address Models

Berry and Pakes (2007) consider a *pure characteristics* model which is a mixture over deterministic utility functions. (You can also think of this as a limit of mixed polynomial logit representations with the noise parameter going to zero). For example, random expected utility from Chapter 4 is a pure characteristics model. Pure characteristics is explicitly an RU representation (a randomization over utility functions). In contrast, random coefficients is only implicitly RU (a randomization over logits, each being itself a randomization over utility functions). Broadly speaking, random coefficients and pure characteristics models are similar, the key difference being that in former there is positive demand for dominated products. A formal connection was drawn by Lu and Saito (2022).

Hotelling (1929) assumed that each agent has a deterministic utility with a blisspoint. The address models, which generalize the idea of a blisspoint, are reviewed in Chapter 4 of Anderson, de Palma, and Thisse (1992).

10.6.3 Complementarities?

While random coefficients models can help us avoid some unrealistic patterns of substitution, all goods are still gross substitutes. This is basically because those models can be written as IARU that are quasilinear in prices. Here v function is deterministic (the average of the mixing distribution) and all the preference heterogeneity is hidden in the distribution of $\tilde{\epsilon}$. By condition (iv) of the WDZ theorem, the derivative of demand for good x with respect to the price of good y is negative. Are there models where goods are complements? The following simple example, due to Nicola Rossaia, shows that models of attention (such as in Chapter 6) can have this property.

Example 10.9 (Attention creates complementarities). Suppose there are three goods $X = \{x_1, x_2, x_3\}$, and two states $S = \{s_1, s_2\}$. The utility of good x_i in state s_j equals $v(x_i, s_j) - p_i$, where p_i is the price of good i. The function v is defined in Table 10.1.

The agent can pay a cost $\frac{1}{2}$ of observing the true state (or remain with their uniform prior at no cost). Suppose that initially the price of all three goods is zero. The agent chooses to learn the state and the observed (unconditional) choice probabilities are $\left(\frac{1}{2}, \frac{1}{2}, 0\right)$. Suppose that the price of good x_2 increases

Table 10.1 *Payoffs in Example 10.9.*

	$v(x, s_1)$	$v(x, s_2)$
x_1	4	0
x_2	0	4
x_3	3	3

by one. The agent now chooses not to observe the state and the choice probabilities are $(0, 0, 1)$, so demand for good 1 went down as price of good 2 went up. The same conclusion obtains when demand is observed conditional on the state: when prices are $(0, 0, 0)$ demand in state s_1 is $(1, 0, 0)$ and when prices are $(0, 1, 0)$, demand in state s_1 is $(0, 0, 1)$.[10]   △

10.7   DEALING WITH ENDOGENEITY*

So far, we have been maintaining the assumption that the distribution over preference shocks is independent of the attribute ξ. However, this assumption is often violated. A common example is when there are demand shocks that influence the equilibrium prices.

Suppose that the analyst observes K independent markets.[11] In each market k we observe a vector of prices p^k and non-price attributes ξ^k. Let $\tilde{\eta}_x^k$ be the (unobservable to the analyst) *demand shifter*. The random utility equals $\tilde{U}(x, p_x, \xi_x) = \langle \beta, \xi_x \rangle - p_x + \tilde{\eta}_x + \tilde{\gamma}_x$, where the realization of $\tilde{\eta}_x$ is constant within each market but i.i.d. across markets whereas $\tilde{\gamma}_x$ are i.i.d. within and across markets, independent of $(\tilde{\xi}, \tilde{p}, \tilde{\eta})$ and distributed TIEV.

It is useful to write the random utility as $\tilde{U}(x, p_x, \xi_x) = \tilde{\delta}_x + \tilde{\gamma}_x$, where

$$\tilde{\delta}_x = \langle \beta, \xi_x \rangle - p_x + \tilde{\eta}_x. \tag{10.1}$$

Each market is large enough so that the observed market share of good x equals the theoretical choice probability:

$$s_x^k(p^k) = \frac{e^{\tilde{\delta}_x^k}}{\sum_{y \in A} e^{\tilde{\delta}_y^k}}.$$

Given the invertibility of logit, the analyst can recover δ^k from s^k up to a normalization. Let $0 \in X$ be the outside good and set $\delta_0^k := 0$ and

$$\delta_x^k := \log s_x^k - \log s_0^k. \tag{10.2}$$

In principle, this could work for any invertible model (see Section 10.3).

To see what can go wrong with the naive approach, suppose that whenever there is a positive demand shock, firms can capture all the benefits from it by increasing prices, so that $p_x^k = \tilde{\pi}_x^k + \tilde{\eta}_x^k$, where $\tilde{\pi}_x^k$ is unobservable to the analyst and independent of everything else. Equation (10.1) then implies that $\delta_x^k = \langle \beta, \xi_x^k \rangle - \tilde{\pi}_x^k$. So an analyst who naively regresses market shares on prices will "estimate" a zero own-price elasticity.

---

[10] The cost of attention in this example takes a very specific form. Fosgerau, Melo, De Palma, and Shum (2020) study a general class of Bregman divergences and show that they lead to behavior equivalent to a form of RU.

[11] The independence assumption is often relaxed (see, e.g., the discussion on pp. 617–618 of Berry, Linton, and Pakes (2004)).

To do inference correctly, we need to use instrumental variables. Suppose that we have an independent source of variation in prices, for example, shocks to firm's costs. We will say that z is an *instrumental variable* if:

- z is correlated with p (instrument relevance)
- $\mathbb{E}[\tilde{\eta}|z] = 0$ (instrument validity).

Because of the same inversion argument, the analyst can deduce δ^k from market shares s^k, so for any choice of β she can impute a value of η^k using Equations (10.2) and (10.1). The optimal value of $\hat{\beta}$ minimizes the sample correlation between imputed η^k and observed z^k (as k varies over the markets).

The IV approach can also be combined with other models. Berry (1994) discusses nested logit (recall Section 3.4) and vertical differentiation models. Berry, Levinsohn, and Pakes (1995) combine it with random coefficients (Section 10.6.1). Here

$$\tilde{\delta}_x = \langle \tilde{\beta}, \xi_x \rangle - \tilde{\alpha} p_x + \tilde{\eta}_x, \tag{10.3}$$

so that the coefficients $\tilde{\alpha}$ and $\tilde{\beta}$ are random (vary within each market) and independent of $(\tilde{\eta}, \tilde{\xi}, \tilde{p})$. There is a large literature on estimation of BLP, with many applications to various settings.[12] The IV approach can also be combined with the *pure characteristics* model (Berry and Pakes, 2007).

10.8 PERTURBED UTILITY*

Recall perturbed utility from Section 3.8. Now, instead of menu-variation, we will consider attribute-variation. This version of PU was used in game theory by Hofbauer and Sandholm (2002), Mattsson and Weibull (2002), and van Damme and Weibull (2002). This class can be characterized by a weakening of the WDZ conditions (Theorem 10.5): dropping alternating signs and weakening gross substitutes to positive definiteness. Thus, this is a weaker model than simple ARU, but still has quite a bit of bite. (Recall that with menu-variation the general form of PU had no bite.)

Definition 10.10. We say that $\rho \sim$ *simple PU* if $\rho(\cdot, v)$ solves

$$\max_{p \in \text{int } \Delta(X)} \sum_{x \in X} v(x)p(x) - c(p),$$

where $c : \text{int}(\Delta(X)) \to \mathbb{R}$ is such that at each point the Jacobian of c is positive definite on $\{v \in \mathbb{R}^n : \sum_x v(x) = 0\}$ and the norm of its gradient approaches infinity near the boundary of $\Delta(X)$.

---

[12] See, for example, Nevo (2000), Ackerberg, Benkard, Berry, and Pakes (2007), and Shum (2016). For identification results, see Berry and Haile (2009, 2014). See also Berry and Haile (2021) for a review.

Theorem 10.11 (Hofbauer and Sandholm, 2002). *Suppose that $\rho : \mathbb{R}^X \to \Delta(X)$ is continuously differentiable. $\rho \sim$ simple PU if and only if it satisfies translation invariance, zero limit demand, symmetric partials, and positive definiteness.*

A recent study of identification of PU with attributes is Allen and Rehbeck (2019). In their model each individual solves

$$\max_{p \in \Delta(X)} \sum_{x \in X} p(x) v_x(\xi_x) - c(p, \epsilon),$$

where ξ_x are observed attributes of good x and ϵ is unobservable heterogeneity. This is observationally equivalent to

$$\max_{p \in \Delta(X)} \sum_{x \in X} p(x) v_x(\xi_x) - \bar{c}(p),$$

which enables them to prove a generalization of the WDZ lemma from which they are able to identify utility indices, changes in average indirect utility, and obtain bounds for counterfactuals.

CHAPTER 11

Random Consideration

11.1 INTRODUCTION

So far, the agent was considering all the items on the menu. In this very short chapter the agent will pay attention only to a subset of the menu, called the *consideration set*. Here "attention" is exogenous to the agent – it is perhaps determined by advertising.[1] Another interpretation is random product availability (unobservable to the analyst).

The consideration set is randomly drawn from some distribution. This distribution can depend on the menu offered and/or on attributes ξ, such as prices, branding, advertising, and so on. We will start with the menu-variation literature and talk about attribute-variation later in this chapter. Technically, we could have discussed menu-variation already in Chapter 3, but I wanted to present it side by side with attribute-variation (even though the two literatures don't talk to each other as much as they might want to).[2]

11.2 MODELS WITH MENU VARIATION

Typically, in this literature one selected item is the *status quo* or the outside option. Choosing this item, denoted $o \in X$, means falling back on the status quo: not making a choice at all and sticking with the default. Here $\mathcal{A}^o$ is the collection of all menus that contain the staus quo.

Definition 11.1 (Random Consideration Set). A *random consideration set* is a probability space $(\Omega, \mathcal{F}, \mathbb{P})$ and a random mapping $\tilde{\Gamma} : \Omega \times \mathcal{A}^o \to \mathcal{A}^o$ such that $\mathbb{P}(\tilde{\Gamma}(A) \subseteq A) = 1$ for all $A \in \mathcal{A}^o$. We will define its distribution by $m_A(C) := \mathbb{P}(\tilde{\Gamma}(A) = C)$.

---

[1] In Chapter 6, "attention" was a margin of choice: The agent paid attention only if it made sense to do it given the cost. A recent paper of Caplin, Dean, and Leahy (2019) builds a link between these two approaches.

[2] A third literature exists where the consideration set is a deterministic function of the menu (see, e.g., Hauser and Wernerfelt (1990), Masatlioglu, Nakajima, and Ozbay (2012), Bordalo, Gennaioli, and Shleifer (2013) and citations therein).

This definition assumes that o is always considered; Horan (2019) explores models of choice with default when the no-choice behavior is unobservable. For each possible realization of the consideration set $\tilde{\Gamma}(A)$, the agent maximizes a random utility function $\tilde{U}$ on the set $\tilde{\Gamma}(A)$.

Definition 11.2 (Random Consideration). $\rho \sim RC$ if there exists a random consideration set $\tilde{\Gamma}$ and a random utility function $\tilde{U}$ such that

$$\rho(x, A) = \mathbb{P}\left(x \in \tilde{\Gamma}(A) \text{ and } \tilde{U}(x) = \max_{y \in \tilde{\Gamma}(A)} \tilde{U}(y)\right).$$

As recognized by Manski (1977), this model does not have any bite because all the randomness in choice can be attributed to the randomness of the consideration set. Unless we impose more assumptions, it will be impossible to separately identify the variation in utility and consideration. For simplicity many decision-theoretic models assume that utility is deterministic and focus the analysis entirely on $\tilde{\Gamma}$.

Various assumptions about $\tilde{\Gamma}$ are being made. Manzini and Mariotti (2014) assumed that items belong to $\tilde{\Gamma}$ independently of each other: Each $x \in A$ belongs to $\tilde{\Gamma}(A)$ with probability γ_x, independently over x.

Definition 11.3 (Independent Random Consideration). $\rho \sim IRC$ if $\rho \sim RC$ with

$$m_A(C) = \prod_{x \in C} \gamma_x \prod_{x \in A \setminus C} (1 - \gamma_x)$$

for each $C \in \mathcal{A}^o$ such that $C \subseteq A$, where the numbers $(\gamma_x)_{x \in X}$ are all between zero and one and independent of the menu A and $\gamma_o = 1$.

In particular, under IRC the probability that the consideration set consists just of the default option equals $\prod_{x \in A \setminus \{o\}} (1 - \gamma_x)$.

The independence assumption seems strong. In particular, it rules out the following simple example.

Example 11.4 (Sleeping Agent). The agent is in one of two states (asleep, or awake). When asleep, they only pay attention to o. When awake, they consider the whole menu A. The probability α that the agent wakes up is independent of the menu. $\triangle$

The above example is a special case of a more general model of Aguiar (2017), where a set $\widetilde{B} \in \mathcal{A}^o$ of options gets generated at random and the consideration set equals the intersection of $\widetilde{B}$ with the menu. In the above example $\widetilde{B} = X$ with probability α and $\widetilde{B} = \{o\}$ with probability $1 - \alpha$.

Definition 11.5 (Constant Random Consideration). $\rho \sim CRC$ if $\rho \sim RC$ with $\tilde{\Gamma}(A) = \tilde{B} \cap A$ for some random menu $\tilde{B} : \Omega \to \mathcal{A}^o$.

Proposition 11.6. *Any ρ with an IRC representation has a CRC representation. Any ρ with a CRC representation has an RU representation.*

Another way to relax IRC was proposed by Brady and Rehbeck (2016). Here, the distribution of $\tilde{\Gamma}$ is defined by a Luce-type formula over the collection of menus.

Definition 11.7 (Luce-Random Consideration). ρ has an *LRC* representation if it has an RC representation with

$$m_A(C) = \frac{\alpha_C}{\sum_{C' \subseteq A} \alpha_{C'}}$$

for each set $C \in \mathcal{A}^o$ and the numbers $(\alpha_C)_{C \in \mathcal{A}^o}$ are positive and independent of the menu A.

Kovach and Suleymanov (2021) show that a given representation $\tilde{\Gamma}$ is of the IRC variety if and only if it is at the same time CRC and LRC representation. It can be further shown that this propagates to the level of primitives: $\rho \sim IRC$ if it has a $\rho \sim CRC$ and $\rho \sim LRC$ (Suleymanov, 2023).

Proposition 11.8. *A ρ satisfies Definition 11.3 if and only if it satisfies Definitions 11.5 and 11.7.*

IRC, CRC, and LRC have been axiomatized respectively by Manzini and Mariotti (2014), Aguiar (2017), and Brady and Rehbeck (2016). Here is the uniqueness result.

Proposition 11.9. *Suppose $\rho \sim RC$ as in Definition 11.2 and suppose that the utility function is deterministic and ranks the object o in the last place. Then:*

(i) *If ρ has an IRC representation, then the utility function is ordinally unique and the set of probabilities $(\gamma_x)_{x \in X}$ is unique.*

(ii) *If ρ has a CRC representation, then the utility function is ordinally unique and the distribution of $\tilde{C}$ is unique.*

(iii) *If ρ has an LRC representation, then the utility function is ordinally unique and the distribution α is unique.*

The assumption that ρ is defined on all menus $\mathcal{A}^o$ can be somewhat relaxed. In part (i) the domain of ρ needs to contain sets of the form $\{x, y, z, o\}$ and be closed under set-inclusion, In part (iii) the domain of ρ needs to contain sets of the form $\{x, y, o\}$ and be closed under set-inclusion.

Remark 11.10. Uniqueness obtains only within these classes. Since IRC and CRC also have RU representations, all the choice variation could be attributed to taste variation. Thus, a ρ can have an RC representation with some deterministic utility function v and at the same time an RU representation with a random utility $\tilde{U}$. In this situation, the analyst is not in the position of deciding which representation is the "true" one, unless she makes some assumptions about unobservables, for example, insists that there is absolutely no taste variation. We will see that this is different with attribute-variation. △

Cattaneo, Ma, Masatlioglu, and Suleymanov (2020) further relax the properties of $\tilde{\Gamma}$, while keeping the assumption that preferences are deterministic (They drop the status quo from the domain.) The only restriction they impose on attention is a form of regularity.

Definition 11.11 (Monotone-Random Consideration). $\rho \sim MRC$ if $\rho \sim RC$ with $\tilde{\Gamma}$ such that for any $C \subseteq A$ and $x \in A \setminus C$ we have

$$m_A(C) \leq m_{A \setminus \{x\}}(C).$$

This assumption is satisfied by the IRC, CRC, and LRC models and many other examples discussed by Cattaneo, Ma, Masatlioglu, and Suleymanov (2020). This class of representations provides further insight into the issue of identification. The paper defines revealed preference by a violation of regularity: $x \succ^* y$ if adding y to a menu causes x to be chosen strictly more often from that menu. They show that in the MRC class $x \succ^* y$ if and only if for all monotone representations the utility of x is above y. Moreover, they show that the MRC class is characterized by acyclicity of $\succ^*$.

All the papers above assume that utility is deterministic, which leaves no room for preference heterogeneity. Aguiar, Boccardi, Kashaev, and Kim (2023) and Kashaev and Aguiar (2021) relax the deterministic utility assumption and study uniqueness properties of various subclasses of MRC. They also construct statistical tests and design an experiment to tell various classes apart. Gibbard (2021) also studies uniqueness in the model where both utility and consideration are random.

11.3   MODELS WITH ATTRIBUTE VARIATION

In the applied literature the menu is fixed to be X and instead what varies are the attributes of each alternative, for example, in Chapter 10. Let $\mathcal{E}$ be the set of possible attribute profiles which determine the random consideration set and the random utility function.

Definition 11.12. $\rho \sim RCwithattributes$ if there exists a random consideration set $\tilde{\Gamma} : \Omega \times \mathcal{E} \to M^o$ and a random utility function $\tilde{U} : \Omega \to \mathbb{R}^{X \times \mathcal{E}}$, such that

$$\rho(x, \xi) = \mathbb{P}\left(\tilde{U}(x, \xi) = \max_{y \in \tilde{\Gamma}(\xi)} \tilde{U}(y, \xi) \right).$$

Like with menu-variation, the general model has no bite, so various restrictions have been studied. For an overview of this literature, see Crawford, Griffith, and Iaria (2021).

Historically, the first special case is nested logit (Section 3.4). Here the nest is randomly drawn according to Luce probabilities and then choice from each nest is also Luce. Intuitively, this involves two assumptions: (1) The consideration sets form a partition of X. (2) The probabilities of drawing different consideration sets and the probabilities of choosing from those consideration sets are driven by the same underlying function v. A number of models have been proposed that relax the first assumption but keep the second one: Swait (2001), Wen and Koppelman (2001) and Cascetta and Papola (2001), Cantillo and de Dios Ortúzar (2005), and Calastri, Hess, Choudhury, Daly, and Gabrielli (2019).

Other models relax both assumptions. A version of independent random consideration (IRC) with attributes was studied by Swait and Ben-Akiva (1987), Ben-Akiva and Boccara (1995), Goeree (2008), and Van Nierop, Bronnenberg, Paap, Wedel, and Franses (2010). Here $\gamma_x(\xi_x)$ is a function only of the characteristics of item x but not the other items. For example, in Goeree (2008) γ can depend on the level of advertising.

A version of the "sleeping agent" model (Example 11.4) was studied by Ho, Hogan, and Scott Morton (2017), Hortaçsu, Madanizadeh, and Puller (2017), and Heiss, McFadden, Winter, Wuppermann, and Zhou (2016). Here the probability of waking up is a function only of the characteristics of the status quo (but not the other items).

Abaluck and Adams-Prassl (2021) study identification properties of a hybrid of those two models, under the assumption that utility is quasilinear in prices. While the standard IARU model (Definition 10.2) satisfies the symmetry of the partials condition (Theorem 10.5), they show that nontrivial attention leads to asymmetric partials. In fact, they show that attention can be identified from those asymmetries. Their paper contains an interesting proof-of-concept experiment. Imagine that for each menu A the analyst randomly draws a set $C \subseteq A$ with probability $m_A(C)$ and makes sure that the agent considers all of these items before making a choice according to ρ (none of the items in $A \setminus C$ are shown to the agent). If we now average over all C, the recorded stochastic choices will be

$$\rho^*(x, A) = \sum_{C \subseteq A} \rho(x, C) m_A(C).$$

Abaluck and Adams-Prassl (2021) run such an experiment and confirm that when ρ^* is fed to the model the correct set of weights m_A is estimated.

Barseghyan, Molinari, and Thirkettle (2021) and Barseghyan, Coughlin, Molinari, and Teitelbaum (2021) study nonparametric restrictions on the consideration set distribution. They allow for arbitrary correlation between consideration sets and preferences and only restrict the cardinality of the consideration set from below. In general, their approach is computationally challenging because of the presence of an infinitely dimensional nuisance parameter $m_X(\cdot|\xi)$.

11.4   OTHER "BEHAVIORAL" MODELS

Kovach and Tserenjigmid (2022b) study a model where items in the consideration set receive a boost in utility, but items outside of that set can still be chosen.

Echenique, Saito, and Tserenjigmid (2018) study a model where the agent processes alternatives in several batches and within each batch chooses using a modified Luce rule.

Manzini and Mariotti (2018) axiomatize a model where the distribution over preferences depends directly on the menu without the intermediation of the consideration set. They assume that $\mu_A = \alpha_A \delta_u + (1 - \alpha_A)\delta_v$, where $u, v :$ $X \rightarrow \mathbb{R}$ are independent of the menu and α_A is menu-dependent; see also Manzini, Mariotti, and Petri (2019).

In Simon (1956) the agent is *satisficing*: They go through a menu in some order and stop the first time they hit an item that is "good enough" (see also Rubinstein and Salant, 2006). Aguiar, Boccardi, and Dean (2016) study a model where this order is random and unobservable to the analyst. Here, with a deterministic preference and threshold, all the choice variability is attributed to this random order.

Tversky (1972a, 1972b) studies a model of *elimination by aspects* (EBA).[3] In this model, each alternative is described by binary characteristics (aspects). The agent randomly picks an aspect and eliminates all items from the menu that do not posses this aspect. The process continues with a randomly picked aspect until there is only one item left or all items have the same aspects and such a tie is broken uniformly. EBA is a special case of RU, but there are no known axiomatizations of it. Gul, Natenzon, and Pesendorfer (2014) axiomatize a closely-related attribute rule.

Limited memory is similar to limited consideration (Yegane, 2021). There is an active literature in behavioral economics (Bordalo, Gennaioli, and Shleifer, 2020) and in psychology (Kahana, 2012).

---

[3] Becker, DeGroot, and Marschak (1963) sketched a version of this model where a subset of aspects can be considered at the same time.

CHAPTER 12

Dynamic Discrete Choice

12.1 PANEL DATA

In Chapter 7 we studied dynamic choices of a "myopic" agent, whose utility is given by some stochastic process. That exposition focused on the case with menu variation. In econometrics, the menu is fixed but there is variation in the attributes of each good. For completeness, I will now briefly describe this model. I will use ξ_{xt} to denote the vector of attributes and ξ_t will stand for stacked vector. Following the static definition (Definition 10.2), we have

$$\tilde{U}_t(x_t, \xi_t) = v(x_t, \xi_{xt}) + \tilde{\epsilon}_t(x_t).$$

Here, the function v is just like in the static model (deterministic, typically linear or polynomial, with coefficients identical for all agents). The stochastic process $(\tilde{\epsilon}_t)$ can be either i.i.d. or involve *permanent unobservable heterogeneity*:

$$\tilde{\epsilon}_t(x) = \tilde{\alpha}(x) + \tilde{\eta}_t(x), \tag{12.1}$$

where $\tilde{\alpha}$ is drawn once for the agent at the beginning of time, and $\tilde{\eta}_t$ is i.i.d. and independent of α. This approach allows for unobserved heterogeneity, but only in the levels (the coefficients of v are not random).

As discussed in Chapter 7 the econometric problem with panel data is nontrivial because past choices of the agent may appear as if they influence future choices, even if in reality they simply carry information about their unobservable type (which here is $\tilde{\alpha}$).

Estimation and identification are covered in Hsiao (2022). Chamberlain (1984) showed that if η_t are TIEV i.i.d. over time and alternatives, then the linear coefficients of v are identified without imposing any restrictions on the distribution of $\tilde{\alpha}$ conditional on ξ. Manski (1987) relaxed the i.i.d. assumption to full support and stationarity (i.e., conditional on ξ_t and $\tilde{\alpha}$ the distribution of $\tilde{\epsilon}_t$ is the same in each time period, but allowed to be serially correlated). He showed that inference is possible if there is enough variation in ξ. Chamberlain (2010) showed that having enough variation in ξ is necessary for inference, and even under this assumption inference is slow unless we are in the TIEV family.

12.2 MARKOV DECISION PROBLEMS

In Chapter 8 we introduced forward-looking agents, who anticipate their future choices. Their utility satisfies the Bellman equation that ties together $\widetilde{U}_t$ and $\widetilde{U}_{t+1}$. In Section 8.2 we showed that such agents like bigger menus because such menus give them more option value. There, we used the domain of decision trees (Section 7.5), which is a dynamic extension of menu variation. The econometric approach uses Markov Decision Problems, which can be thought of as a dynamic extension of both menu variation and attribute variation. The model is richer than the panel data model from Section 12.1 because the action today controls the future distribution of (ξ_t, ϵ_t). Their utility is forward-looking and takes this possibility into account.

This model was introduced by Rust (1994); for exposition see Aguirre-gabiria and Mira (2010) and Abbring (2010). In a *Markov Decision Problem* (MDP) in each period t the state $s_t \in S$ is revealed to the agent. The set of available actions in state s_t is given by $A(s_t)$. The agent has a state-dependent utility $v_t(x_t, s_t)$. There is a transition probability over s_{t+1} that depends on the current action x_t and the current state s_t. Thus, choices made in period t affect both the current payoffs as well as the distribution over future states (and therefore future menus and future utilities). The transition probability is known by the agent and estimated by the analyst under a set of assumptions.

The MDP is partially observed by the analyst. The state has two components $s_t = (\xi_t, \epsilon_t)$ where ξ_t is observed by the analyst while ϵ_t is private to the agent. The menu in period t depends only on the observable part of the state, ξ_t. The transition probability satisfies the conditional independence (CI) assumption:

$$\mathbb{P}[\xi_{t+1}, \epsilon_{t+1} | \xi_t, \epsilon_t, x_t] = \mathbb{P}[\epsilon_{t+1} | \xi_{t+1}] \cdot \mathbb{P}[\xi_{t+1} | \xi_t, x_t]. \tag{CI}$$

This means two things: (1) conditional on the current decision and current observable state variable, the next period observable state variable is independent of the current ϵ, (2) conditional on the current observable state variable, the current ϵ is independent of the past ϵ.

Observed choice probabilities are given by

$$\rho(x_t, \xi_t) = \mathbb{P}\left[\widetilde{U}_t(x_t, \xi_t) = \max_{y_t \in A(\xi_t)} \widetilde{U}_t(y_t, \xi_t) \,\Big|\, \xi_t\right], \tag{12.2}$$

where the utility of action x_t equals

$$\widetilde{U}_t(x_t, \xi_t) = v(x_t, \xi_t) + \tilde{\epsilon}_t(x_t) + \delta\mathbb{E}\left[\max_{x_{t+1} \in A(\tilde{\xi}_{t+1})} \widetilde{U}_{t+1}(x_{t+1}, \tilde{\xi}_{t+1}) \,\Big|\, x_t, \xi_t\right]. \tag{12.3}$$

Notice that because CI rules out persistence in unobservables, the choice probability can be written without conditioning on the history of past choices, that is, observed choices are history-independent (c.f. Example 7.1). Thanks to CI we can also drop the subscript on U_t; I kept it above for greater clarity.

The literature typically couples CI with the i.i.d. assumption

$$\epsilon_t(x) \text{ and } \epsilon_t(y) \text{ are i.i.d. and independent of } \xi_t \qquad \text{(i.i.d.)}$$

Rust (1987) introduced *dynamic logit*, which combines CI and i.i.d. with the additional parametric TIEV assumption on ϵ_t. Due to its tractability, this model is a workhorse for estimation.[1].

Example 12.1 (Bus Engine Replacement). Rust (1987) studied the choices of Harold Zurcher, the superintendent of a bus company. Zurcher is managing a fleet of buses, each characterized by current milage $\xi_t \in [0, \infty]$. In each period for each bus, Zurcher can make a replacement decision. Replacing the engine, $x_t = 1$, means resetting the current mileage to zero, at a cost *RC*. Not replacing, $x_t = 0$, preserves the current mileage. There is a maintenance cost $c(\xi_t)$. Let θ be the vector of parameters of c that also includes RC. The state variable next period is $\xi_{t+1} = \xi_t(1 - x_t) + \eta_{t+1}$, where the mileage increments, η_{t+1}, are random and independent of the current decision. Since ξ is observable, this process can be separately estimated by the econometrician. Zurcher's utility function solves:

$$\tilde{U}_t(0, \xi_t; \theta) = -c(\xi_t; \theta) + \tilde{\epsilon}_t(0) + \delta\mathbb{E}[\max_{x_{t+1}} U_{t+1}(x_{t+1}, \xi_t + \tilde{\eta}_{t+1}; \theta)],$$

$$\tilde{U}_t(1, \xi_t; \theta) = -c(0; \theta) - RC(\theta) + \tilde{\epsilon}_t(1) + \delta\mathbb{E}[\max_{x_{t+1}} U_{t+1}(x_{t+1}, \tilde{\eta}_{t+1}; \theta)],$$

where $\epsilon_t(1)$ and $\epsilon_t(0)$ are i.i.d. TIEV. $\triangle$

Rust's original approach was to use dynamic programming to compute $U(\cdot; \theta)$ for each value of θ to obtain $\rho(\cdot; \theta)$ and then estimate θ. This was later simplified by Hotz and Miller (1993) and Hotz, Miller, Sanders, and Smith (1994) using an inversion argument (Section 10.3). Roughly speaking, by the WDZ Lemma (Lemma 10.4) the continuation value can be directly computed by integrating the choice probabilities. This method works for general i.i.d. models. See, for example, Shum (2016) for exposition. A related result in decision theory is Theorem 3 of Lu (2016).

12.3 SERIAL CORRELATION OF $\tilde{\varepsilon}$

The CI assumption rules out persistent unobservables. One simple way to relax this assumption is to assume permanent unobservable heterogeneity, which can be thought of as a time-1 mixture of i.i.d. models. Here, the utility in each period depends on the agent's "type" (which they privately learn in period 1), but each type of agent is also subject to i.i.d. shocks, exactly like in the panel data formulation (12.1). Such a formulation was used, for example, by Lee (2013).

---

[1] See, for example, Miller (1984), Rust (1989), Hendel and Nevo (2006), and Gowrisankaran and Rysman (2012).

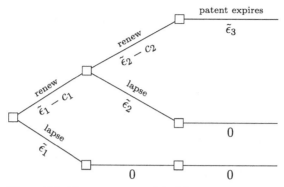

Figure 12.1 The patent renewal decision tree.

The so called *Eckstein–Keane–Wolpin* models combine permanent unobserved heterogeneity with transitory shocks that are allowed to be correlated across actions (see, e.g., Example 2 of Aguirregabiria and Mira (2010)).

Pakes (1986) relaxed CI in another way by endowing (ϵ_t) with a Markov structure.

Example 12.2. Figure 12.1 illustrates a simple example of patent renewal. The firm can renew the patent ($x_t = 1$) at cost c_t. The instant reward for renewing is $\tilde{\epsilon}_t$. Not renewing the patent ($x_t = 0$) makes it lapse forever. Thus, renewing gives an immediate payoff of $\tilde{\epsilon}_t - c_t$ plus the option value of renewing in the future.

The econometrician knows c_t and wants to estimate the option value assuming that the distribution of rewards (ϵ_t) follows a first-order Markov process. The agent's utility is $\tilde{U}_t(0) = 0$ and

$$\tilde{U}_t(1) = \tilde{\epsilon}_t - c_t + \delta \mathbb{E}[\max_{x_{t+1}} \tilde{U}_{t+1}(x_{t+1})|\tilde{\epsilon}_t]\}.$$

There is actually no state variable in this model, except for t. Pakes (1986) shows that the solution involves a decreasing sequence of deterministic thresholds such that in period t it is optimal for the agent to renew iff ϵ_t is above the threshold. Based on this he formulates a maximum likelihood estimator.   △

Finally, general models of unobservable serially correlated state variables go beyond the Markov assumption and impose almost no structure on $\tilde{\epsilon}$ (Norets, 2009; Hu and Shum, 2012).

12.4   IDENTIFICATION

In general, under CI the value of δ is not identified (Manski, 1993; Rust, 1994). This is because we can define a new utility function $\hat{v}(x, \xi) := v(x, \xi) + \delta \mathbb{E}[\max_{x'} U(x', \xi')|x, \xi]$ and set $\hat{\delta} = 0$.

To identify v, it is assumed that δ is known to the analyst. Let k be the cardinality of $\mathcal{E}$ and n be the cardinality of X. There are kn utility parmeters. Because CI imposes history-independence, we observe kn conditional choice probabilities. Since they have to sum up to one for each ξ, to get point identification we need to make k normalizing assumptions.

One typical approach is to fix an alternative x_0 and set $v(x_0, \xi) = 0$ for all ξ. Other normalizations include: exclusion restrictions (setting some elements of v equal to each other) or parametric restrictions. A vast literature on identification both under CI and with serial correlation, which includes Hotz and Miller (1993), Taber (2000), Magnac and Thesmar (2002), Norets and Tang (2013), and Kasahara and Shimotsu (2009) and is summarized by Abbring (2010)

Abbring and Daljord (2020) show that *local point identification* holds. Under an exclusion restriction, a range of δ is identified and for each δ there is a unique v. Other partial identification approaches involve imposing shape restrictions on v, for example, monotonicity, concavity, supermodularity, or obtaining bounds on parameter values (Honoré and Tamer, 2006). Even if parameters are partially identified, it is sometimes possible to point-identify the counterfactuals (Kalouptsidi, Scott, and Souza-Rodrigues, 2021; Kalouptsidi, Kitamura, Lima, and Souza-Rodrigues, 2021).

12.5 DYNAMIC LOGIT

It is relatively easy to axiomatically characterize dynamic logit if we dispense with the observable states ξ_t. Let each action be identified with a payoff today and a continuation menu tomorrow, that is, $x_t = (z_t, A_{t+1})$. This is just like deterministic decision trees from Section 7.5. On this domain, the MDP (12.3) becomes what I will call *Additive Dynamic Random Utility* (ADRU).

$$
\tilde{U}_t(z_t, A_{t+1}) = v_t(z_t) + \delta \mathbb{E}\left[\max_{x_{t+1} \in A_{t+1}} \tilde{U}_{t+1}(x_{t+1})\right] + \tilde{\epsilon}_t(z_t, A_{t+1}),
$$
$$(12.4)$$

with deterministic utility functions $v_t \in \mathbb{R}^Z$, discount factor $\delta \in [0, 1]$, and random payoff shock $\tilde{\epsilon}_t : \Omega^t \to \mathbb{R}^{X_t}$.

Note that in ADRU δ is not identified because we represent the same choices with $\delta' = 0$ and

$$
\epsilon'_t(z_t, A_{t+1}) = \delta \mathbb{E}\left[\max_{x_{t+1} \in A_{t+1}} \tilde{U}_{t+1}(x_{t+1})\right] + \epsilon_t(z_t, A_{t+1}).
$$

Dynamic logit is ADRU plus the i.i.d. and TIEV assumptions. Fudenberg and Strzalecki (2015) showed that the main axiomatic consequences of these assumptions are Luce's IIA (Axiom 3.3, period by period) and the analogues of Preference for Flexibility (Axiom 8.4) and Sophistication (Axiom 8.14).

Axiom 12.3 (Weak Preference for Flexibility). For all t if $B_{t+1} \supsetneq A_{t+1}$ and $A_t := \{(z_t, B_{t+1}), (z_t, A_{t+1})\}$

$$0 < \rho_t((z_t, A_{t+1}), A_t) < \frac{1}{2}.$$

Weak Preference for Flexibility holds for all i.i.d. representations with unbounded support. Compared with Preference for Flexibility (Axiom 8.4), which says that in pairwise choice (z_t, B_{t+1}) is chosen with probability one, here this probability is strictly less than one (because the support of $\tilde{\epsilon}_t$ is unbounded).

Axiom 12.4 (Recursivity). For all t, z_t, A_{t+1}, B_{t+1} and $A_t := \{(z_t, B_{t+1}), (z_t, A_{t+1})\}$

$$\rho_t((z_t, A_{t+1}), A_t) \geq \rho_t((z_t, B_{t+1}), A_t)$$

$$\Updownarrow$$

$$\sum_{x_{t+1} \in A_{t+1}} \rho_{t+1}(x_{t+1}, A_{t+1} \cup B_{t+1}) \geq \sum_{x_{t+1} \in B_{t+1}} \rho_{t+1}(x_{t+1}, A_{t+1} \cup B_{t+1}).$$

Recursivity says that (z_t, A_{t+1}) is chosen more frequently at time t than (z_t, B_{t+1}) if and only if an alternative from A_{t+1} is chosen more frequently at time $t+1$ than an alternative from B_{t+1}. This leverages the "log-sum" expression (3.2) and is specific to the TIEV assumption and does not hold for all i.i.d. models.

Fudenberg and Strzalecki (2015) also show that all the parameters of the model, that is, δ and v are identified under a stationarity assumption on v. I think this result extends to all of i.i.d. models. This sharp result comes from the rich variation in intertemporal problems that may be absent in the field, but can be easily incorporated in experimental settings.

A number of recent decision theory papers use dynamic logit as a building block, such as the dynamic attribute rule of Gul, Natenzon, and Pesendorfer (2014). Other papers view $\tilde{\epsilon}_t$ as errors, not utility shocks. In Fudenberg and Strzalecki (2015), errors lead to "choice aversion" (each menu is penalized by a function of its size). This makes the agent averse to bigger menus and leads to stochastic versions of the Set-Betweenness axiom which is studied in the literature on temptation and self-control (Gul and Pesendorfer, 2001; Dekel, Lipman, and Rustichini, 2009). Ke (2018) offers a dynamic model of mistakes (agent evaluates each menu by the expectation of the utility under her own SCF).

12.6   CONSEQUENCES OF THE I.I.D. ASSUMPTION

In this section we will further explore the consequences of the i.i.d. assumption in the simplified framework without observable attributes. The part of i.i.d. that we will be focusing on is that ϵ is i.i.d. across alternatives. (Once we eliminate the covariates, i.i.d. over time is guaranteed by CI.)

The consequences described here hold not only for i.i.d. $\tilde{\epsilon}_t$, but also under certain forms serial correlation, for example, with permanent unobserved heterogeneity, where we have a mixture of i.i.d. models that inherits its properties.

12.6.1 Preference for Flexibility

Under the i.i.d. assumption each alternative $x_t = (z_t, A_{t+1})$ gets its own realization of the ϵ-shock. In particular even if $B_{t+1} \supsetneq A_{t+1}$, the two random variables $\tilde{\epsilon}_t(z_t, A_{t+1})$ and $\tilde{\epsilon}_t(z_t, B_{t+1})$ are i.i.d. Thus, as Weak Preference for Flexibility (Axiom 12.3) says, dominated choices will be made with positive probability. Mechanically this makes sense because small menus sometimes get a shock that outweighs their lower option value. Yet, from a theoretical point of view, it seems reasonable to assume that smaller menu gets chosen with probability zero, as asserted by Preference for Flexibility (Axiom 8.4). However, as discussed by Rust (1987), models that predict zero choice probabilities for some alternatives will be impossible to estimate, so this can be an issue for applications.

The i.i.d. assumption is a solution to a practical problem, but is it the right solution? Consider what happens if we increase the variance of ϵ. Intuitively, increasing the variance of shocks in period $t + 1$ should increase the attractiveness of the bigger menu, as it now offers more option value. For example, suppose that $v_{t+1}(x) = 0$ for all x and consider a singleton menu versus a menu of two items. If ϵ_{t+1} are i.i.d. normal with mean zero and standard deviation λ, then the expected value of the first one is zero, whereas the expected value of the second one is $\frac{\lambda}{\sqrt{\pi}}$, which is increasing in the variance; intuitively, if we increase the noise, the chance that we get at least one favorable draw gets higher. Given this logic, one would expect that the bigger menu gets chosen with a higher probability as λ increases.

However, there is another effect: Increasing λ automatically brings today's choice probabilities closer to a half because we are also increasing the variance of ϵ_t. This is happening because under the i.i.d. assumption each option (z_1, A_1) and (z_1, B_1) gets its own independent shock even though the consumption today is the same. It turn out that this second effect is stronger.

Proposition 12.5 (Frick, Iijima, and Strzalecki, 2019). *Suppose that there are two periods and ϵ are i.i.d. and scaled multiplicatively by $\lambda > 1$. Let $A_2 = \{z_2\}$, $B_2 = \{z_2, z_2'\}$, and $A_1 = \{(z_1, A_2), (z_1, B_2)\}$ for some fixed z_1, z_2, z_2' such that $v(z_2') > v(z_2)$. Then the probability $\rho_1((z_1, A_2), A_1)$ strictly increases in λ.*

As you recall, the i.i.d. assumption also leads to unrealistic predictions about substitution patterns (Section 10.6) and about choices over lotteries (Section 4.6). In the static setting these problems can be fixed by appropriately disciplining the $\tilde{\epsilon}$, such as in the random characteristics model and random expected utility model. In the dynamic setting the model from Chapter 8 is imposing similar discipline.

To summarize Chapter 8: If we think of ϵ as representing shocks to utilities, then continuation menus cannot directly impact today's utility (as they do in the i.i.d. model). They can do so only indirectly, via the expectation of tomorrow's utility. Becase of this, shocks to continuation menus cannot be arbitrary and should be carried by the conditional expectation operator. This is the maintained assumption in some dynamic discrete choice papers, notably Pakes (1986) and Taber (2000).

12.6.2 Postponing Decisions

The implications of the i.i.d. assumption can be seen perhaps even more starkly if we consider a slight variation of the above problem and focus on the timing of choices.

Suppose that you are packing your bag for a trip that starts on Saturday. Right now is Friday morning ($t = 1$) and you can decide to pack the bag today after checking the weather forecast ($t = 2$), or wait and pack on Saturday morning ($t = 3$).

Suppose that the objects you can pack are your sun glasses g or your rain coat c (but not both). If you decide to pack today, then the menu you are choosing is $A_2^{now} = \{\{g\}, \{c\}\}$, that is, in period $t = 2$ you will be choosing between $\{g\}$ and $\{c\}$. If instead you decide to pack on Saturday, then in period $t = 2$ you will face the menu $A_2^{later} = \{\{g, c\}\}$, that is, you will not be making any choices in $t = 2$. Your period $t = 1$ choice, illustrated in Figure 12.2, is between those two menus. Let $A_1 := \{A_2^{now}, A_2^{later}\}$, that is, there is no intermediate consumption; suppose further that packing is not a costly activity.

The agent from Chapter 8 will deterministically choose A_2^{later} To see that, note that we have

$$\tilde{U}_1(A_2^{later}) = \mathbb{E}\left[\mathbb{E}\left[\max\left\{\tilde{u}_3(g), \tilde{u}_3(c)\right\}|\omega^2\right]|\omega^1\right]$$
$$\geq \mathbb{E}\left[\max\left\{\mathbb{E}[\tilde{u}_3(g)|\omega^2], \mathbb{E}[\tilde{u}_3(c)|\omega^2]\right\}|\omega^1\right] = \tilde{U}_1(A_2^{now}).$$

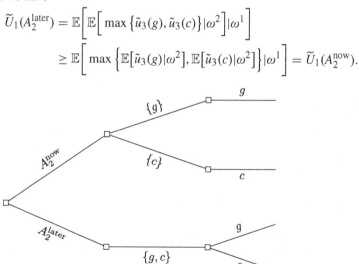

Figure 12.2 Early and late decisions.

This holds because of conditional Jensen's inequality, which is exactly the same reason why the agent has preference for flexibility, cf. Example 8.2. (The agent may be indifferent if they think that the accuracy of Friday's forecast is perfect, that is, that there is no information gained between $t = 2$ and $t = 3$.)

Instead, the i.i.d. agent packs early with probability bigger than a half.

Proposition 12.6 (Fudenberg and Strzalecki, 2015; Frick, Iijima, and Strzalecki, 2019). *If (ρ_t) has an i.i.d. representation with $\delta < 1$, then*

$$\frac{1}{2} < \rho_1\left(A_2^{\text{now}}, A_1\right) < 1.$$

Moreover, if ε is scaled by $\lambda > 1$, then $\rho_1(A_2^{\text{now}}, A_1)$ strictly increases (modulo ties).

This is mechanically true under i.i.d. because the agent receives the ϵ not at the time of consumption, but at the time of decision, even if the decision has only delayed consequences. Thus, in a sense, making decisions early allows them to get the max ϵ earlier. To illustrate that, consider the special case where $v_3(g) = v_3(c) = v$. Here, we have

$$V(A_2^{\text{later}}) = \delta^2 v + \delta^2 \mathbb{E}[\max\{\tilde{\epsilon}_3(g), \tilde{\epsilon}_3(c)\}]$$
$$\leq \delta^2 v + \delta \mathbb{E}[\max\{\tilde{\epsilon}_2(g), \tilde{\epsilon}_2(c)\}] = V(A_2^{\text{now}}),$$

so by (3.3) the probability of packing now is more than a half.[2]

Such behavior is suggestive of a preference for commitment, which is usually associated with choice overload or self-control problems (see the discussion after Theorem 8.6). One might argue that consumers do suffer from such behavioral issues, but perhaps in that case we might prefer to have a structural model of their preference for commitment, along the lines of Strotz (1955) and Gul and Pesendorfer (2001), instead of commitment being a mechanical side-effect of the i.i.d. assumption? Another issue is that dynamic discrete choice models are often applied to choices of profit-maximizing firms. Do we want to argue that firms also suffer from such behavioral biases?

The above examples hinge on somewhat artificial situations, where the agent is offered a direct choice between two nested menus, or offered an option to defer choice at no cost. My remarks may thus be only of theoretical interest. However, I think some caution may be warranted when applying the i.i.d. assumption to practical situations. For example, Frick, Iijima, and Strzalecki (2019) show how i.i.d. models can lead to biased parameter estimates even more realistic stopping problems.

---

[2] Fudenberg and Strzalecki (2015) show that a modification of dynamic logit leads to the opposite prediction: Late choices are more frequent. However this coincides with the agent liking smaller menus more, so does not address the issues discussed in Section 12.6.1.

Additional Material and Proof Sketches

A.1   CHAPTER 1

Example A.1 (Positivity does not imply positive density). This example is
due to Ricky Li. Let $X = \{x, y, z\}$ and let ρ be represented by distribution over
preferences

$$\mu(x \succ y \succ z) = \mu(y \succ x \succ z) = \mu(z \succ x \succ y) = \frac{1}{3}.$$

It is easy to verify that ρ satisfies Positivity. Moreover, notice that $\rho(z, \{y, z\}) =
\rho(z, \{x, y, z\})$.

Suppose that ρ has an ARU representation with a positive density for some
$v : X \to \mathbb{R}$. Let

$$E := \{\epsilon \in \mathbb{R}^X : v(x) + \epsilon(x) > v(z) + \epsilon(z) > v(y) + \epsilon(y)\}.$$

Notice that this is a set of positive Lebesgue measure; however, we have

$$0 = \rho(z, \{y, z\}) - \rho(z, \{x, y, z\}) = \mathbb{P}(E),$$

which is a contradiction. $\triangle$

A.3   CHAPTER 3

A.3.1   GEV

Let $X = \{x_1, \ldots, x_n\}$. The joint CDF equals

$$G(\epsilon) = \exp(-H(e^{-\epsilon_1}, \ldots, e^{-\epsilon_n})),$$

where the function $H : \mathbb{R}_+^n \to \mathbb{R}_+$ is:

- homogenous of degree α for some $\alpha > 0$
- satisfies $t_x \to \infty$ with fixed t_{-x} implies $H(t) \to \infty$
- for any distinct $x_1, \ldots, x_k$ the crosspartial $\frac{\partial^k H}{\partial t_{x_1}, \cdots, \partial t_{x_k}}$ is positive for
  odd k and negative for even k.

The advantage of this class is that the choice probabilities are given in closed form by

$$\rho(x, X) = \alpha^{-1} \frac{\partial}{\partial v_x} \ln H(e^{v_1}, \ldots, e^{v_n}).$$

This is because the formula for consumer surplus under GEV is $V(X) = \log H(e^{v_1}, \ldots, e^{v_n})$ and by the WDZ lemma (Lemma 10.4), the choice probabilities are the gradient of consumer surplus.

We get logit by setting $H(t_1, \ldots, t_n) := \sum_{i=1}^n t_i^\alpha$. We get nested logit by setting $H(t_1, \ldots, t_n) := \sum_{i=1}^k \left(\sum_{x \in B_i} t_x^{\alpha_2} \right)^{\frac{\alpha_1}{\alpha_2}}$ where $\{B_1, \ldots B_k\}$ the nest structure (a partition of X). When $\alpha_1 < \alpha_2$, then this H satisfies the above conditions, which shows that nested logit with such parameters has an RU representation.

For more on this class, see Section 2.7.2 of Anderson, de Palma, and Thisse (1992) and Section 4.6 of Train (2009).

A.3.2   Proof of Proposition 3.10

Note that we have two Fechnerian representations (v_1, F_1) and (v_2, F_2) that satisfy Richness (Axiom 3.20). By Theorem 3.21, there exists $\alpha > 0$ and $\beta \in \mathbb{R}$ such that $v_2 = \alpha v_1 + \beta$ and $F_2(\alpha t) = F_1(t)$ for all $t \in D_1$.   □
Weaker results can be obtained in the finite X case:

(i) If $F_1 = F_2$, then there exists $\beta \in \mathbb{R}$ such that $v_2(x) = v_1(x) + \beta$ for all $x \in X$.
(ii) If $v_1 = v_2$, then F_1 and F_2 coincide on the set $\{v(x) - v(y) : x, y \in X\}$.

To prove (i), let F be the shared CDF of $\tilde{\epsilon}_x - \tilde{\epsilon}_y$ for $x \neq y$. We have

$$\rho(x, y) = F(v_1(x) - v_1(y)) = F(v_2(x) - v_2(y)),$$

for all $x \neq y$. The function F is strictly increasing since $\tilde{\epsilon}$ has a positive density (why?), so

$$v_1(x) - v_1(y) = v_2(x) - v_2(y),$$

for all $x \neq y$. Thus, $v_1(x) - v_2(x)$ is a constant function of x.
To prove (ii), we have

$$F_1(v(x) - v(y)) = \rho(x, y) = F_2(v(x) - v(y)).$$

Part (i) says that if we know that the distribution of ϵ is the same, then v is pinned down uniquely up to an additive constant. Similarly, part (ii) says that if we know that v is the same, then the distribution of ϵ differences is the same (on the relevant domain).

Example A.2 (Fechnerian that is not i.i.d. ARU). This example is due to Jetlir Duraj. Suppose that $X = \left[-\frac{1}{2}, \frac{1}{2} \right]$ and $\rho(x, y) = \frac{1}{2}(1 + x - y)$. This ρ

has a Fechnerian representation where $v(x) = x$ and F is the CDF of a uniform distribution on $[-1, 1]$. Moreover, it can be checked that ρ in our example satisfies the Richness condition in Theorem 3.21, so F is pinned down up to the scale factor. But F cannot be the CDF of the difference of two i.i.d. random variables. The characteristic function of the difference of two i.i.d. random variables is a real and nonnegative function $|\varphi(t)|^2$, where φ is the characteristic function of one of them. But the characteristic function of F equals $\sin(t)/t$, which takes negative values. $\triangle$

A.3.3 Proof of Theorem 3.21

The necessity of the quadruple condition is trivial. Sufficiency follows from Debreu's (1958) theorem, which says that there exists $v : X \to \mathbb{R}$ such that for any $x, y, z, w \in X$

$$\rho(x, y) \geq \rho(z, w) \iff v(x) - v(y) \geq v(z) - v(w). \tag{A.1}$$

It remains to conjure up the F function. Expression (A.1) defines a preference $\succsim$ on $X \times X$ with two representations $(x, y) \mapsto \rho(x, y)$ and $(x, y) \mapsto v(x) - v(y)$. By ordinal uniqueness (Proposition 1.3) there exists a strictly increasing function $F : D \to \mathbb{R}$ such that $\rho(x, y) = F(v(x) - v(y))$.

The existence of $\alpha > 0$ and $\beta \in \mathbb{R}$ such that $v_2 = \alpha v_1 + \beta$ follows from Debreu (1958). This implies that $F_1(v_1(x) - v_1(y)) = \rho(x, y) = F_2(v_2(x) - v_2(y)) = F_2(\alpha(v_1(x) - v_1(y)))$.

To prove that F is continuous, we need to prove a converse to the intermediate value theorem that every increasing function with the "intermediate value property" is continuous. This is a known result but we will prove it from scratch because at this point in the proof we don't know if D is an interval.

Toward contradiction, suppose that F is discontinuous at some point $d \in D$. This means there is a sequence $d_n \to d$ such that $F(d_n)$ does not converge to $F(d)$. Without loss we can restrict attention to a subsequence such that $d_n < d_{n+1} < d$ for all n.

Since F is increasing, the sequence $F(d_n)$ is increasing and bounded from above by $F(d)$, so it has a limit. Let $q := \lim_n F(d_n)$. Pick any number $q^* \in (q, F(d))$. We will invoke the Richness axiom to show that there must exist d^* for which $F(d^*) = q^*$. This means that $d_n < d^* < d$ for all n which is a contradiction because $d_n \to d$.

So it just remains to invoke Richness and find d^*. Let $d_1 = v(x_1) - v(y_1)$ and $d = v(x) - v(y)$. If either $v(x_1) = v(x)$ or $v(y_1) = v(y)$ then apply Richness directly. Otherwise, are four cases to check:

(1) $v(x_1) < v(x)$ and $v(y_1) < v(y)$. Then $v(x_1) - v(y_1) < v(x) - v(y) < v(x) - v(y_1)$, so $\rho(x_1, y_1) < q^* < \rho(x, y_1)$ and by Richness there exists $x^* \in X$ such that $\rho(x^*, y_1) = q^*$. Define $d^* := v(x^*) - v(y_1)$.

(2) $v(x_1) > v(x)$ and $v(y_1) < v(y)$. Then $v(x_1) - v(y_1) < v(x) - v(y) < v(x_1) - v(y)$, so $v(y_1) - v(x_1) < v(y) - v(x_1)$ and $F(v(y_1) - v(x_1)) <$

$1 - q^* < F(v(y) - v(x_1))$, so by Richness there exists $y^* \in X$ such that $\rho(y^*, x_1) = 1 - q^*$. Define $q^* := v(x_1, y^*)$.

(3) $v(x) > v(x_1)$ and $v(y_1) > v(y)$. Then there are two subcases:

(a) $v(x_1) - v(y) < v(x) - v(y_1)$. Then either $\rho(x_1, y) < q^* < \rho(x, y)$ or $\rho(x_1, y_1) < q^* < \rho(x, y_1)$ (or both). Each of those subcases can be dealt with analogously to case 1.

(b) $v(x) - v(y_1) < v(x_1) - v(y)$. Then again there are two subcases, which can be dealt with analogously to case 2.

(4) $v(x_1) < v(x)$ and $v(y_1) > v(y)$. This can be dealt with analogously to case 3.   □

A.3.4   Proof of Proposition 3.23

Sufficiency follows from Scott's (1964) theorem, which says that there exists $v : X \to \mathbb{R}$ such that for any $x, y, z, w \in X$

$$\rho(x, y) \geq \rho(z, w) \Longleftrightarrow v(x) - v(y) \geq v(z) - v(w). \tag{A.2}$$

It remains to conjure up the F function. This is done exactly like in Appendix A.3.3.   □

A.4   CHAPTER 4

A.4.1   Proof of Proposition 4.23

Let $X = \Delta^s(Z)$. By Theorem 3.5, ρ has a Luce representation

$$\rho(p, A) = \frac{w(p)}{\sum_{q \in A} w(q)}$$

for some function $w : X \to \mathbb{R}_{++}$. In particular, the function w represents $\succsim^*$. By Theorem 4.5, $\succsim^*$ has an EU representation $U(p) = \mathbb{E}_p v$ for some $v : Z \to \mathbb{R}$. Let $U(X)$ denote the range of U. By ordinal uniqueness, there exists a strictly increasing function $h : U(X) \to \mathbb{R}$ such that $w(p) = h(\mathbb{E}_p v)$.   □

A.5   CHAPTER 5

A.5.1   Proof of Proposition 5.6

Bayes $\Rightarrow$ obedience: Fix A and suppose that $(\rho^s) \sim \text{Bayes}(p, \beta, v)$. Then

$$\rho^s(x, A) = \beta(M_x|s), \tag{A.3}$$

where

$$M_x = \{m \in M : \sum_{s \in S} v(x, s)p(s|m) \geq \sum_{s \in S} v(y, s)p(s|m) \text{ for all } y \in A\}.$$

Consider now the action recommendation $x \in A$. Upon hearing it, the agent's posterior is the average of all the posteriors in M_x:

$$p(s|M_x) = \frac{p(s, M_x)}{p(M_x)} = \frac{\sum_{m \in M_x} p(s|m)p(m)}{p(M_x)} = \sum_{m \in M_x} p(s|m)\lambda(m),$$

where $\lambda(m) = \frac{p(m)}{p(M_x)}$. Thus, taking the average of the inequalities in the definition of M_x with weights $\lambda(m)$ gives us

$$\sum_{s \in S} v(x, s)p(s|M_x) \geq \sum_{s \in S} v(y, s)p(s|M_x) \text{ for all } y \in Y. \qquad (A.4)$$

Notice that $p(s|M_x) = \frac{\beta(E_x|s)p(s)}{D_x}$, where $D_x = \sum_{s' \in S} \beta(E_x, s')p(s')$. Plugging in (A.3) gives us

$$p(s|M_x) = \frac{\rho^s(x, A)p(s)}{D_x}.$$

Substituting to (A.4) and multiplying both sides by D_x gives us obedience.

Obedience $\Rightarrow$ Bayes: Fix menu A and define $M := A$ and $\beta(x|s) := \rho^s(x, A)$. Obedience implies that upon hearing x the agent wants to choose x, so modulo ties in the Bayes representation the set M_x equals $\{x\}$. Thus the Bayes representation implies that the probability of choosing $x \in A$ in state s equals $\beta(x|s)$, which as we know is the actual choice probability $\rho^s(x, A)$.

As mentioned in the text, to deal with ties we need to allow a different tiebreaker after each message: If $x, y \in M_x$ then the tiebreaker needs to put probability zero on choosing y. $\qquad \square$

A.6 CHAPTER 6

A.6.1 Proof Sketch of Proposition 6.11

Fix $s \in S$ and let p_n be such that $p_n(s) \to 1$. Fix an experiment β and let $\mu_n := p_n \oplus \beta$. Notice that we have $\mu_n \to \delta_{\delta_s}$ (in the weak* topology). If c is prior independent, then $c(p \oplus \beta) = c(p_n \oplus \beta)$ for all n. We will now show that under UPS, the right hand side converges to zero, which means that $c(p \oplus \beta) = 0$ and since β was arbitrary, this implies that c is identically equal to zero.

Suppose that c is UPS. We have $c(\mu_n) = \int [L(q) - L(p_n)]\mu_n(dq)$. Consider first the expression $\int L(q)\mu_n(dq)$. Since $\mu_n \to \delta_{\delta_s}$ we have that $\int L(q)\mu_n(dq) \to L(\delta_s)$, assuming that L is bounded. Likewise, $L(p_n) \to L(\delta_s)$ since L is continuous.

A.6.2 The Blackwell Theorem

There are many equivalences known as the Blackwell theorem. Most of them characterize an incomplete ranking of experiments $\beta \geq \beta'$. Others characterize a ranking of distributions over posteriors $\mu \geq \mu'$. The two orders are connected, which is why I am using the same symbol to denote them. There is a vast literature on this topic, starting with Bohnenblust, Shapley, and Sherman (1949) and Blackwell (1951, 1953). A nice summary of the Blackwell theorem is given by Le Cam (1996). Torgersen (1991) is a very very dense book on this topic.

This section collects results from many sources and is incomplete. We assume that M is rich enough so that by varying β we can trace out all μ. The set S is finite; all measures are Borel.

First, we introduce the notion of a *garbling* that lets us compare two experiments. Intuitively, β' is a garbling of β if we can first generate the signal m according to β and then add "noise" to it.

Definition A.6.1 (Garbling). $\beta' : S \to \Delta(M')$ is a *garbling* of $\beta : S \to \Delta(M)$ if there exists a probability kernel $G : M \to \Delta(M')$ such that for every measurable set $E' \subseteq M'$

$$\beta'(E'|s) = \int_M G(E'|m)\beta(dm|s).$$

The key here is that the distribution $G(\cdot|m)$ is independent of the state, so it does not carry any additional information: It is pure noise.

Next, we need a notion of *dilation* that lets us compare two distributions over posteriors. Intuitively, μ' is a dilation of μ if it is a mean-preserving spread of it: We generate q according to μ and then in its place plug in a distribution over posteriors that averages to q.

Definition A.6.2 (Dilation). μ' is a *dilation* of μ if for some probability kernel $D : \Delta(S) \to \Delta(\Delta(S))$ such that $q = \int_{\Delta(S)} q'D(dq'|q)$ for all q and for every measurable set $B \subseteq \Delta(S)$

$$\mu'(B) = \int_{\Delta(S)} D(B|q)\mu(dq).$$

Definition A.6.3 (Achievable Payoff Profiles). For any menu A define a *behavioral strategy* to be a mapping from signals to mixed actions $\sigma : M \to \Delta(A)$. Let Σ be the set of behavioral strategies; the advantage of considering mixtures is that this set is now convex. The expected payoff of σ (given β) in state s is

$$v(\sigma, s; \beta) := \left\{ \int_M \sum_{x \in A} v(x, s)\sigma(x|m)\beta(dm|s) \right\}$$

and let $\vec{v}(\sigma; \beta)$ be the profile of such payoffs as s ranges over S. Let $AEP(\beta) := \{\vec{v}(\sigma; \beta) : \sigma \in \Sigma\}$ be the set of *achievable expected payoff profiles* given β.

Theorem A.6.4 (Blackwell).

> (1) *The following are all equivalent definitions of $\beta \geq \beta'$:*
> >   (i) *β' is a garbling of β.*

    (ii) $V_p^A(\beta) \geq V_p^A(\beta')$ *for any decision problem A, v, p.*

    (iii) *For any decision problem* $AEP(\beta) \supseteq AEP(\beta')$.

    (iv) $\sum_{s \in S} \int_M \phi(q_m)\beta(dm|s)p(s) \geq \sum_{s \in S} \int_M \phi(q_m)\beta'(dm|s)p(s)$
    for any convex and continuous function $\phi : \Delta(S) \to \mathbb{R}$ *and*
    any prior p.

(2) *The following are equivalent definitions of* $\mu \geq \mu'$:

    (i) μ *is a dilation of* μ'.

    (ii) $V^A(\mu) \geq V^A(\mu')$ *for any decision problem A, v.*

    (iii) $\int_{\Delta(S)} \phi(q)\mu(dq) \geq \int_{\Delta(S)} \phi(q)\mu'(dq)$ *for any convex and*
    continuous function $\phi : \Delta(S) \to \mathbb{R}$.

(3) *Moreover, the following are equivalent:*

    (i) $\beta \geq \beta'$.

    (ii) $p \oplus \beta \geq p \oplus \beta'$ *for some full support* $p \in \Delta(S)$.

    (iii) $p \oplus \beta \geq p \oplus \beta'$ *for all full support* $p \in \Delta(S)$.

Notice that the Blackwell ordering of informativeness is expressed in opposite ways for μ and for β. To make β less informative we need to apply a *garbling*, that is, also add risk to it. Intuitively, this makes sense: Adding uncorrelated noise makes the message less informative. To make μ *more* informative we need to apply a *dilation*, that is, also add risk to it. (Recall the concave order over lotteries. Condition 2(iii) is a multidimensional extension of the convex order.) This may seem at first confusing, but recall that in the world of distributions over posteriors having no information means a point mass on some p and adding information means splitting that mass point into a random posterior. A perfectly informative signal splits p into the vertices of the simplex.

A.7   CHAPTER 7

Definition A.7.1. If (ρ_1, ρ_2) has a DRU representation, then it satisfies Bounded History Dependence and therefore α-History Independence.

Proof of Proposition A.7.1

I thank Ricky Li for helping sharpen this proof. Let $E := N(x_2, A_1)$, $F := N(x_1, A_1)$, and $G := N(x_1, B_1)$. The axiom implies that $G \subseteq F$. Let $H := F \backslash G$. We have

$$
\begin{aligned}
|P(E|F) - P(E|G)| &= |P(E|G)P(G|F) + P(E|H)P(H|F) - P(E|G)| \\
&= |P(E|G)(P(G|F) - 1) + P(E|H)P(H|F)| \\
&= |-P(E|G)P(H|F) + P(E|H)P(H|F)| \\
&= P(H|F)|P(E|H) - P(E|G)| \\
&\leq P(H|F) = 1 - P(G|F) = 1 - \frac{P(G)}{P(F)}. \qquad \square
\end{aligned}
$$

A.9   CHAPTER 9

A.9.1   A Calculation behind Example 9.14

Let $w^x := e^{v(x)}$. Let Y_t^x be independent Poisson processes with intensities w^x respectively. Let $Y_t := \sum_{x \in A} Y_t^x$. The stopping time is the first time the process Y_t hits value 1. By Theorem 18.2 of Gravner (2017), Y_t is a Poisson process with intensity $w^A := \sum_{x \in A} w^x$. By Proposition 18.1 the distribution of the stopping time is exponential with parameter w^A. By Example 18.5 of Gravner (2017), the conditional choice probabilities are of the Luce form.   □

A.10   CHAPTER 10

A.10.1   More about Theorem 10.5

This theorem is usually stated with more generality by not assuming continuous differentiability: Theorem 5.1 of McFadden (1981), Theorem 3.1 of Anderson, de Palma, and Thisse (1992), Theorem 3 of Koning and Ridder (2003), Corollary 8 of Fosgerau, McFadden, and Bierlaire (2013), or Theorem 1 of Yang and Kopylov (2023).

Continuous differentiability of ρ simplifies exposition as it saves us yet another condition, which implies that the distribution of $\tilde{\epsilon}$ is in some sense smooth.

Formally, Theorem 10.5 follows from Theorem 3.1 of Anderson, de Palma, and Thisse (1992) because if ρ is continuously differentiable, then conditions (iv) and (v) imply their condition P1, their condition P2 is our (iii), their condition P3 is our (i), and their P4 is our (ii).   □

A.10.2   Proof of Proposition 10.7

Let G be the CDF of $\tilde{\epsilon}_x$. By definition, we can write for any $x \in X$ and any $p \in \mathbb{R}^X$

$$\rho(x, p) = \mathbb{P}\big(w(x) - p_x + \tilde{\epsilon}_x \geq w(x') - p_{x'} + \tilde{\epsilon}_{x'} \ \forall \ x' \neq x\big)$$
$$= \int_{e_x = -\infty}^{e_x = +\infty} \prod_{x' \neq x} G(w(x) - p_x + e_x - w(x') + p_{x'}) g(e_x) de_x.$$

This formula implies that if $\rho(x, \bar{p}) = \rho(y, \bar{p})$ for some $x, y \in X$ and $\bar{p} \in \mathbb{R}^X$, then $w(x) - \bar{p}_x = w(y) - \bar{p}_y$.

This in turn implies that, $\rho(x, (\bar{p}_{-z}, p_z)) = \rho(y, (\bar{p}_{-z}, p_z))$ as a function of p_z for a fixed value of $\bar{p}_{-z}$; thus their derivatives in p_z must coincide as well.   □

A.10.3   Cyclic Monotonicity

Blume (2008) attributes the concept of cyclic monotonicity to Hotelling (1929). Rockafellar (1966) showed that a correspondence satisfies cyclic monotonicity if and only if it is a subdifferential of a proper convex function. What follows is a simpler result, for functions, as opposed to correspondences. An analogous result for deterministic demand systems with quasilinear utility was obtained by Nocke and Schutz (2017).

Theorem A.10.1. *Suppose that* $\rho : \mathbb{R}^X \to \Delta(X)$ *is continuously differentiable. The following conditions are equivalent:*

(a) ρ *satisfies cyclic monotonicity*

(b) ρ *satisfies symmetric partials and the Jacobian of* ρ *is positive semi-definite*

(c) $\rho = \nabla V$ *for some convex and differentiable function* $V : \mathbb{R}^X \to \mathbb{R}$.

Moreover, the equivalence of (a) and (c) holds for any continuous function.

Proof.

(c)$\Rightarrow$ (b) Symmetric partials follows from Schwartz's theorem (also known as Young's theorem), Theorem 9.41 of Rudin (1976). Positive semi-definiteness follows from Theorem 35 of Fenchel (1953).

(b)$\Rightarrow$ (c) By Theorem 10.9 of Apostol (1969), condition (iii) $\rho = \nabla V$ for some potential function $V : \mathbb{R}^X \to \mathbb{R}$. Thus the Jacobian of ρ is the Hessian of V. By Theorem 35 of Fenchel (1953), if the Hessian is positive semidefinite, then V is a convex function.

(c)$\Rightarrow$ (a) Follows from Theorem 24.8 of Rockafellar (1970).

(a)$\Rightarrow$ (c) I thank Terry Rockafellar for helping me with this part. By Theorem 24.8 of Rockafellar (1970), cyclic monotonicity implies that $\rho \subseteq \nabla V$ for some closed, proper convex function $V : \mathbb{R}^X \to \mathbb{R}$. By Theorem 12.17 of Rockafellar and Wets (2009), the mapping $\nabla V : \mathbb{R}^n \to \mathbb{R}^n$ is monotone according to their Definition 12.1. By their Example 12.17 a continuous function is maximally monotone, which implies that $\rho = \nabla V$. The conclusion follows from Theorem 25.1 of Rockafellar (1970). $\square$

Bibliography

Abaluck, J., and A. Adams-Prassl (2021): "What do consumers consider before they choose? Identification from asymmetric demand responses," *The Quarterly Journal of Economics*, 136(3), 1611–1663. 145, 155

Abbring, J. H. (2010): "Identification of dynamic discrete choice models," *Annual Review of Economy*, 2(1), 367–394. 158, 161

Abbring, J. H., and Ø. Daljord (2020): "Identifying the discount factor in dynamic discrete choice models," *Quantitative Economics*, 11(2), 471–501. 161

Abdulkadiroglu, A., J. D. Angrist, Y. Narita, and P. A. Pathak (2017): "Research design meets market design: Using centralized assignment for impact evaluation," *Econometrica*. Vol. 85, No. 5 (September, 2017), 1373–1432. 108

Ackerberg, D., C. L. Benkard, S. Berry, and A. Pakes (2007): "Econometric tools for analyzing market outcomes," *Handbook of Econometrics*, 6, 4171–4276. 149

Afriat, S. N. (1967): "The construction of utility functions from expenditure data," *International Economic Review*, 8(1), 67–77. 140

Agranov, M., P. J. Healy, and K. Nielsen (2023): "Stable randomisation," *The Economic Journal*, 133, 2553–2579. 9

Agranov, M., and P. Ortoleva (2017): "Stochastic choice and preferences for randomization," *Journal of Political Economy*, 125(1), 40–68. 9, 60

(in press): "Ranges of preferences and randomization," *Review of Economics and Statistics*. 60

Aguiar, V. H. (2017): "Random categorization and bounded rationality," *Economics Letters*, 159, 46–52. 152, 153

Aguiar, V. H., M. J. Boccardi, and M. Dean (2016): "Satisficing and stochastic choice," *Journal of Economic Theory*, 166, 445–482. 156

Aguiar, V. H., M. J. Boccardi, N. Kashaev, and J. Kim (2023): "Random utility and limited consideration," *Quantitative Economics*, 14(1), 71–116. 154

Aguirregabiria, V., and P. Mira (2010): "Dynamic discrete choice structural models: A survey," *Journal of Econometrics*, 156(1), 38–67. 158, 160

Ahn, D., R. Iijima, T. Sarver, and Y. L. Yaouanq (2019): "Behavioral characterizations of Naiveté for time-inconsistent preferences," *Review of Economic Studies*, 86, 2319–2355. 119

Ahn, D. S., R. Iijima, and T. Sarver (2020): "Naivete about temptation and self-control: Foundations for recursive naive quasi-hyperbolic discounting," *Journal of Economic Theory*, 189, 105087. 119

Ahn, D. S., and T. Sarver (2013): "Preference for flexibility and random choice," *Econometrica*, 81(1), 341–361. 55, 56, 117, 118, 119

Ahumada, A., and L. Ülkü (2018): "Luce rule with limited consideration," *Mathematical Social Sciences*, 93, 52–56. 30

Allais, M. (1953): "Le Comportment de l'Homme Rational devant le Risque, Critique des Postulates et Axiomes de l'Ecole Americaine," *Econometrica*, 21, 803–815. 51

Allen, R., and J. Rehbeck (2019): "Revealed stochastic choice with attributes," *Econometrica*, 87(3), 1021–1054. 150

Alós-Ferrer, C., E. Fehr, and N. Netzer (2021): "Time will tell: Recovering preferences when choices are noisy," *Journal of Political Economy*, 129(6), 1828–1877. 133

Anderson, S., A. de Palma, and J. Thisse (1992): *Discrete Choice Theory of Product Differentiation*. MIT Press, Cambridge, MA. 42, 147, 168, 174

Angrist, J., P. Hull, P. A. Pathak, and C. Walters (2017): "Leveraging lotteries for school value-added: Testing and estimation," *Quarterly Journal of Economics*. Volume 132, Issue 2, 871–919. 108

Anscombe, F. J., and R. J. Aumann (1963): "A definition of subjective probability," *The Annals of Mathematical Statistics*, 34(1), 199–205. 74

Apesteguia, J., and M. A. Ballester (2017a): "Stochastic representative agent," Working Paper. 34

Apesteguia, J., and M. A. Ballester (2017b): "Monotone stochastic choice models: The case of risk and time preferences," *Journal of Political Economy*, 126(1), 74–106. 59

Apesteguia, J., M. A. Ballester, and J. Lu (2017): "Single-crossing random utility models," *Econometrica*. 43

Apostol, T. M. (1969): *Calculus*, vol. 2. John Wiley & Sons, New York, 2nd edn. 144, 175

Arrow, K. J. (1959): "Rational choice functions and orderings," *Economica*, 26(102), 121–127. 5

Arrow, K. J., D. Blackwell, and M. Girshick (1949): "Bayes and minimax solutions of sequential decision problems," *Econometrica*, 17, 213–244. 125

Audley, R. (1960): "A stochastic model for individual choice behavior," *Psychological Review*, 67(1), 1. 132

Aumann, R. J., and L. Savage (1987): "Letter from Robert Aumann to Leonard Savage and Letter from Leonard Savage to Robert Aumann," in *Essays on Economic Decisions under Uncertainty*, ed. by J. H. Drèze, pp. 76–78. Cambridge University Press, Cambridge. 74

Auster, S., Y.-K. Che, and K. Mierendorff (2022): "Prolonged learning and Hasty Stopping: The Wald Problem with Ambiguity," 133

Baldassi, C., S. Cerreia-Vioglio, F. Maccheroni, M. Marinacci, and M. Pirazzini (2020): "A behavioral characterization of the drift diffusion model and its multialternative extension for choice under time pressure," *Management Science*, 66(11), 5075–5093. 134

Ballinger, T. P., and N. T. Wilcox (1997): "Decisions, error and heterogeneity," *The Economic Journal*, 107(443), 1090–1105. 9, 61

Bandyopadhyay, T., I. Dasgupta, and P. K. Pattanaik (1999): "Stochastic revealed preference and the theory of demand," *Journal of Economic Theory*, 84(1), 95–110. 4

Barberá, S., and P. Pattanaik (1986): "Falmagne and the rationalizability of stochastic choices in terms of random orderings," *Econometrica*, 54(3), 707–715. 15, 26

Barlow, H. B. (1961): "Possible principles underlying the transformation of sensory messages," *Sensory Communication*, 1(01). 74

Barseghyan, L., M. Coughlin, F. Molinari, and J. C. Teitelbaum (2021): "Heterogeneous choice sets and preferences," *Econometrica*, 89(5), 2015–2048. 155

Barseghyan, L., F. Molinari, T. O'Donoghue, and J. C. Teitelbaum (2013): "The nature of risk preferences: Evidence from insurance choices," *American Economic Review*, 103(6), 2499–2529. 61

——— (2018): "Estimating risk preferences in the field," *Journal of Economic Literature*, 56(2), 501–64. 59

Barseghyan, L., F. Molinari, and M. Thirkettle (2021): "Discrete choice under risk with limited consideration," *American Economic Review*, 111(6), 1972–2006. 155

Becker, G. M., M. H. DeGroot, and J. Marschak (1963): "Stochastic models of choice behavior," *Behavioral Science*, 8(1), 41–55. 52, 57, 59, 156

——— (1964): "Measuring utility by a single-response sequential method," *Behavioral Science*, 9(3), 226–232. 52

Becker, G. S., and K. M. Murphy (1988): "A theory of rational addiction," *The Journal of Political Economy*, pp. 675–700. 105

Ben-Akiva, M., and B. Boccara (1995): "Discrete choice models with latent choice sets," *International Journal of Research in Marketing*, 12(1), 9–24. 155

Ben-Akiva, M., and S. R. Lerman (1985): *Discrete Choice Analysis*. MIT Press, Cambridge, MA. 42

Bergemann, D., and S. Morris (2016): "Bayes correlated equilibrium and the comparison of information structures in games," *Theoretical Economics*, 11(2), 487–522. 68

Bergemann, D., and J. Välimäki (2002): "Information acquisition and efficient mechanism design," *Econometrica*, 70(3), 1007–1033. 84

Berry, S., J. Levinsohn, and A. Pakes (1995): "Automobile prices in market equilibrium," *Econometrica*, 63(4), 841–890. 142, 149

Berry, S., O. B. Linton, and A. Pakes (2004): "Limit theorems for estimating the parameters of differentiated product demand systems," *The Review of Economic Studies*, 71(3), 613–654. 148

Berry, S., and A. Pakes (2007): "The pure characteristics demand model," *International Economic Review*, 48(4), 1193–1225. 147, 149

Berry, S. T. (1994): "Estimating discrete-choice models of product differentiation," *The RAND Journal of Economics*, 242–262. Discussion paper number 15276. 140, 142, 149

Berry, S. T., and P. A. Haile (2009): "Nonparametric identification of multinomial choice demand models with heterogeneous consumers," Discussion paper, National Bureau of Economic Research. 149

——— (2014): "Identification in differentiated products markets using market level data," *Econometrica*, 82(5), 1749–1797. 149

——— (2021): "Foundations of demand estimation," in *Handbook of Industrial Organization*, eds. Ho, K., Hortacsu, A., & Lizzeri, A., Elsevier North-Holland. 145, 149

Blackwell, D. (1951): "Comparison of experiments, proceedings of the second berkeley symposium on mathematical statistics and probability," ed. by J. Neyman vol. 4, pp. 1–62. Elsevier, University of California Press Berkeley and Los Angeles. 64, 77, 84, 172

——— (1953): "Equivalent comparisons of experiments," *The Annals of Mathematical Statistics*, 44(11), 265–272. 172

Blavatskyy, P. R. (2008): "Stochastic utility theorem," *Journal of Mathematical Economics*, 44(11), 1049–1056. 57

Block, D., and J. Marschak (1960): "Random orderings and stochastic theories of responses," in *Contributions to Probability and Statistics*, pp. 97–132, ed. by G. Olkin, M. Hoeffding Stanford University Press, Stanford. 12, 21, 23, 24, 26, 52

Bloedel, A. W., and W. Zhong (2021): "The cost of optimally-acquired information," *mimeo*. 91, 93

Blume, L. E. (2008): "Duality," in *The New Palgrave Dictionary of Economics*. New York: Palgrave Macmillan. Available at: www.dictionaryofeconomics.com/article. 174

Bogacz, R., E. Brown, J. Moehlis, P. Holmes, and J. D. Cohen (2006): "The physics of optimal decision making: A formal analysis of models of performance in two-alternative forced-choice tasks," *Psychological Review*, 113(4), 700. 7, 131, 133

Bohnenblust, H. F., L. S. Shapley, and S. Sherman (1949): *Reconnaissance in Game Theory*. Rand Corporation, Santa Monica, CA. 84, 172

Bordalo, P., N. Gennaioli, and A. Shleifer (2012): "Salience theory of choice under risk," *Quarterly Journal of Economics*, 127, 1243–1285. 8

——— (2013): "Salience and consumer choice," *Journal of Political Economy*, 121(5), 803–843. 151

——— (2020): "Memory, attention, and choice," *The Quarterly Journal of Economics*, 1399, 1399–1442. 156

Boyd, J. H., and R. E. Mellman (1980): "The effect of fuel economy standards on the US automotive market: An hedonic demand analysis," *Transportation Research Part A: General*, 14(5–6), 367–378. 146

Brady, R. L., and J. Rehbeck (2016): "Menu-dependent stochastic feasibility," *Econometrica*, 84(3), 1203–1223. 153

Branco, F., M. Sun, and J. M. Villas-Boas (2012): "Optimal search for product information," *Management Science*, 58(11), 2037–2056. 133

Brehm, J. W. (1956): "Postdecision changes in the desirability of alternatives," *The Journal of Abnormal and Social Psychology*, 52(3), 384. 106

Brown, S. D., and A. Heathcote (2008): "The simplest complete model of choice response time: Linear ballistic accumulation," *Cognitive Psychology*, 57(3), 153–178. 133

Brownstone, D., and K. Train (1998): "Forecasting new product penetration with flexible substitution patterns," *Journal of Econometrics*, 89(1–2), 109–129. 146

Bucher, S., and A. Brandenburger (2021): "Divisive normalization is an efficient code for multivariate Pareto-distributed environments," in *50th Annual Meeting of the Society for Neuroscience (Neuroscience 2021)*. 74

Buchholz, N., L. Doval, J. Kastl, F. Matějka, and T. Salz (2020): "The value of time: Evidence from auctioned cab rides," Discussion paper, National Bureau of Economic Research. 139

Busemeyer, J. R., and J. T. Townsend (1993): "Decision field theory: A dynamic-cognitive approach to decision making in an uncertain environment," *Psychological Review*, 100(3), 432. 133

Calastri, C., S. Hess, C. Choudhury, A. Daly, and L. Gabrielli (2019): "Mode choice with latent availability and consideration: Theory and a case study," *Transportation Research Part B: Methodological*, 123, 374–385. 155

Callaway, F., A. Rangel, and T. L. Griffiths (2020): "Fixation patterns in simple choice reflect optimal information sampling," *PLoS Computational Biology*, 17(3), e1008863. 132

Camerer, C. F. (1989): "An experimental test of several generalized utility theories," *Journal of Risk and Uncertainty*, 2(1), 61–104. 9

Campbell, J. Y., and J. H. Cochrane (1999): "By force of habit: A consumption-based explanation of aggregate stock market behavior," *Journal of Political Economy*, 107, 205–251. 105

Cantillo, V., and J. de Dios Ortúzar (2005): "A semi-compensatory discrete choice model with explicit attribute thresholds of perception," *Transportation Research Part B: Methodological*, 39(7), 641–657. 155

Caplin, A. (2016): "Measuring and modeling attention," *Annual Review of Economics*, 8, 379–403. 95

Caplin, A., and M. Dean (2013): "Behavioral implications of rational inattention with shannon entropy," Discussion paper, National Bureau of Economic Research. 89

——— (2015): "Revealed preference, rational inattention, and costly information acquisition," *The American Economic Review*, 105(7), 2183–2203. 93, 94, 95

Caplin, A., M. Dean, and J. Leahy (2017): "Rationally inattentive behavior: Characterizing and generalizing Shannon entropy," Working Paper 23652, National Bureau of Economic Research. 94, 95

——— (2019): "Rational inattention, optimal consideration sets, and stochastic choice," *The Review of Economic Studies*, 86(3), 1061–1094. 151

——— (2022): "Rationally inattentive behavior: Characterizing and generalizing Shannon entropy," *Journal of Political Economy*, 130(6), 000–000. 90, 95

Caplin, A., and D. Martin (2015): "A testable theory of imperfect perception," *The Economic Journal*, 125(582), 184–202. 68

——— (2016): "The dual-process drift diffusion model: Evidence from response times," *Economic Inquiry*, 54(2), 1274–1282. 121

Cardell, N. S., and F. C. Dunbar (1980): "Measuring the societal impacts of automobile downsizing," *Transportation Research Part A: General*, 14(5–6), 423–434. 146

Cascetta, E., and A. Papola (2001): "Random utility models with implicit availability/perception of choice alternatives for the simulation of travel demand," *Transportation Research Part C: Emerging Technologies*, 9(4), 249–263. 155

Cattaneo, M. D., X. Ma, Y. Masatlioglu, and E. Suleymanov (2020): "A random attention model," *Journal of Political Economy*, 128(7), 2796–2836. 153, 154

Cerreia-Vioglio, S., D. Dillenberger, and P. Ortoleva (2015): "Cautious expected utility and the certainty effect," *Econometrica*, 83(2), 693–728. 52

Cerreia-Vioglio, S., D. Dillenberger, P. Ortoleva, and G. Riella (2019): "Deliberately stochastic," *American Economic Review*, 109(7), 2425–45. 60

Cerreia-Vioglio, S., F. Maccheroni, M. Marinacci, and A. Rustichini (2017): "Multinomial logit processes and preference discovery: Inside and outside the black box." *The Review of Economic Studies* 90(3): 1155–1194. 30

Chade, H., and E. Schlee (2002): "Another look at the Radner–Stiglitz nonconcavity in the value of information," *Journal of Economic Theory*, 107(2), 421–452. 86

Chamberlain, G. (1984): "Panel data," *Handbook of Econometrics*, 2, 1247–1318. 157

——— (1993): "Feedback in panel data models," Discussion paper, *mimeo*, Harvard University. 105

——— (2010): "Binary response models for panel data: Identification and information," *Econometrica*, 78(1), 159–168. 157

Chambers, C. P., and F. Echenique (2016): *Revealed Preference Theory*, vol. 56. Cambridge University Press, Cambridge. 25, 26

Chambers, C. P., C. Liu, and J. Rehbeck (2020): "Costly information acquisition," *Journal of Economic Theory*, 186, 104979. 95

Chambers, C. P., Y. Masatlioglu, and C. Turansick (2021): "Correlated choice," *arXiv preprint arXiv:2103.05084*. 102, 105

(in press): "Correlated choice," *Theoretical Economics*. 102, 103

Chang, H., Y. Narita, and K. Saito (2022): "Approximating choice data by discrete choice models," *mimeo*. 146

Che, Y.-K., and K. Mierendorff (2019): "Optimal dynamic allocation of attention," *American Economic Review*, 109(8), 2993–3029. 91, 135

Chen, M. K. (2008): "Rationalization and cognitive dissonance: Do choices affect or reflect preferences?" *Cowles Foundation Discussion Paper No. 1669*. 106

Chen, M. K., and J. L. Risen (2010): "How choice affects and reflects preferences: Revisiting the free-choice paradigm," *Journal of Personality and Social Psychology*, 99(4), 573. 106

Chernoff, H. (1954): "Rational selection of decision functions," *Econometrica*, 22(4), 422–443. 5

(1961): "Sequential tests for the mean of a normal distribution," in *Proceedings of the Fourth Berkeley Symposium on Mathematical Statistics and Probability*, vol. 1, pp. 79–91. University of California Press, Berkeley, CA. 130

Chew, S. H. (1983): "A generalization of the quasilinear mean with applications to the measurement of income inequality and decision theory resolving the Allais paradox," *Econometrica*, 51(4), 1065–1092. 52

Chew, S. H., L. G. Epstein, and U. Segal (1991): "Mixture symmetry and quadratic utility," *Econometrica*, 59(1), 139–163. 52

Chiong, K., M. Shum, R. Webb, and R. Chen (2018): "Split-second decision-making in the field: Response times in mobile advertising," *Available at SSRN*. 132

Chiong, K. X., A. Galichon, and M. Shum (2016): "Duality in dynamic discrete-choice models," *Quantitative Economics*, 7(1), 83–115. 142

Cicchini, G. M., G. Anobile, and D. C. Burr (2014): "Compressive mapping of number to space reflects dynamic encoding mechanisms, not static logarithmic transform," *Proceedings of the National Academy of Sciences*, 111(21), 7867–7872. 72

Clark, S. A. (1996): "The random utility model with an infinite choice space," *Economic Theory*, 7(1), 179–189. 25, 26

Clithero, J. A., and A. Rangel (2013): "Combining Response times and choice data using a neuroeconomic model of the decision process improves out-of-sample predictions," *mimeo*. 127

Cohen, M., and J.-C. Falmagne (1990): "Random utility representation of binary choice probabilities: A new class of necessary conditions," *Journal of Mathematical Psychology*, 34(1), 88–94. 41

Cohen, M. A. (1980): "Random utility systems – The infinite case," *Journal of Mathematical Psychology*, 22(1), 1–23. 13, 26

Constantinides, G. M. (1990): "Habit formation: A resolution of the equity premium puzzle," *Journal of Political Economy*, 98(3), 519–543. 105

Cooke, K. (2017): "Preference discovery and experimentation," *Theoretical Economics*, 12(3), 1307–1348. 121

Cover, T. M., and J. A. Thomas (2006): *Elements of Information Theory*. John Wiley and Sons, New York, 2nd edn. 88, 89, 93

Crawford, G. S., R. Griffith, and A. Iaria (2021): "A survey of preference estimation with unobserved choice set heterogeneity," *Journal of Econometrics*, 222(1), 4–43. 154

Crawford, G. S., and M. Shum (2005): "Uncertainty and learning in pharmaceutical demand," *Econometrica*, 73(4), 1137–1173. 106

Dagsvik, J. K. (1995): "How large is the class of generalized extreme value random utility models?" *Journal of Mathematical Psychology*, 39(1), 90–98. 36

—— (2008): "Axiomatization of stochastic models for choice under uncertainty," *Mathematical Social Sciences*, 55(3), 341–370. 57

—— (2015): "Stochastic models for risky choices: A comparison of different axiomatizations," *Journal of Mathematical Economics*, 60, 81–88. 57

Daly, A., and S. Zachary (1975): "Commuters' values of time," *LGORU Report T55, Reading.* 146

—— (1979): "Improved multiple choice models," in *Identifying and Measuring the Determinants of Mode Choice*, ed. by D. Hensher, and Q. Dalvi, pp. 335–357. Teakfield, London. 142

van Damme, E. (1991): *Stability and Perfection of Nash Equilibria.* Springer, New York. 41

van Damme, E., and J. Weibull (2002): "Evolution in games with endogenous mistake probabilities," *Journal of Economic Theory*, 106(2), 296–315. 149

Davidson, D., and J. Marschak (1959): "Experimental tests of stochastic decision theory," in *Measurement Definitions and Theories*, ed. by C. W. Churchman. John Wiley & Sons. 38

De Clippel, G., and K. Rozen (2021): "Bounded rationality and limited data sets," *Theoretical Economics*, 16(2), 359–380. 21

De Jong, G., A. Daly, M. Pieters, and T. Van der Hoorn (2007): "The logsum as an evaluation measure: Review of the literature and new results," *Transportation Research Part A: Policy and Practice*, 41(9), 874–889. 31

de Oliveira, H. (2019): "Axiomatic foundations for entropic costs of attention," Discussion paper, *mimeo*. 84

De Oliveira, H., T. Denti, M. Mihm, and M. K. Ozbek (2016): "Rationally inattentive preferences and hidden information costs," *Theoretical Economics*, 12(2), 2–14. 84, 95

De Palma, A., M. Ben-Akiva, D. Brownstone, C. Holt, T. Magnac, D. McFadden, P. Moffatt, N. Picard, K. Train, and P. Wakker (2008): "Risk, uncertainty and discrete choice models," *Marketing Letters*, 19(3–4), 269–285. 61

Dean, M., and N. L. Neligh (2023): "Experimental tests of rational inattention," *Journal of Political Economy*, 131(12), 3415–3461. 7, 83, 85, 95

Debreu, G. (1958): "Stochastic choice and cardinal utility," *Econometrica*, 26(3), 440–444. 38, 169

Debreu, G. (1960): "Review of RD Luce, individual choice behavior: A theoretical analysis," *American Economic Review*, 50(1), 186–188. 32

Dekel, E. (1986): "An axiomatic characterization of preferences under uncertainty: Weakening the independence axiom," *Journal of Economic Theory*, 40(2), 304–318. 52

Dekel, E., B. Lipman, and A. Rustichini (2001): "Representing preferences with a unique subjective state space," *Econometrica*, 69(4), 891–934. 116

Dekel, E., B. L. Lipman, and A. Rustichini (2009): "Temptation-driven preferences," *The Review of Economic Studies*, 76(3), 937–971. 162

Dekel, E., B. L. Lipman, A. Rustichini, and T. Sarver (2007): "Representing preferences with a unique subjective state space: A corrigendum," *Econometrica*, 75(2), 591–600. 116

DellaVigna, S. (2018): "Structural Behavioral Economics," in *Handbook of Behavioral Economics: Applications and Foundations 1*, vol. 1, pp. 613–723, ed. by B. Douglas Bernheim, Stefano DellaVigna, and David Laibson. Elsevier, Amsterdam. 61

Deming, D. J. (2011): "Better schools, less crime?" *The Quarterly Journal of Economics*, 126(4), 2063–2115 qjr036. 108

Deming, D. J., J. S. Hastings, T. J. Kane, and D. O. Staiger (2014): "School choice, school quality, and postsecondary attainment," *The American Economic Review*, 104(3), 991–1013. 108

Denti, T. (2022): "Posterior-separable cost of information," Discussion paper. 69, 95

Denti, T. (2023): *Private Communication*. 95

Denti, T., M. Marinacci, and A. Rustichini (2022a): "Experimental cost of information," *American Economic Review*, 112, 3106–3123. 66, 91

(2022b): "The experimental order on random posteriors," *mimeo*. 93

Dew, R., A. Ansari, and Y. Li (2020): "Modeling dynamic heterogeneity using Gaussian processes," *Journal of Marketing Research*, 57(1), 55–77. 101

Dillenberger, D., J. S. Lleras, P. Sadowski, and N. Takeoka (2014): "A theory of subjective learning," *Journal of Economic Theory*, 152, 287–312. 117

Doval, L. (2018): "Whether or not to open Pandora's box," *Journal of Economic Theory*, 175, 127–158. 121

Doya, K., S. Ishii, A. Pouget, and Rajesh P. N. Rao (eds) (2007): *Bayesian Brain: Probabilistic Approaches to Neural Coding*. The MIT Press, Cambridge, MA.

Drugowitsch, J., R. Moreno-Bote, A. K. Churchland, M. N. Shadlen, and A. Pouget (2012): "The cost of accumulating evidence in perceptual decision making," *The Journal of Neuroscience*, 32(11), 3612–3628. 7, 130

Dubé, J.-P., G. J. Hitsch, and P. E. Rossi (2010): "State dependence and alternative explanations for consumer inertia," *The RAND Journal of Economics*, 41(3), 417–445. 101

Duraj, J. (2018): "Dynamic random subjective expected utility," Discussion paper. 77

Duraj, J., and Y.-H. Lin (2019): "Costly information and random choice," Discussion paper. 134

(2021): "Identification and welfare evaluation in sequential sampling models," *Theory and Decision* 92, 407–431. 134

Dwenger, N., D. Kübler, and G. Weizsäcker (2018): "Flipping a coin: Evidence from university applications," *Journal of Public Economics*, 167, 240–250. 60

Echenique, F., and K. Saito (2019): "General Luce model," *Economic Theory*, 68(4), 811–826. 30

Echenique, F., K. Saito, and G. Tserenjigmid (2018): "The perception-adjusted Luce model," *Mathematical Social Sciences*, 93, 67–76. 156

Edwards, W. (1965): "Optimal strategies for seeking information: Models for statistics, choice reaction times, and human information processing," *Journal of Mathematical Psychology*, 2(2), 312–329. 126

Einav, L., A. Finkelstein, S. P. Ryan, P. Schrimpf, and M. R. Cullen (2013): "Selection on moral hazard in health insurance," *American Economic Review*, 103(1), 178–219. 59

Ellis, A. (2018): "Foundations for optimal inattention," *Journal of Economic Theory*, 173, 56–94. 95

Enke, B., and T. Graeber (2019): "Cognitive uncertainty," Discussion paper, National Bureau of Economic Research. 81

Epstein, L. G., and S. Ji (2020): "Optimal learning under robustness and time-consistency," *Operations Research*, 70(3), 1317–1329. 133

Epstein, L. G., and S. Zin (1989): "Substitution, risk aversion, and the temporal behavior of consumption and asset returns: A theoretical framework," *Econometrica*, 57(4), 937–969. 119

Erdem, T., and M. P. Keane (1996): "Decision-making under uncertainty: Capturing dynamic brand choice processes in turbulent consumer goods markets," *Marketing Science*, 15(1), 1–20. 106

Ergin, H. (2003): "Costly contemplation," *mimeo*. 84

Ergin, H., and T. Sarver (2010): "A unique costly contemplation representation," *Econometrica*, 78(4), 1285–1339. 84

Falmagne, J. (1978): "A representation theorem for finite random scale systems," *Journal of Mathematical Psychology*, 18(1), 52–72. 26, 27

Falmagne, J.-C. (1983): "A random utility model for a belief function," *Synthese*, 57(1), 35–48. 14

Fechner, Gustav, T. (1860): *Elemente der psychophysik*, 2 Vols. Breitkopf und Haïtel, Leipzig. 7

Fehr, E., and A. Rangel (2011): "Neuroeconomic foundations of economic choice – Recent advances," *The Journal of Economic Perspectives*, 25(4), 3–30. 120

Feldman, P., and J. Rehbeck (2022): "Revealing a preference for mixtures: An experimental study of risk," *Quantitative Economics*, 13(2), 761–786. 57

Feller, W. (1957): *An Introduction to Probability Theory and Its Applications*, vol. 2. John Wiley & Sons, New York, 2nd edn. 32, 127

Fenchel, W. (1953): *Convex cones, sets, and functions*. Lecture notes, Princeton University, Department of Mathematics. From notes taken by D. W. Blackett, Spring 1951. 144, 175

Fiorini, S. (2004): "A short proof of a theorem of Falmagne," *Journal of Mathematical Psychology*, 48(1), 80–82. 24, 26

Fishburn, P. (1970): *Utility Theory for Decision Making*, John Wiley & Sons, Inc. New York. 74

——— (1998): "Stochastic utility," in *Handbook of Utility Theory: Volume 1: Principles*, p. 273, ed. by Salvador Barbera, Peter Hammond, and Christian Seidl. Springer, Amsterdam. 27

Flynn, J. P., and K. A. Sastry (2023): "Strategic mistakes," *Journal of Economic Theory*, 212, 105704. 43

Fosgerau, M., D. McFadden, and M. Bierlaire (2013): "Choice probability generating functions," *Journal of Choice Modelling*, 8, 1–18. 144, 174

Fosgerau, M., E. Melo, A. De Palma, and M. Shum (2020): "Discrete choice and rational inattention: A general equivalence result," *International Economic Review*, 61(4), 1569–1589. 148

Fox, J. T., K. il Kim, S. P. Ryan, and P. Bajari (2011): "A simple estimator for the distribution of random coefficients," *Quantitative Economics*, 2(3), 381–418. 146

Fox, J. T., K. il Kim, S. P. Ryan, and P. Bajari (2012): "The random coefficients logit model is identified," *Journal of Econometrics*, 166(2), 204–212. 146

Fox, J. T., K. il Kim, and C. Yang (2016): "A simple nonparametric approach to estimating the distribution of random coefficients in structural models," *Journal of Econometrics*, 195(2), 236–254. 146

Frick, M. (2016): "Monotone threshold representations," *Theoretical Economics*, 11(3), 757–772. 37

Frick, M., R. Iijima, and T. Strzalecki (2019): "Dynamic random utility," *Econometrica*, 87(6), 1941–2002. 56, 105, 110, 119, 163, 165

Frydman, C., and L. J. Jin (2022): "Efficient coding and risky choice," *The Quarterly Journal of Economics*, 137(1), 161–213. 81

Fudenberg, D., R. Iijima, and T. Strzalecki (2014): "Stochastic choice and revealed perturbed utility," Working Paper version. 36, 43

——— (2015): "Stochastic choice and revealed perturbed utility," *Econometrica*, 83(6), 2371–2409. 29, 43

Fudenberg, D., and D. K. Levine (1995): "Consistency and cautious fictitious play," *Journal of Economic Dynamics and Control*, 19, 1065–1089. 41

Fudenberg, D., and D. K. Levine (1998): *The Theory of Learning in Games*. MIT Press, Cambridge, MA. 15

Fudenberg, D., W. Newey, P. Strack, and T. Strzalecki (2020): "Testing the drift-diffusion model," *Proceedings of the National Academy of Sciences*, 117(52), 33141–33148. 134

Fudenberg, D., P. Strack, and T. Strzalecki (2015): "Stochastic choice and optimal sequential sampling," *arXiv preprint arXiv:1505.03342*. 127

——— (2018): "Speed, accuracy, and the optimal timing of choices," *American Economic Review*, 108, 3651–3684. 129, 130, 131, 135

Fudenberg, D., and T. Strzalecki (2015): "Dynamic logit with choice aversion," *Econometrica*, 83(2), 651–691. 161, 162, 165

Gabaix, X., and D. Laibson (2017): "Myopia and Discounting," 81

Gaia Lombardi, Ernst Fehr, T. H. (2020): "Attentional foundations of framing effects," *mimeo*. 132

Gentzkow, M., and E. Kamenica (2014): "Costly persuasion," *American Economic Review: Papers & Proceedings*, 104(5), 457–62. 91

Gescheider, G. (1997): *Psychophysics: The Fundamentals*. L. Erlbaum Associates, Mahwah, NJ. 8, 71

Gibbard, P. (2021): "Disentangling preferences and limited attention: Random-utility models with consideration sets," *Journal of Mathematical Economics*, 94, 102468. 154

Gilboa, I. (1990): "A necessary but insufficient condition for the stochastic binary choice problem," *Journal of Mathematical Psychology*, 34(4), 371–392. 41

Gilboa, I., and A. Pazgal (2001): "Cumulative discrete choice," *Marketing Letters*, 12(2), 119–130. 105

Gilboa, I., A. Postlewaite, and L. Samuelson (2016): "Memorable consumption," *Journal of Economic Theory*, 165, 414–455. 106

Gilboa, I., and D. Schmeidler (1989): "Maxmin expected utility with non-unique prior," *Journal of Mathematical Economics*, 18(2), 141–153. 85

Gittins, J., K. Glazebrook, and R. Weber (2011): *Multi-armed Bandit Allocation Indices*. John Wiley & Sons, New York. 121

Gittins, J. C. (1979): "Bandit processes and dynamic allocation indices," *Journal of the Royal Statistical Society: Series B (Methodological)*, 41(2), 148–164. 121

Goeree, M. S. (2008): "Limited information and advertising in the US personal computer industry," *Econometrica*, 76(5), 1017–1074. 155

Gold, J. I., and M. N. Shadlen (2007): "The neural basis of decision making," *Annual Review of Neuroscience*, 30, 535–574. 120

Gonczarowski, Y. A., S. D. Kominers, and R. I. Shorrer (2020): "Infinity and beyond: Scaling economic theories via logical compactness," 26, 95

Gowrisankaran, G., and M. Rysman (2012): "Dynamics of consumer demand for new durable goods," *mimeo*. 159

Grandmont, J.-M. (1972): "Continuity properties of a von Neumann-Morgenstern utility," *Journal of Economic Theory*, 4(1), 45–57. 48

Gravner, J. (2017): *Lecture Notes for Introductory Probability*. 174

Green, D. M., and J. A. Swets (1966): *Signal Detection Theory and Psychophysics*, vol. 1. Wiley, New York. 71

Greenwald, A. G., D. E. McGhee, and J. L. Schwartz (1998): "Measuring individual differences in implicit cognition: The implicit association test," *Journal of Personality and Social Psychology*, 74(6), 1464. 120

Griliches, Z. (1961): "Hedonic Price Indexes for Automobiles: An Econometric of Quality Change," in *The Price Statistics of the Federal Government*, pp. 173–196. NBER, Cambridge, MA. 139

Gul, F. (1991): "A theory of disappointment aversion," *Econometrica*, 59(3), 667–686. 52

Gul, F., P. Natenzon, and W. Pesendorfer (2014): "Random choice as behavioral optimization," *Econometrica*, 82(5), 1873–1912. 29, 31, 34, 35, 36, 156, 162

Gul, F., and W. Pesendorfer (2001): "Temptation and self-control," *Econometrica*, 69(6), 1403–1435. 115, 162, 165

(2004): "Self-control and the theory of consumption," *Econometrica*, 72(1), 119–158. 109

(2006): "Random expected utility," *Econometrica*, 74(1), 121–146. 14, 53, 55, 56

(2007): "Harmful addiction," *The Review of Economic Studies*, 74(1), 147–172. 105

(2013): "Random utility maximization with indifference," *mimeo*. 15

Handel, B. R. (2013): "Adverse selection and inertia in health insurance markets: When nudging hurts," *The American Economic Review*, 103(7), 2643–2682. 59

Hanes, D. P., and J. D. Schall (1996): "Neural control of voluntary movement initiation," *Science*, 274(5286), 427–430. 73

Hansen, L. P., and T. J. Sargent (2008): *Robustness*. Princeton University Press, Princeton. 85

Harless, D. W., and C. F. Camerer (1994): "The predictive utility of generalized expected utility theories," *Econometrica*, 62(6), 1251–1289. 37, 61

Harmon-Jones, E. E., and J. E. Mills (1999): "Cognitive dissonance: Progress on a pivotal theory in social psychology," in *Scientific Conferences Program, 1997, U Texas, Arlington, TX, US; This volume is based on papers presented at a 2-day conference at the University of Texas at Arlington, Winter 1997*. American Psychological Association. 106

Harsanyi, J. (1973a): "Games with randomly disturbed payoffs: A new rationale for mixed-strategy equilibrium points," *International Journal of Game Theory*, 2(1), 1–23. 9

(1973b): "Oddness of the number of equilibrium points: A new proof," *International Journal of Game Theory*, 2(1), 235–250. 42

Hauser, J. R., and B. Wernerfelt (1990): "An evaluation cost model of consideration sets," *Journal of Consumer Research*, 16(4), 393–408. 151

Hausman, J. A., and D. McFadden (1984): "Specification tests for the multinomial logit model, Econometrica 52(5), 1219–1240. 30, 139

Hausman, J. A., and D. A. Wise (1978): "A conditional probit model for qualitative choice: Discrete decisions recognizing interdependence and heterogeneous preferences," *Econometrica*, 46(2), 403–426. 146

He, J., and P. Natenzon (2024): "Moderate utility," *American Economic Review: Insights*, 6(2), 176–195. 40, 41

Hébert, B., and M. Woodford (2017): "Rational inattention and sequential information sampling," Discussion paper, National Bureau of Economic Research. 134

  (2021): "Neighborhood-based information costs," *American Economic Review*, 111(10), 3225–3255. 93

Heckman, J. J. (1981): "Heterogeneity and state dependence," in *Studies in Labor Markets*, pp. 91–140, ed. by Sherwin Rosen. University of Chicago Press, Chicago. 105, 107

Heiss, F., D. McFadden, J. Winter, A. Wuppermann, and B. Zhou (2016): "Inattention and switching costs as sources of inertia in medicare Part D," Discussion paper, National Bureau of Economic Research. 155

Hendel, I., and A. Nevo (2006): "Measuring the implications of sales and consumer inventory behavior," *Econometrica*, 74(6), 1637–1673. 159

Hey, J. D., and E. Carbone (1995): "Stochastic choice with deterministic preferences: An experimental investigation," *Economics Letters*, 47(2), 161–167. 60

Hey, J. D., and C. Orme (1994): "Investigating generalizations of expected utility theory using experimental data," *Econometrica*, 62(6), 1291–1326. 9, 61

Ho, K., J. Hogan, and F. Scott Morton (2017): "The impact of consumer inattention on insurer pricing in the Medicare Part D program," *The RAND Journal of Economics*, 48(4), 877–905. 155

Ho, K., and R. S. Lee (2017): "Insurer competition in health care markets," *Econometrica*, 85(2), 379–417. 59

Ho, K., and R. S. Lee (2020): "Health Insurance menu design for large employers," Working Paper 27868, National Bureau of Economic Research. 59

Hofbauer, J., and W. Sandholm (2002): "On the global convergence of stochastic fictitious play," *Econometrica*, 70(6), 2265–2294. 15, 144, 149, 150

Honoré, B. E., and E. Kyriazidou (2000): "Panel data discrete choice models with lagged dependent variables," *Econometrica*, 68(4), 839–874. 105

Honoré, B. E., and E. Tamer (2006): "Bounds on parameters in panel dynamic discrete choice models," *Econometrica*, 74(3), 611–629. 161

Horan, S. (2019): "Random consideration and choice: A case study of 'default' options," *Mathematical Social Sciences*, 102, 73–84. 152

  (2021): "Stochastic semi-orders," *Journal of Economic Theory*, 192, 105–171. 30

Hortaçsu, A., S. A. Madanizadeh, and S. L. Puller (2017): "Power to choose? An analysis of consumer inertia in the residential electricity market," *American Economic Journal: Economic Policy*, 9(4), 192–226. 155

Hotelling, H. (1929): "Stability in competition," *The Economic Journal*, 39(153), 41–57. 9, 147, 174

  (1932): "Edgeworth's taxation paradox and the nature of demand and supply functions," *Journal of Political Economy*, 40(5), 577–616. 143

Hotz, V. J., and R. A. Miller (1993): "Conditional choice probabilities and the estimation of dynamic models," *The Review of Economic Studies*, 60(3), 497–529. 142, 159, 161

Hotz, V. J., R. A. Miller, S. Sanders, and J. Smith (1994): "A simulation estimator for dynamic models of discrete choice," *The Review of Economic Studies*, 61(2), 265–289. 159

Hsiao, C. (2022): *Analysis of Panel Data*. Cambridge University Press, Cambridge. 157

Hu, Y., and M. Shum (2012): "Nonparametric identification of dynamic models with unobserved state variables," *Journal of Econometrics*, 171(1), 32–44. 160

Huber, J., J. W. Payne, and C. Puto (1982): "Adding asymmetrically dominated alternatives: Violations of regularity and the similarity hypothesis," *Journal of Consumer Research*, 9, 90–98. 22

Huber, J., J. W. Payne, and C. P. Puto (2014): "Let's be honest about the attraction effect," *Journal of Marketing Research*, 51(4), 520–525. 22

Hyogo, K. (2007): "A subjective model of experimentation," *Journal of Economic Theory*, 133(1), 316–330. 121

Iyengar, S. S., and M. R. Lepper (2000): "When choice is demotivating: Can one desire too much of a good thing?" *Journal of Personality and Social Psychology*, 79(6), 995–1006. 22

Jaffe, S., and E. G. Weyl (2010): "Linear demand systems are inconsistent with discrete choice," *The BE Journal of Theoretical Economics*, 10(1) (Advances), Article 52. 141

Jazayeri, M., and M. N. Shadlen (2010): "Temporal context calibrates interval timing," *Nature Neuroscience*, 13(8), 1020. 81

Jeuland, A. P. (1979): "Brand choice inertia as one aspect of the notion of brand loyalty," *Management Science*, 25(7), 671–682. 101

Jones, M., and E. N. Dzhafarov (2014): "Unfalsifiability and mutual translatability of major modeling schemes for choice reaction time," *Psychological Review*, 121(1), 1. 127, 133

Jung, C. G. (1910): "The association method," *The American Journal of Psychology*, 21(2), 219–269. 120

Kahana, M. J. (2012): *Foundations of Human Memory*. Oxford University Press USA, New York. 156

Kahneman, D. (2011): *Thinking, Fast and Slow*. Farrar, Straus and Giroux, New York. 121

Kahneman, D., and A. Tversky (1979): "Prospect theory: An analysis of decision under risk," *Econometrica*, 47(2), 263–291. 8, 51, 52

Kallenberg, O. (2001): *Foundations of Modern Probability*. Springer, New York, 2nd edn. 63, 67

Kalouptsidi, M., Y. Kitamura, L. Lima, and E. Souza-Rodrigues (2021): "Counterfactual analysis for structural dynamic discrete choice models," *Review of Economic Studies*. 161

Kalouptsidi, M., P. T. Scott, and E. Souza-Rodrigues (2021): "Identification of counterfactuals in dynamic discrete choice models," *Quantitative Economics*, 12(2), 351–403. 161

Kamenica, E. (2008): "Contextual inference in markets: On the informational content of product lines," *American Economic Review*, 98, 2127–2149. 81

Karni, E., D. Schmeidler, and K. Vind (1983): "On state dependent preferences and subjective probabilities," *Econometrica*, 51(4), 1021–1031. 74

Kasahara, H., and K. Shimotsu (2009): "Nonparametric identification of finite mixture models of dynamic discrete choices," *Econometrica*, 77(1), 135–175. 161

Kashaev, N., and V. H. Aguiar (2021): "A random attention and utility model," *arXiv preprint arXiv:2105.11268*. 154

(2022): "Random rank-dependent expected utility," *Games*, 13(1), 13. 61

Ke, S. (2018): "Rational expectation of mistakes and a measure of error-proneness," *Theoretical Economics*, 13(2), 527–552. 18, 162

Ke, T., and M. Villas-Boas (2016): "Optimal learning before choice," *mimeo*. 135

Ke, T. T., Z.-J. M. Shen, and J. M. Villas-Boas (2016): "Search for information on multiple products," *Management Science*, 62(12), 3576–3603. 134

Keane, M. P. (1997): "Modeling heterogeneity and state dependence in consumer choice behavior," *Journal of Business & Economic Statistics*, 15(3), 310–327. 101

Keller, G., S. Rady, and M. Cripps (2005): "Strategic experimentation with exponential bandits," *Econometrica*, 73(1), 39–68. 121

Khan, S., F. Ouyang, and E. Tamer (2021): "Inference on semiparametric multinomial response models," *Quantitative Economics*, 12(3), 743–777. 142

Khaw, M. W., Z. Li, and M. Woodford (2021): "Cognitive imprecision and small-stakes risk aversion," *The Review of Economic Studies*, 88(4), 1979–2013. 73, 81, 124

Kiani, R., and M. N. Shadlen (2009): "Representation of confidence associated with a decision by neurons in the parietal cortex," *Science*, 324(5928), 759–764. 73

Kitamura, Y., and J. Stoye (2018): "Nonparametric analysis of random utility models," *Econometrica*, 86(6), 1883–1909. 140

Koning, R. H., and G. Ridder (2003): "Discrete choice and stochastic utility maximization," *The Econometrics Journal*, 6(1), 1–27. 28, 141, 145, 174

Koopmans, T. C. (1964): "On the flexibility of future preferences," in *Human Judgments and Optimality*, pp. 243–254, ed. by M. W. Shelly, and G. L. Bryan. John Wiley and Sons, New York. 115

Kovach, M., and E. Suleymanov (2021): "Reference dependence and random attention," *arXiv preprint arXiv:2106.13350*. 153

Kovach, M., and G. Tserenjigmid (2022a): "Behavioral foundations of nested stochastic choice and nested logit," *Journal of Political Economy*, 130(9), 2411–2461. 36

(2022b): "The focal Luce model," *American Economic Journal: Microeconomics*, 14(3), 378–413. 156

Krajbich, I., C. Armel, and A. Rangel (2010): "Visual fixations and the computation and comparison of value in simple choice," *Nature Neuroscience*, 13(10), 1292–1298. 120, 124, 128, 132

Krajbich, I., D. Lu, C. Camerer, and A. Rangel (2012): "The attentional drift-diffusion model extends to simple purchasing decisions," *Frontiers in Psychology*, 3, 193. 128, 132

Krajbich, I., and A. Rangel (2011): "Multialternative drift-diffusion model predicts the relationship between visual fixations and choice in value-based decisions," *Proceedings of the National Academy of Sciences*, 108(33), 13852–13857. 132

Kreps, D., and E. Porteus (1978): "Temporal resolution of uncertainty and dynamic choice theory," *Econometrica*, 46(1), 185–200. 108, 119

Kreps, D. M. (1979): "A representation theorem for 'preference for flexibility'," *Econometrica*, 565–577. 115

(1988): *Notes on the Theory of Choice*, vol. 2. Westview Press, Boulder. 5, 6, 49

Lai, L., and S. J. Gershman (2021): "Policy compression: An information bottleneck in action selection," in *Psychology of Learning and Motivation*, vol. 74, pp. 195–232, ed. by Kara D. Federmeier. Elsevier, New York. 89

Lancaster, K. J. (1966): "A new approach to consumer theory," *Journal of Political Economy*, 74(2), 132–157. 139

Le Cam, L. (1996): "Comparison of experiments: A short review," *Lecture Notes-Monograph Series*, 30, 127–138. 172

Lee, R. S. (2013): "Vertical integration and exclusivity in platform and two-sided markets," *American Economic Review*, 103(7), 2960–3000. 159

Lensman, T. A. (2023): *Private Communication*. 132

Li, R. (2022): "An dynamic random choice," *arXiv:2102.00143v2*. 17, 102, 103

Liang, A., and X. Mu (2020): "Complementary information and learning traps," *The Quarterly Journal of Economics*, 135(1), 389–448. 135

Liang, A., X. Mu, and V. Syrgkanis (2022): "Dynamically aggregating diverse information," *Econometrica*, 90(1), 47–80. 135

Lin, Y.-H. (2018): "Random expected utility with revealed indifference in choice," *mimeo*. 15

———(2019a): "Random non-expected utility: Non-uniqueness," *mimeo*. 61

———(2019b): "Revealed 'Betweenness' preference over lotteries," *mimeo*. 61

———(2022): "Stochastic choice and rational inattention," *Journal of Economic Theory*, 202, 105450. 95

Lipman, B., and W. Pesendorfer (2013): "Temptation," in *Advances in Economics and Econometrics: Tenth World Congress, Volume 1*, pp. 243–288, ed. by Daron Acemoglu, Manuel Arellano, and Eddie Dekel. Cambridge University Press, Cambridge. 115

Loève, M. (1978): "Review: Ju. V. Linnik and I. V. Ostrovskiĭ , Decomposition of random variables and vectors," *Bulletin of the American Mathematical Society*, 84(4), 638–642. 32

Loomes, G. (2005): "Modelling the stochastic component of behaviour in experiments: Some issues for the interpretation of data," *Experimental Economics*, 8(4), 301–323. 58

Loomes, G., and R. Sugden (1995): "Incorporating a stochastic element into decision theories," *European Economic Review*, 39(3–4), 641–648. 55, 57, 59

Lu, J. (2016): "Random choice and private information," *Econometrica*, 84(6), 1983–2027. 15, 76, 79, 95, 159

———(2019): "Bayesian identification: A theory for state-dependent utilities," *American Economic Review*, 109(9), 3192–3228. 76

Lu, J., and K. Saito (2018): "Random intertemporal choice," *Journal of Economic Theory*, 177, 780–815. 119

———(2019): "Repeated choice: A theory of stochastic intertemporal preferences," *mimeo*. 56, 119

———(2022): "Mixed logit and pure characteristics models," *mimeo*. 147

Luce, R. D. (1956): "Semiorders and a theory of utility discrimination," *Econometrica*, 24(2), 178–191. 37

Luce, R. D. (1959): *Individual Choice Behavior*. John Wiley, New York. 29

Luce, R. D. (1986): *Response Times*. Oxford University Press, Oxford. 120, 133

Ma, W. (2018): "Random expected utility theory with a continuum of prizes," *Annals of Operations Research*, 271(2), 787–809. 56

Ma, W. J., K. P. Kording, and D. Goldreich (2022): *Bayesian Models of Perception and Action*. The MIT Press, Cambridge, MA.

Maccheroni, F., M. Marinacci, and A. Rustichini (2006): "Ambiguity aversion, robustness, and the variational representation of preferences," *Econometrica*, 74(6), 1447–1498. 85

Machina, M. J. (1982): "'Expected Utility' analysis without the independence axiom," *Econometrica*, 50(2), 277–323. 52

Machina, M. J. (1985): "Stochastic choice functions generated from deterministic preferences over lotteries," *The Economic Journal*, 95(379), 575–594. 59

Mackowiak, B., F. Matejka, and M. Wiederholt (2018): "Rational inattention: A disciplined behavioral model," *mimeo*, Goethe University Frankfurt. 95

Magnac, T., and D. Thesmar (2002): "Identifying dynamic discrete decision processes," *Econometrica*, 70(2), 801–816. 161

Manski, C. F. (1977): "The structure of random utility models," *Theory and Decision*, 8(3), 229–254. 140, 152

(1987): "Semiparametric analysis of random effects linear models from binary panel data," *Econometrica*, 357–362. 157

(1988): "Identification of binary response models," *Journal of the American Statistical Association*, 83(403), 729–738. 28, 142

(1993): "Dynamic choice in social settings: Learning from the experiences of others," *Journal of Econometrics*, 58(1–2), 121–136. 160

(2003): *Partial Identification of Probability Distributions*. Springer Science & Business Media, New York. 20

(2007): "Partial identification of counterfactual choice probabilities," *International Economic Review*, 48(4), 1393–1410. 20

Manzini, P., and M. Mariotti (2014): "Stochastic choice and consideration sets," *Econometrica*, 82(3), 1153–1176. 29, 152, 153

(2018): 'Dual random utility maximisation,' *Journal of Economic Theory*, 177, 162–182. 156

Manzini, P., M. Mariotti, and H. Petri (2019): "Corrigendum to 'Dual random utility maximisation' [J. Econ. Theory 177 (2018) 162–182]," *Journal of Economic Theory*, 184, 104944. 156

Marley, A. (1989): "A random utility family that includes many of the 'classical' models and has closed form choice probabilities and choice reaction times," *British Journal of Mathematical and Statistical Psychology*, 42(1), 13–36. 133

(1990): "A historical and contemporary perspective on random scale representations of choice probabilities and reaction times," *Journal of Mathematical Psychology*, 34(1), 81–87. 41

(1997): "Probabilistic choice as a consequence of nonlinear (sub) optimization," *Journal of Mathematical Psychology*, 41(4), 382–391. 61

Marley, A. A. J., and H. Colonius (1992): "The 'horse race' random utility model for choice probabilities and reaction times, and its compering risks interpretation," *Journal of Mathematical Psychology*, 36(1), 1–20. 133

Marschak, J. (1959): "Binary choice constraints on random utility indicators," Cowles Foundation Discussion Papers 74, Cowles Foundation for Research in Economics, Yale University. 37, 41

Martins, A., and R. Astudillo (2016): "From softmax to sparsemax: A sparse model of attention and multi-label classification," in *International Conference on Machine Learning*, pp. 1614–1623. PMLR. 42

Mas-Colell, A., M. D. Whinston, J. R. Green, et al. (1995): *Microeconomic Theory*, vol. 1. Oxford University Press, New York. 5

Masatlioglu, Y., D. Nakajima, and E. Y. Ozbay (2012): "Revealed attention," *The American Economic Review*, 102(5), 2183–2205. 151

Matejka, F., and A. McKay (2015): "Rational inattention to discrete choices: A new foundation for the multinomial logit model," *The American Economic Review*, 105(1), 272–298. 89, 95

Mattsson, L.-G., and J. W. Weibull (2002): "Probabilistic choice and procedurally bounded rationality," *Games and Economic Behavior*, 41, 61–78. 149

Matzkin, R. L. (1992): "Nonparametric and distribution-free estimation of the binary threshold crossing and the binary choice models," *Econometrica*, 60(2), 239–270. 142

(1993): "Nonparametric identification and estimation of polychotomous choice models," *Journal of Econometrics*, 58(1–2), 137–168. 142

(2013): "Nonparametric identification in structural economic models," *Annual Review of Economics*, 5(1), 457–486. 142

McAlister, L. (1982): "A dynamic attribute satiation model of variety-seeking behavior," *Journal of Consumer Research*, 9(2), 141–150. 106

McClellon, M. (2015): "Unique random utility representations," Discussion paper. 27

McFadden, D. (1973): "Conditional logit analysis of qualitative choice behavior," in *Frontiers in Econometrics*, pp. 105–142 ed. by P. Zarembka. Institute of Urban and Regional Development, University of California, New York. 15, 17, 18, 139, 141

(1974): "The measurement of urban travel demand," *Journal of Public Economics*, 3(4), 303–328. 7

(1975): "On independence, structure, and simultaneity in transportation demand analysis," Discussion paper. 142

(1978): 'Modeling the choice of residential location', in A. Karlqvist, L. Lundqvist, F. Snickars, and J. Weibull, eds., *Spatial Interaction Theory and Planning Models*, North-Holland, Amsterdam, pp. 75–96. 35

(1981): "Econometric models of probabilistic choice," in *Structural Analysis of Discrete Data*, pp. 198–272 ed. by C. Manski, and D. McFadden. MIT Press, Cambridge, Massachusetts. 35, 36, 140, 142, 144, 174

McFadden, D., and M. Richter (1971): "On the extension of a set function on a set of events to a probability on the generated Boolean σ-algebra," Working Paper, University of California, Berkeley. 25, 26

McFadden, D., and M. Richter (1990): "Stochastic rationality and revealed stochastic preference," in *Preferences, Uncertainty, and Optimality, Essays in Honor of Leo Hurwicz*, pp. 161–186, ed. by J. S. Chipman, D. McFadden, and M. K. Richter, pp. 161–186. Westview Press Inc., Boulder, CO. 25, 26

McFadden, D., and K. Train (2000): "Mixed MNL models for discrete response," *Journal of Applied Econometrics*, 15, 447–470. 34, 146

McFadden, D. L. (2005): "Revealed stochastic preference: A synthesis," *Economic Theory*, 26(2), 245–264. 26, 140

Melkonyan, T., and Z. Safra (2016): "Intrinsic variability in group and individual decision making," *Management Science*, 62(9), 2651–2667. 61

Mellers, B. A., and K. Biagini (1994): "Similarity and choice," *Psychological Review*, 101(3), 505. 58

Mensch, J. (2018): "Cardinal representations of information," *Available at SSRN 3148954*. 91

Miao, J., and H. Xing (2023): "Dynamic discrete choice under rational inattention," *Economic Theory*, 77(3), 1–56. 135

Miller, R. (1984): "Job matching and occupational choice," *The Journal of Political Economy*, 92, 1086–1120. 108, 159

Milosavljevic, M., J. Malmaud, A. Huth, C. Koch, and A. Rangel (2010): "The drift diffusion model can account for value-based choice response times under high and low time pressure," *Judgement & Decision Making*, 5, 437–449. 128

Monderer, D. (1992): "The stochastic choice problem: A game-theoretic approach," *Journal of Mathematical Psychology*, 36(4), 547–554. 26

Morris, S., and P. Strack (2019): "The Wald Problem and the equivalence of sequential sampling and static information costs," *mimeo*. 93, 134

Mosteller, F., and P. Nogee (1951): "An experimental measurement of utility," *Journal of Political Economy*, 59(5), 371–404. 9, 52

Myerson, R. B. (1982): "Optimal coordination mechanisms in generalized principal–agent problems," *Journal of Mathematical Economics*, 10(1), 67–81. 68

Natenzon, P. (2019): "Random choice and learning," *Journal of Political Economy*, 127(1), 419–457. 80

Nevo, A. (2000): "A practitioner's guide to estimation of random-coefficients logit models of demand," *Journal of Economics & Management Strategy*, 9(4), 513–548. 149

Newsome, W. T., K. H. Britten, and J. A. Movshon (1989): "Neuronal correlates of a perceptual decision," *Nature*, 341(6237), 52–54. 7

Nocke, V., and N. Schutz (2017): "Quasi-linear integrability," *Journal of Economic Theory*, 169, 603–628. 175

Norets, A. (2009): "Inference in dynamic discrete choice models with serially orrelated unobserved state variables," *Econometrica*, 77(5), 1665–1682. 160

Norets, A., and X. Tang (2013): "Semiparametric Inference in dynamic binary choice models," *The Review of Economic Studies*, 81(3), 1229–1262. 161

Ok, E. (2014): *Elements of Order Theory*. 6

Ok, E. A., and G. Tserenjigmid (2022): "Indifference, indecisiveness, experimentation, and stochastic choice," *Theoretical Economics*, 17(2), 651–686. 6

Osborne, M. J., and A. Rubinstein (2020): *Models in Microeconomic Theory*. Open Book Publisher, Cambridge. 5

Oud, B., I. Krajbich, K. Miller, J. H. Cheong, M. Botvinick, and E. Fehr (2016): "Irrational time allocation in decision-making," *Proceedings of the Royal Society B: Biological Sciences*, 283(1822), 20151439. 124, 131

Pakes, A. (1986): "Patents as options: Some estimates of the value of holding European patent stocks," *Econometrica*, 54, 755–784. 108, 160, 164

——— (2010): "Alternative models for moment inequalities," *Econometrica*, 78(6), 1783–1822. 142

Pakes, A., J. Porter, K. Ho, and J. Ishii (2015): "Moment inequalities and their application," *Econometrica*, 83(1), 315–334. 142

Pakes, A., J. Porter, M. Shepard, and S. Calder-Wang (2020): "Unobserved heterogeneity, state dependence, and health plan choices," *mimeo*. 106

Pavan, A., I. Segal, and J. Toikka (2014): "Dynamic mechanism design: A myersonian approach," *Econometrica*, 82(2), 601–653. 112

Persico, N. (2000): "Information acquisition in auctions," *Econometrica*, 68(1), 135–148. 84

Petzschner, F. H., and S. Glasauer (2011): "Iterative Bayesian estimation as an explanation for range and regression effects: A study on human path integration," *Journal of Neuroscience*, 31(47), 17220–17229. 72

Piermont, E., and R. Teper (2018): "Disentangling strict and weak choice in random expected utility models," 15

——— (2019): "Exploration and correlation," *Games and Economic Behavior*, 116, 96–104. 121

Pike, A. (1966): "Stochastic models of choice behaviour: Response probabilities and latencies of finite Markov chain systems 1," *British Journal of Mathematical and Statistical Psychology*, 19(1), 15–32. 132

Podczeck, K. (2010): "On existence of rich Fubini extensions," *Economic Theory*, 45(1), 1–22. 57

Polanía, R., M. Woodford, and C. C. Ruff (2019): "Efficient coding of subjective value," *Nature Neuroscience*, 22(1), 134–142. 74

Pollard, D. (2002): *A User's Guide to Measure Theoretic Probability*, vol. 8. Cambridge University Press, Cambridge. 25

Pomatto, L., P. Strack, and O. Tamuz (2023): "The cost of information," *American Economic Review*, 113, 1360–1393. 92, 93

Quiggin, J. (1982): "A theory of anticipated utility," *Journal of Economic Behavior & Organization*, 3(4), 323–343. 52

Radner, R., and J. Stiglitz (1984): "A nonconcavity in the value of information," *Bayesian Models in Economic Theory*, 5(3), 33–52. 86

Raiffa, H. (1968): *Decision Analysis. Introductory Lectures on Choices Under Uncertainty*. Addison-Wesley, Reading, MA. 107

Raiffa, H., and R. Schlaifer (1961): *Applied Statistical Decision Theory*. Division of Research, Harvard Business School, Boston. 84

Rambachan, A. (2021): "Identifying prediction mistakes in observational data," in press, *The Quarterly Journal of Economics*. 70, 71

Ratcliff, R. (1978): "A theory of memory retrieval," *Psychological Review*, 85(2), 59. 126, 131

Ratcliff, R., A. Cherian, and M. Segraves (2003): "A comparison of macaque behavior and superior colliculus neuronal activity to predictions from models of two-choice decisions," *Journal of Neurophysiology*, 90(3), 1392–1407. 73

Ratcliff, R., and G. McKoon (2008): "The diffusion decision model: Theory and data for two-choice decision tasks," *Neural Computation*, 20(4), 873–922. 120, 131

Ratcliff, R., and P. L. Smith (2004): "A comparison of sequential sampling models for two-choice reaction time," *Psychological Review*, 111(2), 333. 131

Regenwetter, M., C. P. Davis-Stober, S. H. Lim, Y. Guo, A. Popova, C. Zwilling, Y.-S. Cha, and W. Messner (2014): "QTest: Quantitative testing of theories of binary choice," *Decision*, 1(1), 2. 61

Regenwetter, M., and A. Marley (2001): "Random relations, random utilities, and random functions," *Journal of Mathematical Psychology*, 45(6), 864–912. 12

Reutskaja, E., R. Nagel, C. F. Camerer, and A. Rangel (2011): "Search dynamics in consumer choice under time pressure: An eye-tracking study," *The American Economic Review*, 101(2), 900–926. 120, 128

Rieskamp, J., J. R. Busemeyer, and B. A. Mellers (2006): "Extending the bounds of rationality: Evidence and theories of preferential choice," *Journal of Economic Literature*, 44(3), 631–661. 41

Rockafellar, R. T. (1966): "Characterization of the subdifferentials of convex functions," *Pacific Journal of Mathematics*, 17(3), 497–510. 174

Rockafellar, R. T. (1970): *Convex Analysis*, no. 28. Princeton University Press, Princeton. 42, 175

Rockafellar, R. T., and R. J.-B. Wets (2009): *Variational Analysis*, vol. 317. Springer Science & Business Media, New York. 175

Roe, R. M., J. R. Busemeyer, and J. T. Townsend (2001): "Multialternative decision field theory: A dynamic connectionist model of decision making," *Psychological Review*, 108(2), 370. 128

Rosenthal, A. (1989): "A bounded-rationality approach to the study of noncooperative games," *International Journal of Game Theory*, 18, 273–292. 42

Roy, R. (1947): "La distribution du revenu entre les divers biens," *Econometrica*, 15(3), 205–225. 143

Rozen, K. (2010): "Foundations of intrinsic habit formation," *Econometrica*, 78(4), 1341–1373. 105

Rubinstein, A. (2007): "Instinctive and cognitive reasoning: A study of response times," *The Economic Journal*, 117(523), 1243–1259. 121

Rubinstein, A., and Y. Salant (2006): "A model of choice from lists," *Theoretical Economics*, 1(1), 3–17. 156

Rudin, W. (1976): *Principles of Mathematical Analysis (3rd edition)*, vol. 3. McGraw-hill, New York. 175

Rust, J. (1987): "Optimal replacement of GMC bus engines: An empirical model of Harold Zurcher," *Econometrica*, 55(5) 999–1033. 108, 159, 163

——— (1989): "A dynamic programming model of retirement behavior," in *The Economics of Aging*, ed. by D. Wise, pp. 359–398. University of Chicago Press, Chicago. 159

——— (1994): "Structural estimation of Markov decision processes," *Handbook of Econometrics*, 4, 3081–3143. 158, 160

Rustichini, A., K. E. Conen, X. Cai, and C. Padoa-Schioppa (2017): "Optimal coding and neuronal adaptation in economic decisions," *Nature Communications*, 8(1), 1–14. 74

Rustichini, A., and P. Siconolfi (2014): "Dynamic theory of preferences: Habit formation and taste for variety," *Journal of Mathematical Economics*, 55, 55–68. 106

Ryan, M. (2015): "A strict stochastic utility theorem," *Economics Bulletin*, 35(4), 2664–2672. 57

Safonov, E. (2017): "Random choice with framing effects: A Bayesian model," *mimeo*. 80, 81

Saito, K. (2018): "Axiomatizations of the mixed Logit model," 146

Samuelson, P. A. (1938): "A note on the pure theory of consumer's behaviour," *Economica*, 5(17), 61–71. 4

Savage, L. J. (1972): *The Foundations of Statistics*. Courier Corporation. 74

Scott, D. (1964): "Measurement structures and linear inequalities," *Journal of Mathematical Psychology*, 1(2), 233–247. 38, 170

Seetharaman, P. (2004): "Modeling multiple sources of state dependence in random utility models: A distributed lag approach," *Marketing Science*, 23(2), 263–271. 101

Sen, A. K. (1971): "Choice functions and revealed preference," *The Review of Economic Studies*, 38(3), 307–317. 5

Shadlen, M. N., T. D. Hanks, A. K. Churchland, R. Kiani, and T. Yang (2006): "The speed and accuracy of a simple perceptual decision: A mathematical primer," in *Bayesian Brain: Probabilistic Approaches to Neural Coding*, pp. 209–237, ed. by Kenji Doya, Shin Ishii, Alexandre Pouget, and Rajesh P. N. Rao. The MIT Press Cambridge, MA. 120

Shaked, M., and J. G. Shanthikumar (2007): *Stochastic Orders*. Springer Science & Business Media, New York. 50

Shi, X., M. Shum, and W. Song (2018): "Estimating semi-parametric panel multinomial choice models using cyclic monotonicity," *Econometrica*, 86(2), 737–761. 143, 145

Shum, M. (2016): *Econometric Models for Industrial Organization*, World Scientific, Singapore. 149, 159

Simon, H. A. (1956): "Rational choice and the structure of the environment," *Psychological Review*, 63(2), 129. 156

Simonson, I. (1989): "Choice based on reasons: The case of attraction and compromise effects," *Journal of Consumer Research*, 16(2), 158–174. 22

Sims, C. A. (2003): "Implications of rational inattention," *Journal of Monetary Economics*, 50(3), 665–690. 84

(2006): "Rational inattention: Beyond the linear-quadratic case," *The American Economic Review*, 96(2), 158–163. 84

(2010): "Rational inattention and monetary economics," in *Handbook of Monetary Economics*, vol. 3, pp. 155–181, ed. By Benjamin M. Friedman and Michael Woodford. Elsevier, Amsterdam. 84

Smeulders, B., L. Cherchye, and B. D. Rock (2021): "Nonparametric analysis of random utility models: Computational tools for statistical testing," *Econometrica*, 89(1). 140

Smith, P. L. (1990): "A note on the distribution of response times for a random walk with Gaussian increments," *Journal of Mathematical Psychology*, 34(4), 445–459. 127

Smith, P. L., and D. Vickers (1988): "The accumulator model of two-choice discrimination," *Journal of Mathematical Psychology*, 32(2), 135–168. 133

Smith, T. E. (1984): "A choice probability characterization of generalized extreme value models," *Applied Mathematics and Computation*, 14(1), 35–62. 145

Soerensen, J. R.-V., and M. Fosgerau (2020): "How McFadden met Rockafellar and learnt to do more with less," Discussion paper. 142

Sopher, B., and J. M. Narramore (2000): "Stochastic choice and consistency in decision making under risk: An experimental study," *Theory and Decision*, 48(4), 323–350. 57

Sprumont, Y. (2020): "The triangular inequalities are su¢ cient for regularity," *mimeo*. 41

Stahl, D. O. (1990): "Entropy control costs and entropic equilibria," *International Journal of Game Theory*, 19, 129–138. 41

Steiner, J., C. Stewart, and F. Matějka (2017): "Rational inattention dynamics: Inertia and delay in decision-making," *Econometrica*, 85(2), 521–553. 89, 134

Stone, M. (1960): "Models for choice-reaction time," *Psychometrika*, 25(3), 251–260. 126

Stoye, J. (2019): "Revealed stochastic preference: A one-paragraph proof and generalization," *Economics Letters*, 177, 66–68. 25, 26

Strack, P., and D. Taubinsky (2021): "Dynamic preference 'Reversals' and time inconsistency," *mimeo*. 119

Strotz, R. H. (1955): "Myopia and inconsistency in dynamic utility maximization," *The Review of Economic Studies*, 23(3), 165–180. 18, 115, 165

Suleymanov, E. (2023): *Private Communication*. 153

Sun, Y. (2006): "The exact law of large numbers via Fubini extension and characterization of insurable risks," *Journal of Economic Theory*, 126(1), 31–69. 57

Swait, J. (2001): "Choice set generation within the generalized extreme value family of discrete choice models," *Transportation Research Part B: Methodological*, 35(7), 643–666. 155

Swait, J., and M. Ben-Akiva (1987): "Incorporating random constraints in discrete models of choice set generation," *Transportation Research Part B: Methodological*, 21(2), 91–102. 155

Swensson, R. G. (1972): "The elusive tradeoff: Speed vs accuracy in visual discrimination tasks," *Perception & Psychophysics*, 12(1), 16–32. 120

Swets, J. A. (1973): "The relative operating characteristic in psychology: A technique for isolating effects of response bias finds wide use in the study of perception and cognition," *Science*, 182(4116), 990–1000. 71

Taber, C. R. (2000): "Semiparametric identification and heterogeneity in discrete choice dynamic programming models," *Journal of Econometrics*, 96(2), 201–229. 161, 164

Tajima, S., J. Drugowitsch, N. Patel, and A. Pouget (2019): "Optimal policy for multi-alternative decisions," *Nature Neuroscience*, 22(9), 1503–1511. 130

Tanner, W. P., and J. A. Swets (1954): "A decision-making theory of visual detection," *Psychological Review*, 61(6), 401. 71

Terry, A., A. Marley, A. Barnwal, E.-J. Wagenmakers, A. Heathcote, and S. D. Brown (2015): "Generalising the drift rate distribution for linear ballistic accumulators," *Journal of Mathematical Psychology*, 68, 49–58. 133

Thurstone, L. (1927): "A law of comparative judgment," *Psychological Review*, 34(4), 273. 7, 9, 17

Todd, P. E., and K. I. Wolpin (2006): "Assessing the impact of a school subsidy program in Mexico: Using a social experiment to validate a dynamic behavioral model of child schooling and fertility," *American Economic Review*, 96(5), 1384–1417. 108

Torgersen, E. (1991): *Comparison of Statistical Experiments*, no. 36. Cambridge University Press, Cambridge. 91, 172

Train, K. (1986): *Choice Analysis: Theory, Econometrics, and an Application to Automobile Demand*, MIT Press, Cambridge, MA. 142

Train, K. (2009): *Discrete Choice Methods with Simulation*. Cambridge University Press, Cambridge, 2nd edn. 36, 168

Turansick, C. (2021): "Identification in the random utility model," *arXiv preprint arXiv:2102.05570*. 27

Tversky, A. (1969): "Intransitivity of preferences," *Psychological Review*, 76, 31–48. 9
    (1972a): "Choice by elimination," *Journal of Mathematical Psychology*, 9, 341–367. 156
    (1972b): "Elimination by aspects: A theory of choice," *Psychological Review*, 79(4), 281–299. 156

Tversky, A., and D. Kahneman (1992): "Advances in prospect theory: Cumulative representation of uncertainty," *Journal of Risk and Uncertainty*, 5(4), 297–323. 52

Tversky, A., and J. E. Russo (1969): "Substitutability and similarity in binary choice," *Journal of Mathematical Psychology*, 6, 1–12. 40

Tversky, A., and R. H. Thaler (1990): "Anomalies: Preference reversals," *Journal of Economic Perspectives*, 4(2), 201–211. 124

Van Lint, J. H., and R. M. Wilson (2001): *A Course in Combinatorics*. Cambridge University Press, Cambridge. 24

Van Nierop, E., B. Bronnenberg, R. Paap, M. Wedel, and P. H. Franses (2010): "Retrieving unobserved consideration sets from household panel data," *Journal of Marketing Research*, 47(1), 63–74. 155

Van Zandt, T. (1996): "Hidden information acquisition and static choice," *Theory and Decision*, 40(3), 235–247. 95

Verstynen, T., and P. N. Sabes (2011): "How each movement changes the next: An experimental and theoretical study of fast adaptive priors in reaching," *Journal of Neuroscience*, 31(27), 10050–10059. 72

Vickers, D. (1970): "Evidence for an accumulator model of psychophysical discrimination," *Ergonomics*, 13(1), 37–58. 132

Von Neumann, J., and O. Morgenstern (1944): *Theory of Games and Economic Behavior*. Princeton University Press, Princeton, NJ. 49

Wald, A. (1947): "Foundations of a general theory of sequential decision functions," *Econometrica*, 15(4), 279. 84

Webb, R. (2019): "The (neural) dynamics of stochastic choice," *Management Science*, 65(1), 230–255. 133

Weitzman, M. L. (1979): "Optimal search for the best alternative," *Econometrica*, 47(3), 641–654. 121

Wen, C.-H., and F. S. Koppelman (2001): "The generalized nested logit model," *Transportation Research Part B: Methodological*, 35(7), 627–641. 155

Wilcox, N. T. (2008): "Stochastic models for binary discrete choice under risk: A critical primer and econometric comparison," in *Risk Aversion in Experiments*, vol. 12, pp. 197–292, ed. by James C. Cox and G. W. Harrison. Emerald Group Publishing Limited, Bingley, UK. 59

——— (2011): "'Stochastically more risk averse:' A contextual theory of stochastic discrete choice under risk," *Journal of Econometrics*, 162(1), 89–104. 59

Williams, D. (1991): *Probability with Martingales*. Cambridge University Press, Cambridge. 73

Williams, H. C. (1977): "On the formation of travel demand models and economic evaluation measures of user benefit," *Environment and Planning A*, 9(3), 285–344. 142

Woodford, M. (2012): "Inattentive valuation and reference-dependent choice," https://doi.org/10.7916/D8VD6XVK. 91, 93

——— (2014): "An optimizing neuroeconomic model of discrete choice," *Working Paper, Columbia University*. 134

——— (2020): "Modeling imprecision in perception, valuation, and choice," *Annual Review of Economics*, 12, 579–601. 81

Woodrow, H. (1933): "Weight-discrimination with a varying standard," *The American Journal of Psychology*, 45(3), 391–416. 8

Yaari, M. E. (1987): "The dual theory of choice under risk," *Econometrica*, 55(1), 95–115. 52

Yang, E., and Kopylov, I. (2023). "Random quasi-linear utility," *Journal of Economic Theory*, 209, 105650. 174

Yegane, E. (2021): "Stochastic choice with limited memory," *mimeo*. 156

Zhong, W. (2022): "Optimal dynamic information acquisition," *Econometrica*, 90(4), 1537–1582. 135

Zwilling, C. E., D. R. Cavagnaro, M. Regenwetter, S. H. Lim, B. Fields, and Y. Zhang (2019): "QTest 2.1: Quantitative testing of theories of binary choice using Bayesian inference," *Journal of Mathematical Psychology*, 91, 176–194. 61

Index

action-recommendation, 68, 93
acyclicity
  cyclic monotonicity, 144, 174
  for APU, 42
  for Fechnerian, 38
  no improving action cycles, 94
  rational mixing, 60
additive perturbed utility
    (APU), 42
additive random expected utility, 52
additive random utility (ARU), 15
  i.i.d. ARU, 16, 31
  independent ARU (IARU), 140
  simple IARU, 141
Ahn–Sarver Theorem, 118
Anscombe–Aumann
  representation of SCF, 76
  theorem, 75
Anscombe–Aumann (AA)
  representation of preferences, 74
attention, 83, 151
attributes, 139

Bayes
  average Bayes representation, 66
  consistency, 77, 94
  plausibility, 65
  representation, 64
  rule, 63
  rule in the Normal-Normal model, 73
Bellman equation, 112
Blackwell theorem, 171
Block–Marschak (BM)
  Axiom, 24
  Polynomials, 24

  Theorem, 24
blue bus–red bus, 32

character recognition, 71
Chernoff model, 130
choice function
  deterministic, 4, 123
  stochastic, see stochastic choice
    function
chronometric function, 127
conditional logit, 141
consideration set, 151, 154
cost
  of waiting, 123, 131
  over experiments, 86, 90, 134
  cyclic monotonicity, see acyclicity

decision tree, 108
Dekel–Lipman–Rustichini (DLR)
  representation, 116
  theorem, 116
diminishing sensitivity, 8
discrete choice, 7, 139
distribution over posteriors, 65
  representation, 66
drift-diffusion model (DDM), 126
dynamic
  logit, 159, 161
  random expected utility (DREU), 104
  random utility (DRU), 101

entropy, 41, 88
expected utility
  non-expected utility, 51, 59
expected utility (EU), 47, 63, 113

Other titles in the series (*continued from page iii*)

Printed in the United States
by Baker & Taylor Publisher Services